The Way of Wisdom

Job, Proverbs, Ecclesiastes, the Song of Solomon

(Latin-English Interlinear Translation)

The Way of Wisdom

Job, Proverbs, Ecclesiastes, Song of Solomon
(Latin-English Interlinear Translation)

Searchlight Press
Who Are You Looking For?
5634 Ledgestone Drive
Dallas, Texas 75214-2026 USA
888-896-6081
ISBN 978-0-9644609-7-3
Manufactured in the United States of America

Ad maiorem dei gloriam

Table of Contents

About the Vulgate **5**

Job **7**
- Introduction to Job 8
- The Book of Job 10

About Solomon 166

Proverbs 167
- Introduction to Proverbs 167
- The Book of Proverbs 170

Ecclesiastes 301
- Introduction to Ecclesiastes 301
- Solomon's Birth 301
- How Solomon Became David's Heir 305
- Solomon's Path to Kingship 308
- Solomon's Views of Women 310
- Solomon's Authorship 313
- Seven Pillars of Solomon's Theology 315
- What is the Value of Ecclesiastes? 319
- The Book of Ecclesiastes 322

The Song of Solomon 367
- Introduction to the Song of Solomon 367
- The Book of the Song of Solomon 371

About *The Vulgate*

Biblia Sacra Iuxta Vulgatam Versionem is a carefully-restored version of what was long the official Bible translation, into Latin, of Roman Catholicism. The version I use in my translation came through BibleWorks, an excellent software tool for serious students of scripture. The German Bible Society holds the copyright to this particular version, and has graciously allowed me to use it in these translations.

Eusebius Hieronymus, known to history as Saint Jerome, was born 347 C.E., died 419/420 C.E. A"biblical translator and monastic leader, traditionally regarded as the most learned of the Latin Fathers,"[1] Jerome combined a love of scripture with a vast knowledge of Classical learning. His translation grew out of his own longing for holiness and a Christian vocation. His life, mired as it was in controversy and struggle, set the stage for the preservation of scripture through the dark centuries following the collapse of Rome's Empire in the West.

In 382 [C.E.], Pope Damasus commissioned Jerome, the leading biblical scholar of his day, to produce an acceptable Latin version of the Bible from the various translations then being used. His revised Latin translation of the Gospels appeared about 383. Using the Septuagint Greek version of the Old Testament, he produced new Latin translations of the Psalms (the so-called Gallican Psalter), the Book of Job, and some other books. Later, he decided that the Septuagint was unsatisfactory and began translating the entire Old Testament from the original Hebrew versions, a process that he completed about 405.[2]

Rather than translating the Bible into the literary Latin of his day, he translated it into so-called Vulgar Latin, the language of ordinary people, intending that the Bible be read and understood as widely as possible. The translation draws its English name, "The

---

[1] The New Encyclopaedia Britannica, Volume 6, Micropaedia, Encyclopedia Britannica, Chicago, 1998, pg. 535.

[2] The New Encyclopaedia Britannica, Volume 12, Micropaedia, Encyclopedia Britannica, Chicago, 1998, pg. 438

Vulgate," from this.[3] By the 6th Century after Christ, the Vulgate had become the official translation of the Roman Catholic Church. By means of the Vulgate, scholars transmitted the biblical tradition to the West.[4] In 1455, Johannes Gutenberg printed a version of Jerome's work, making it "the first complete book extant in the West and the earliest printed from movable type."[5]

Jerome's translation is remarkable for both its faithfulness to the originals and the simplicity of its presentation. More than a mere translation, The Vulgate is one of the world's great works of literature and a monument of the world's religions. I offer this translation, convinced of the surpassing value of the Wisdom tradition in the Bible. May others find the same joy reading it as I have found translating it.

Some have asked, Why translate from the Latin, rather than the Hebrew? The Latin language lies at the root of Western learning. The Bible itself existed in the West in Latin, rather than Hebrew, for more than a thousand years. The oldest complete copy of the Bible in Latin, the *Codex Amiatinus,* created in Northumbria, England, dates to shortly after 700 C.E.[6] [7] [8] By contrast, *Codex Aleppo,* oldest extant version of the Hebrew Masoretic Text, dates from the 10th Century of the Common Era.[9]

In no way do I mean to take away from the surpassing value of the work in its original language. I chose to work in the Latin as a tribute to the monumental impact of The Vulgate in its own right. Whether we study the Bible in Hebrew, Latin, Greek,

---

[3] Ibid, pg. 438.

[4] Ibid, pg. 438.

[5] The New Encyclopaedia Britannica, Volume 5, Micropaedia, Encyclopedia Britannica, Chicago, 1998, Pg. 582

[6] Biblia Sacra Iuxta Vulgatam Versionem, IV Editio, Roger Gryson, editor, Deutsche Bibelgesellschaft, Stuttgart, 1994, pg. xxx.

[7] See http://www.newadvent.org/cathen/04081a.htm.

[8] See also http://www.umilta.net/pandect.html and http://en.wikipedia.org/wiki/Codex_Amiatinus.

[9] See http://en.wikipedia.org/wiki/Aleppo_Codex.

English, or any other language, it remains God's Word to us.

The Book of Job

We know for sure neither who wrote the Book of Job, nor where and when it was written. Still, we can say a few things for certain about it. Originally composed in Hebrew, the Book of Job has been included in Jewish scripture at least since the translation of the Old Testament into Greek, in the 3rd Century B.C.E.[10] It was part of Jerome's translation of the Hebrew into Latin, near the end of the 4th Century C.E. It has been praised almost universally as one of the great monuments of human literature, religious and otherwise.

Apart from scholarly debate, what does the Book of Job tell us about its setting in time and space?

- Its inclusion in the canon tells us it is a work considered sacred by Judaism by the 3rd Century B.C.E. at the latest.
- The book does not

---

[10] The New Encyclopedia Britannica: Micropaedia, Volume 10, Encyclopedia Britannica, Chicago, 1998, pg. 643.

mention the Temple, Jerusalem, kings of Israel or Judah, or centralized worship.

- Job and his friends refer frequently to tents as their primary dwelling, indicating a period of nomadic wandering.
- Lack of a concept of individual resurrection points to a time well before Israel accepted such doctrines.
- Job's position in the canon, as the first book of the so-called Writings, before the Book of Psalms, can be taken as an indication that the canon's framers considered it an older work than those that follow it. King David, Israel's second king, is associated with the earliest Psalms. He reigned between 1000 B.C.E. and 962 B.C.E.[11] This suggests a date for Job prior to that.
- If "the family of Ram" referred to at the beginning of Heliu's speech in Job 32:2 is the same Ram mentioned in Ruth 4:19 as an ancestor of David, then the story takes place some four generations before David, circa 1100 B.C.E.

These factors point to a setting prior to the unification of the Israelite tribes under Saul, the first king.[12] The lack of a well-established priesthood, with local chieftains like Job acting as their own priests, points further back toward the time of the Patriarchs. Job presents itself as an account of events taking place during the Patriarchal age, in the Second Millennium before Christ.[13]

Who Is Job?

Job was a prosperous chieftain, with several

[11] The New Encyclopedia Britannica: Micropaedia, Volume 3, Encyclopedia Britannica, Chicago, 1998, pg. 906

[12] See KJV: Judges 21:25 *In those days there was no king in Israel: every man did that which was right in his own eyes.*

[13] The Ryrie Study Bible: New International Version, Charles Ryrie, editor, Moody Press, Chicago, 1986, pg. 675.

children, much wealth in the form of livestock and slaves, and an esteemed place in his culture. Job, allegorically, is Israel in its pilgrimage before God. Job's sufferings, including the loss of wealth, family, home, and respect, echo Israel's losses. Job is also every struggling sufferer who has wondered why bad things happen to good people.

The arguments of Job's friends could be taken verbatim and preached from pulpits today, and few would object. On the other hand, I imagine someone speaking Job's words in contemporary churches would be condemned quickly, however tolerant and liberal the churches consider themselves.

Job's God is not a warm, fuzzy character. His answers to Job's demands are unpleasant in the ear of both ancient and modern readers. His words hint at titanic struggles beyond our understanding. They also remind us of our own mortality, in stark fashion.

Characters in the Story

The following characters have speaking roles in the Book of Job, in order of appearance.

Job
The Lord
Satan
Four of Job's Slaves
Job's Wife
Eliphaz *the* Themanite
Baldad *the* Shuhite
Sophar *the* Naamathite
Heliu.

Chapter 1

God and Satan Agree to Test Job

1:1 *vir erat in terra Hus nomine Iob et erat vir ille simplex et rectus ac timens Deum et recedens a malo*

There was *a* man in *the* land of Uz[14] whose name was Job, and that man was straightforward and upright, fearing God and turning away from evil.[15]

1:2 *natique sunt ei septem filii et tres filiae*

And seven sons and three daughters were born to him.

1:3 *et fuit possessio eius septem milia ovium et tria milia camelorum quingenta quoque iuga boum et quingentae asinae ac familia multa nimis eratque vir ille magnus inter omnes Orientales*

And his property *included* seven thousand sheep, and three thousand camels, and five hundred yoke of oxen, and five hundred donkeys, and *a* large family. And that man was very great among all *the* Orientals.

1:4 *et ibant filii eius et faciebant convivium per domos unusquisque in die suo et mittentes vocabant tres sorores suas ut comederent et biberent cum eis*

And his sons went, and made *a* feast in their homes, each one on his day, and sending *messengers*, called their three sisters, that they might eat and drink with them.

1:5 *cumque in orbem transisissent dies convivii mittebat ad eos Iob et sanctificabat illos consurgensque diluculo offerebat holocausta per singulos dicebat enim ne*

---

[14] The land of Uz is located east of the Jordan River, in the desert region of what is now Jordan and southern Syria.

[15] Use of italic case in the English translation indicates a word added in the translation that is not in the original. The English verb "is" often must be added to make grammatical sense of the Latin. Latin, like Hebrew and Greek before it, often phrased sentences without a verb, where a simple "to be" form is needed in English. The original Latin, translated literally, is "All vanity." Latin, unlike Greek and Hebrew, has neither definite nor indefinite articles (a, an, the). Where these are found in the translations, they are always words that have been added to make better sense of the translation.

forte peccaverint filii mei et benedixerint Deo in cordibus suis sic faciebat Iob cunctis diebus

And when *the* days of feasting ended, Job sent to them, and sanctified them, and, rising early, offered burnt offerings for each. For he said, Perhaps my sons sinned, and had blessed God in their hearts. Thus Job did on all occasions.

1:6 *quadam autem die cum venissent filii Dei ut adsisterent coram Domino adfuit inter eos etiam Satan*

There was *a* certain day, then, when *the* sons of God came, that they might present themselves before *the* Lord. Even Satan presented himself among them,

1:7 *cui dixit Dominus unde venis qui respondens ait circuivi terram et perambulavi eam*

to whom *the* Lord said, Where have you come from?

Satan[16], responding, said, I walked around *the* earth, and wandered over it.

1:8 *dixitque Dominus ad eum numquid considerasti servum meum Iob quod non sit ei similis in terra homo simplex*[17] *et rectus et timens Deum ac recedens a malo?*

And *the* Lord said to him, Have you not considered my slave Job, that *there* is no one on earth like him, *a* straightforward man,[18] and upright, and fearing God, and turning away from evil?

1:9 *cui respondens Satan ait numquid frustra timet Iob Deum*

To whom responding, Satan said, Not for nothing does Job fear God.

---

[16] Literally, "Who."

[17] *Simplex*=simple, straightforward, honest, upright.

[18] The English word "man" translates the Latin *homo*. Many scholars prefer "humanity," to clarify that the word refers to humanity as a whole, not simply to the masculine gender. This is, however, a mistranslation of the number of the original noun. We must take care in introducing an intentional mistranslation into an ancient work, for reasons having to do with contemporary issues. "Man" may be anachronistic in our culture, yet it more closely reflects the Latin *homo* than the plural, generic, English noun, "humanity."

1:10 *nonne tu vallasti eum ac domum eius universamque substantiam per circuitum operibus manuum eius benedixisti et possessio illius crevit in terra*

Do you not surround him, and his house, and all his substance by circuit? You blessed *the* works of his hands and his possession is set apart on earth.

1:11 *sed extende paululum manum tuam et tange cuncta quae possidet nisi in facie tua benedixerit*[19] *tibi*

But extend your hand *a* little, and touch all that he possesses, and see if he does not bless you to your face.

1:12 *dixit ergo Dominus ad Satan ecce universa quae habet in manu tua sunt tantum in eum ne extendas manum tuam egressusque est Satan a facie Domini*

The Lord, therefore, said to Satan, Look, all that he has is in your hand; only do not extend your hand to him.

And Satan went out from *the* face of *the* Lord.

1:13 *cum autem quadam die filii et filiae eius comederent et biberent vinum in domo fratris sui primogeniti*

When, therefore, on a certain day *Job's*[20] sons and daughters ate and drank wine in *the* house of their firstborn brother,

1:14 *nuntius venit ad Iob qui diceret boves arabant et asinae pascebantur iuxta eos*

a messenger came to Job and said, *The* oxen were plowing and the asses grazing alongside them,

1:15 *et inruerunt Sabei tuleruntque omnia et pueros percusserunt gladio et evasi ego solus ut nuntiarem tibi*

And *the* Sabeans[21] attacked them and took all, and struck down *the* helpers with *the* sword, and I alone escaped to

---

[19] Note the use of *benedico,* I bless, rather than its opposite, *maledico,* "I curse."

[20] Literally, "*his* sons and daughters."

[21] The Sabeans were a nation of farmers and traders who lived in southwestern Arabia, near present-day Yemen.

tell you.

fled to tell you.

1:16 *cumque adhuc ille loqueretur venit alter et dixit ignis Dei cecidit e caelo et tactas oves puerosque consumpsit et effugi ego solus ut nuntiarem tibi*

And while he still was speaking, another came and said, *The* fire of God fell from heaven, and, touching *the* sheep and *the* helpers, burned *them* up, and I alone fled to tell you.[22]

1:17 *sed et illo adhuc loquente venit alius et dixit Chaldei fecerunt tres turmas et invaserunt camelos et tulerunt eos necnon et pueros percusserunt gladio et ego fugi solus ut nuntiarem tibi*

And even while he was still speaking, another came and said, *The* Chaldeans[23] made three columns, and came into *the* camels and took them, and struck down *the* helpers with *the* sword, and I alone

1:18 *loquebatur ille et ecce alius intravit et dixit filiis tuis et filiabus vescentibus et bibentibus vinum in domo fratris sui primogeniti*

He was speaking, and, just then, another entered and said, Your sons and daughters were feasting and drinking wine in *the* house of their firstborn brother.

1:19 *repente ventus vehemens inruit a regione deserti et concussit quattuor angulos domus quae corruens oppressit liberos tuos et mortui sunt et effugi ego solus ut nuntiarem tibi*

Suddenly, *a* violent wind came in from *the* desert region, and struck *the* four corners of *the* house, which, collapsing, fell on your children and they are dead. And I alone escaped to tell you.

1:20 *tunc surrexit Iob et scidit tunicam suam et tonso capite corruens in terram adoravit*

---

[22] The *fire of God* is lightning.

[23] The Chaldeans lived between the Tigris and Euphrates rivers, near the Persian Gulf, in what is now southern Iraq. Abraham the Patriarch came from *Ur of the Chaldees* (See Genesis 11:28-31).

Then Job stood up and tore his tunic and, tearing his hair, fell on *the* ground and worshiped,

1:21 *et dixit nudus egressus sum de utero matris meae et nudus revertar illuc Dominus dedit Dominus abstulit sit nomen Domini benedictum*

and said, I came out naked from my mother's womb and I will return there naked.

The Lord gave.

The Lord took away.

May *the* name of *the* Lord be blessed.

1:22 *in omnibus his non peccavit Iob neque stultum quid contra Deum locutus est*

In all these *things*, Job did not sin, nor speak any foolishness against God.

Chapter 2

God and Satan Test Job Again

2:1 *factum est autem cum quadam die venissent filii Dei et starent coram Domino venisset quoque Satan inter eos et staret in conspectu eius*

A certain day came when *the* sons of God came, and stood before *the* Lord. And Satan also came among them, and stood in his sight,

2:2 *ut diceret Dominus ad Satan unde venis qui respondens ait circuivi terram et perambulavi eam*

so that *the* Lord said to Satan, Where have you come from?

Satan,[24] responding, said, I walked around *the* earth, and wandered over it.

2:3 *et dixit Dominus ad Satan numquid considerasti servum meum Iob quod non sit ei similis in terra vir simplex et rectus timens Deum ac recedens a malo et adhuc retinens innocentiam*

---

[24] Literally, "Who."

tu autem commovisti me adversus eum ut adfligerem illum frustra

And *the* Lord said to Satan,

Have you considered my slave Job, that there is no one like him on earth, a straightforward man and upright, fearing God and turning away from evil, and still retaining his innocence?

But you moved me against him, that I might afflict him for no reason.

2:4 *cui respondens Satan ait pellem pro pelle et cuncta quae habet homo dabit pro anima sua*

To whom Satan, responding, said, Skin for skin! All that man has he will give for his life.

2:5 *alioquin mitte manum tuam et tange os eius et carnem et tunc videbis quod in facie benedicat tibi*

If you stretch out your hand another time, and touch his mouth and flesh, and then you will see that he blesses you to your face.

2:6 *dixit ergo Dominus ad Satan ecce in manu tua est verumtamen animam illius serva*

Therefore, the Lord said to Satan, Look, he is in your hand.

Only preserve his life.

2:7 *egressus igitur Satan a facie Domini percussit Iob ulcere pessimo a planta pedis usque ad verticem eius*

Then Satan leaving *the* face of *the* Lord, struck Job with a dismal, ulcerating infection, from *the* soles of his feet to *the* top of his head.[25]

2:8 *qui testa saniem deradebat sedens in sterquilinio*

Job, with *a* scrap of pottery, scraped away *the* discharge from *his* wounds, sitting on *a* manure pile.

2:9 *dixit autem illi uxor sua adhuc tu permanes in simplicitate tua benedic Deo et morere*

---

[25] Again, Satan tests Job using something that Job would face ultimately, whatever the outcome: serious illness.

But his wife said to him, Are you still holding on to your straightforwardness?

Bless God and die!

2:10 *qui ait ad illam quasi una de stultis locuta es si bona suscepimus de manu Domini quare mala non suscipiamus in omnibus his non peccavit Iob labiis suis*

Job[26] said to her, You have spoken like one of *the* fools.

If we accept good from *the* hand of *the* Lord, why can we not accept evil?

In all these *things*, Job did not sin with his lips.[27]

2:11 *igitur audientes tres amici Iob omne malum quod accidisset ei venerunt singuli de loco suo Eliphaz Themanites et Baldad Suites et Sophar Naamathites condixerant enim ut pariter venientes visitarent eum et consolarentur*

[26] Literally, "Who."

[27] Again, Job passes the test. He is truly *simplex*. What does it mean to be faithful when one day you are sure to lose everything you now have?

Then, three friends of Job, hearing all *the* evil that had befallen him, came each one from his home: Eliphaz *the* Themanite,[28] and Baldad *the* Shuhite,[29] and Sophar *the* Naamathite.[30]

For they agreed on coming together, that they might visit him and console *him*.

2:12 *cumque levassent procul oculos suos non cognoverunt eum et exclamantes ploraverunt scissisque vestibus sparserunt pulverem super caput suum in caelum*

And when they lifted up their eyes, they did not recognize him, and, crying out, they wept and tore their clothes, and threw dust over their heads in *the* air.

2:13 *et sederunt cum eo in*

[28] Thema was a town on the Arabian peninsula, halfway between Damascus and Mecca, in present-day Saudi Arabia.

[29] Shuha was an Aramean land on the western side of the Euphrates, in present-day Syria.

[30] Naama was in northwestern Arabia, east of the Sinai peninsula and southeast of the Dead Sea, in what is now Jordan and Saudi Arabia.

terram septem diebus et septem noctibus et nemo loquebatur ei verbum videbant enim dolorem esse vehementem

And they sat with him on *the* ground seven days and seven nights, and no one said *a* word to him, for they saw that his pain was fierce.

Chapter 3

Job Laments His Life

3:1 *post haec aperuit Iob os suum et maledixit diei suo*

After this Job opened his mouth, and cursed his day *of birth*,

3:2 *et locutus est*

and said,

3:3 *pereat dies in qua natus sum et nox in qua dictum est conceptus est homo*

May *the* day
in which I was born perish,
and *the* night
in which it was said,
A man is conceived.

3:4 *dies ille vertatur in tenebras non requirat eum Deus desuper et non inlustret lumine*

May that day
be turned to shadows.
May God not look on it
from above,
and may it not be
illuminated by light.

3:5 *obscurent eum tenebrae*

et umbra mortis occupet eum,
caligo et involvatur
amaritudine

May it be obscured
by shadows,
and may *the* shadow
of death occupy it,
and may gloom wrap it
in bitterness.

3:6 *noctem illam tenebrosus*
turbo possideat non
conputetur in diebus anni nec
numeretur in mensibus

May *a* shadowy tornado
possess that night.
May it not be counted
among *the* days of *the* year,
or numbered among *the*
months.

3:7 *sit nox illa solitaria nec*
laude digna

May that night be solitary,
nor worthy of praise.

3:8 *maledicant ei qui*
maledicunt diei qui parati
sunt suscitare Leviathan

May they curse it,
who curse *the* days
which were prepared
for arousing Leviathan.[31]

3:9 *obtenebrentur stellae*
caligine eius expectet lucem
et non videat nec ortum
surgentis aurorae

May its stars
be overshadowed by gloom.
May it expect light
and not see it,
nor *the* birth of dawn arising,

3:10 *quia non conclusit ostia*
ventris qui portavit me nec
abstulit mala ab oculis meis

because it did not close up
the doors of *the* womb
of *the* one who bore me,
not take away evil from my
eyes.

3:11 *quare non in vulva*
mortuus sum egressus ex
utero non statim perii

Why did I not die
in *the* vulva?
Why did I not
immediately die,
out of *the* uterus?

---

[31] Leviathan may be translated as a "sea monster." Yet Leviathan represents more than that. It is the hidden, overpowering terror that lurks on the fringes of human experience and imagination, beyond our capacity to either predict or restrain.

3:12 *quare exceptus genibus cur lactatus uberibus*

Why *was I* received
by knees?
Why *by* nursing breasts?

3:13 *nunc enim dormiens silerem et somno meo requiescerem*

For now I would be
silent, sleeping,
and I would rest
in my sleep,

3:14 *cum regibus et consulibus terrae qui aedificant sibi solitudines*

with kings
and counselors of *the* earth,
who built solitudes
for themselves,

3:15 *aut cum principibus qui possident aurum et replent domos suas argento*

or with princes
who possess gold,
and fill their houses
with silver.

3:16 *aut sicut abortivum absconditum non subsisterem vel qui concepti non viderunt lucem*

Or, like *a* hidden abortion,
I would not have stood,
even as those
who are conceived
have not seen light.

3:17 *ibi impii cessaverunt a tumultu et ibi requieverunt fessi robore*

There, *the* lawless
cease their tumult,
and there, *those*
drained of strength rest.

3:18 *et quondam vincti pariter sine molestia non audierunt vocem exactoris*

And those chained together,
without aggravation,
do not hear *the* voice
of task-masters.

3:19 *parvus et magnus ibi sunt et servus liber a domino suo*

Small and great are there,
and *a* slave is free
from his master.

3:20 *quare data est misero lux et vita his qui in amaritudine animae sunt*

Why was light given
to *the* miserable,

and life to those who
are in bitterness of soul,

3:21 *qui expectant mortem
et non venit quasi effodientes
thesaurum*

who wait for death,
like those digging
for treasure
and it does not come!

3:22 *gaudentque vehementer
cum invenerint sepulchrum*

They rejoice fiercely
when they find *the* grave;

3:23 *viro cuius abscondita
est via et circumdedit eum
Deus tenebris*

to *a* man whose way
is hidden,
and God surrounds him
with shadows?

3:24 *antequam comedam,
suspiro et quasi inundantes
aquae sic rugitus meus*

Before I eat, I sigh,
and like overflowing waters,
thus is my roar.

3:25 *quia timor quem
timebam evenit mihi et quod
verebar accidit*

Because *the* fear
which I feared
has come to me,
and what I dreaded happened.

3:26 *nonne dissimulavi
nonne silui nonne quievi et
venit super me indignatio*

Did I lie?
Did I keep silence?
Did I rest?

Yet indignation
came over me!

Chapter 4

Eliphaz Speaks
4:1 *respondens autem Eliphaz Themanites dixit*

But Eliphaz *the* Themanite,
responding, said,

4:2 *si coeperimus loqui tibi forsitan moleste accipias sed conceptum sermonem tenere quis possit*

If I begin to talk to you,
perhaps you will
take it badly,
but who can agree
with *the* idea you conceived?

4:3 *ecce docuisti multos et manus lassas roborasti*

Look, you taught many,
and strengthened
weak hands.

4:4 *vacillantes confirmaverunt sermones tui et genua trementia conortasti*

The wavering were
strengthened by your words,
and you comforted
trembling knees.

4:5 *nunc autem venit super te plaga et defecisti tetigit te et conturbatus es*

But now, *the* blow
comes to you
and you are unsettled.
It touched you,
and you are disturbed.

4:6 *timor tuus fortitudo tua patientia tua et perfectio viarum tuarum*

Where is your reverence,
your strength, your patience,
and *the* perfection
of your way?

4:7 *recordare obsecro te quis umquam innocens perierit aut quando recti deleti sint*

Remember, I pray you.
When has *the* innocent
perished,
or when are *the* upright
destroyed?

4:8 *quin potius vidi eos qui operantur iniquitatem et seminant dolores et metunt eos*

On *the* other hand,
I have seen those who
work treachery
and spread sorrow,
and they are mowed down,

4:9 *flante Deo perisse et spiritu irae eius esse consumptos*

perishing by
the breath of God,
and consumed by
the spirit of His anger.

4:10 *rugitus leonis et vox leaenae et dentes catulorum leonum contriti sunt*

The roar of *the* lion
and *the* voice of *the* lioness
and *the* teeth of *the* lion cubs
are broken in pieces.

4:11 *tigris periit eo quod non haberet praedam et catuli leonis dissipati sunt*

The tiger perishes
on account of it,
because it has no prey,
and *the* lion cubs have
starved.

4:12 *porro ad me dictum est verbum absconditum et quasi furtive suscepit auris mea venas susurri eius*

Far away from me
a hidden word was spoken,
and almost furtively
the veins of my ears
hear his whispering,

4:13 *in horrore visionis nocturnae quando solet sopor occupare homines*

in horrible nightmares,
when sleep is in *the* habit
of occupying men.

4:14 *pavor tenuit me et tremor et omnia ossa mea perterrita sunt*

Fear had me, and trembling,
and all my bones were
terrified.

4:15 *et cum spiritus me praesente transiret inhorruerunt pili carnis meae*

And when *a* spirit present
passed over me,
the hairs on my body
stood on end.

4:16 *stetit quidam cuius non agnoscebam vultum imago coram oculis meis et vocem quasi aurae lenis audivi*

The image of someone
whose appearance
I did not know
stood before my eyes,
and I heard *a* voice
like *a* gentle breeze.

4:17 *numquid homo Dei*

conparatione iustificabitur aut factore suo purior erit vir

Can man be justified
in comparison with God,
or will *a* human be purer
than *the one* making him?

4:18 *ecce qui serviunt ei non sunt stabiles et in angelis suis repperit pravitatem*

Look, those who serve him
are not stable,
and he found fault in his
angels.[32]

4:19 *quanto magis hii qui habitant domos luteas qui terrenum habent fundamentum consumentur velut a tinea*

How much more those
who live in houses of clay,
who have foundations
of dirt?
They will be consumed,
if only by worms.

4:20 *de mane usque ad vesperum succidentur et quia nullus intellegit in aeternum peribunt*

From morning to night
they will die,
and because no one
understands,
they perish eternally.

4:21 *qui autem reliqui fuerint auferentur ex eis morientur et non in sapientia*

But those who will be left
will be carried away from
them.
They will die,
and not in wisdom.

---

[32] This statement reflects belief in a primal rebellion in heaven, as in the Babylonian cosmogonies. It is echoed in Luke 10:18 *And he said to them, "I saw Satan fall like lightning from heaven.*

Chapter 5

Eliphaz Continues

5:1 *voca ergo si est qui tibi respondeat et ad aliquem sanctorum convertere*

Call, therefore,
if it is possible
that someone can respond
to you,
and turn to some
of *the* holy ones.

5:2 *vere stultum interficit iracundia et parvulum occidit invidia*

Truly, anger destroys *a* fool,
and envy kills
the inexperienced.

5:3 *ego vidi stultum firma radice et maledixi pulchritudini eius statim*

I saw a fool firmly rooted,
and I immediately cursed his
beauty.

5:4 *longe fient filii eius a salute et conterentur in porta et non erit qui eruat*

His sons will be
far away from safety,
and will be crushed
in *the* gate,[33]
and *there* will be no one
who rescues *them*;

5:5 *cuius messem famelicus comedet et ipsum rapiet armatus et ebibent sitientes divitias eius*

whose harvest
the starving will eat,
and *an* armed man
will plunder him,
and *the* thirsty
will drink up his riches.

5:6 *nihil in terra sine causa fit et de humo non orietur dolor*

Nothing on earth
is done without a reason,
and pain isn't born from dirt.

5:7 *homo ad laborem nascitur et avis ad volatum*

Man is born to labor
as a bird *is born* to flight.

5:8 *quam ob rem ego deprecabor Dominum et ad Deum ponam eloquium meum*

---

[33] A city's main gate was a place of public discourse and decision making similar to today's City Hall or County Courthouse.

From which thing
I pray to *the* Lord,
and direct my eloquence
to God,

5:9 *qui facit magna et inscrutabilia et mirabilia absque numero*

who works great,
unknowable,
and marvelous *things*,
without number;

5:10 *qui dat pluviam super faciem terrae et inrigat aquis universa*

who gives rain
on *the* face of *the* earth,
and irrigates all by waters;

5:11 *qui ponit humiles in sublimi et maerentes erigit sospitate*

who places *the* humble
on high,
and raises *the* grieving
to safety;

5:12 *qui dissipat cogitationes malignorum ne possint implere manus eorum quod coeperant*

who scatters *the* schemes
of *the* malignant,
that their hands cannot
complete what they plot;

5:13 *qui adprehendit sapientes in astutia eorum et consilium pravorum dissipat*

who catches *the* wise
in their cleverness,
and undoes *the* counsel
of *the* twisted.

5:14 *per diem incurrent tenebras et quasi in nocte sic palpabunt in meridie*

By day they meet
with shadows,
and they blink at midday
as if *it* were night.

5:15 *porro salvum faciet a gladio oris eorum et de manu violenti pauperem*

He places safety far away
from *the* sword of their
mouths,
and *the* poor from *the* hands
of *the* violent,

5:16 *et erit egeno spes iniquitas autem contrahet os suum*

and hope will be
to *the* needy,
but lawlessness will draw in

her mouth.

5:17 *beatus homo qui corripitur a Domino increpationem ergo Domini ne reprobes*

The man who is corrected
by *the* Lord is blessed.
Do not, therefore, reject
the Lord's rebuke.

5:18 *quia ipse vulnerat et medetur percutit et manus eius sanabunt*

because He wounds,
and comforts;
He strikes,
and His hands heal.

5:19 *in sex tribulationibus liberabit te et in septima non tanget te malum*

He will free you
from six tribulations,
and in *a* seventh,
harm will not touch you.[34]

5:20 *in fame eruet te de morte et in bello de manu gladii*

In famine He will
pluck you up from death,
and in war from *the* hand
of *the* sword.

5:21 *a flagello linguae absconderis et non timebis calamitatem cum venerit*

You will be hidden
from *the* abuse of *the* tongue,
and you will not fear
calamity when it comes.

5:22 *in vastitate et fame ridebis et bestiam terrae non formidabis*

You will laugh
at destruction and hunger,
and will not fear
the beasts of *the* earth,

5:23 *sed cum lapidibus regionum pactum tuum et bestiae terrae pacificae erunt tibi*

but your pact *will be*
with *the* rocks of *the* region,
and *the* beasts of earth
will be peaceful to you.[35]

5:24 *et scies quod pacem habeat tabernaculum tuum et visitans speciem tuam non peccabis*

---

[34] Compare to Psalm 91:1-16.

[35] Compare verses 19-23 with Psalm 91.

And you will know that
your tent has peace
and, looking over your
appearance, you will not sin.

5:25 *scies quoque quoniam multiplex erit semen tuum et progenies tua quasi herba terrae*

You will know, also,
because your seed
will be multiplied,
and your descendants *will be*
like *the* grass of *the* field.

5:26 *ingredieris in abundantia sepulchrum sicut infertur acervus in tempore suo*

You will go to *the* grave
in abundance,
as *a* treasure is buried
in its time.

5:27 *ecce hoc ut investigavimus ita est quod auditum mente pertracta*

Look, this is so,
as we investigated.
What *you* heard,
let your mind consider.[36]

Chapter 6

Job Responds to Eliphaz

6:1 *respondens autem Iob dixit*

But Job, responding, said,

6:2 *utinam adpenderentur peccata mea quibus iram merui et calamitas quam patior in statera*

If only they might
weigh out my sins
by which I earned wrath,
and *the* calamities
which I suffer in *a* scale!

6:3 *quasi harena maris haec gravior appareret unde et verba mea dolore sunt plena*

This would appear heavier,
than *the* sand of *the* sea.
This is why my words
are full of suffering,

6:4 *quia sagittae Domini in me sunt quarum indignatio ebibit spiritum meum et terrores Domini militant contra me*

because *the* Lord's arrows
are in me!

---

[36] Compare to RSV: "*Lo, this we have searched out; it is true. Hear, and know it for your good.*" In the face of Job's doubts, Eliphaz tries to reinforce that what he has told him is true.

As *a* result,
indignation drinks my spirit,
and *the* Lord's terrors
march against me.

6:5 *numquid rugiet onager cum habuerit herbam aut mugiet bos cum ante praesepe plenum steterit*

Does *a* wild ass bray
when it has grass,
or *an* ox moo when it stands
before *a* full manger?

6:6 *aut poterit comedi insulsum quod non est sale conditum aut potest aliquis gustare quod gustatum adfert mortem*

Or can what
isn't preserved be eaten,
or can someone taste
something that, when tasted,
causes death?

6:7 *quae prius tangere nolebat anima mea nunc prae angustia cibi mei sunt*

What *things* before
my soul did not want
to touch,
now, in *the* face of anguish,
are my food.

6:8 *quis det ut veniat petitio mea et quod expecto tribuat mihi Deus*

Who can allow
that my petition
might come *before Him*,
and that God would give
what I ask,

6:9 *et qui coepit ipse me conterat solvat manum suam et succidat me*

and *the One* who started,
finish destroying me,
loosen His hand,
and cut me down?

6:10 *et haec mihi sit consolatio ut adfligens me dolore non parcat nec contradicam sermonibus Sancti*

And this would be
consolation to me,
that *the* One afflicting me
with pain not restrain
Himself,
nor would I speak against
the words of *the* Holy One.

6:11 *quae est enim fortitudo mea ut sustineam aut quis finis meus ut patienter agam*

For what is my strength,
that I sustain this,

or what is my end,
that I bear *it* patiently?

6:12 *nec fortitudo lapidum fortitudo mea nec caro mea aerea est*

My strength is not
the strength of *a* rock,
nor is my flesh bronze.

6:13 *ecce non est auxilium mihi in me et necessarii quoque mei recesserunt a me*

Look, *there* is
no help for me in me,
and even those I depend on
pull back from me.

6:14 *qui tollit ab amico suo misericordiam timorem Domini derelinquit*

Someone who takes away
mercy from his friend,
abandons fear of *the* Lord.

6:15 *fratres mei praeterierunt me sicut torrens qui raptim transit in convallibus*

My brothers have passed by
me like *a* torrent,
which rushes rapidly
through *the* valleys.

6:16 *qui timent pruinam inruet super eos nix*

Those who fear *the* frost,
snow rushes in upon them.

6:17 *tempore quo fuerint dissipati peribunt et ut incaluerit solventur de loco suo*

In time, they will be
scattered,
they will perish;
as if heated,
they will melt away
from their place.

6:18 *involutae sunt semitae gressuum eorum ambulabunt in vacuum et peribunt*

The ways of their paths
are enveloped.
They walk in *a* void
and perish.

6:19 *considerate semitas Theman itinera Saba et expectate paulisper*

Consider *the* paths
of Theman,
the roads of Saba,
and wait *a* little while.

6:20 *confusi sunt quia speravi venerunt quoque*

usque ad me et pudore
cooperti sunt

They are confused because
I used to hoped.
They came to me, too,
and are overwhelmed
by shame.

6:21 *nunc venistis et modo*
videntes plagam meam
timetis

Now you have come,
and seeing *the* manner
of my trouble,
you are afraid.

6:22 *numquid dixi adferte*
mihi et de substantia vestra
donate mihi

Did I ever say,
Bring me *something*,
or, Use your riches
to help me?

6:23 *vel liberate me de manu*
hostis et de manu robustorum
eruite me

Or, free me from
the hand of *the* enemy,
or snatch me away from
the hand of *the* strong?

6:24 *docete me et ego*
tacebo et si quid forte
ignoravi instruite me

Teach me, and I will shut up.
And if perhaps *there* was
something I didn't know,
show me.

6:25 *quare detraxistis*
sermonibus veritatis cum e
vobis nullus sit qui possit
arguere

Why tear down truth
by words,
when there is no one
who could argue with you?

6:26 *ad increpandum tantum*
eloquia concinnatis et in
ventum verba profertis

You dress up fancy talk
to rebuke that way,
and offer your advice
to *the* wind.

6:27 *super pupillum inruitis*
et subvertere nitimini
amicum vestrum

You rush in *to attack*
the orphan,
and struggle to undermine
your friend.

6:28 *verumtamen quod*
coepistis explete praebete
aurem et videte an mentiar

Still, finish what you started.
Hear me out and see
if I am lying.

6:29 *respondete obsecro absque contentione et loquentes id quod iustum est iudicate*

Answer me, I pray,
without contention,
and saying what is right,
you judge.

6:30 *et non invenietis in lingua mea iniquitatem nec in faucibus meis stultitia personabit*

And you won't find
lies on my tongue,
nor does foolishness
live in my throat.

Chapter 7

7:1 *militia est vita hominis super terram et sicut dies mercennarii dies eius*

The life of *a* man on earth
is *like a* military campaign,
and his days like *the* days
of *a* hired soldier.

7:2 *sicut servus desiderat umbram et sicut mercennarius praestolatur finem operis sui*

As *a* slave desires shade,
and *a* hired soldier waits
for *the* end of his obligation,

7:3 *sic et ego habui menses vacuos et noctes laboriosas enumeravi mihi*

thus also I had empty months,
and have counted out
laborious nights to myself.

7:4 *si dormiero dico quando consurgam et rursum expectabo vesperam et replebor doloribus usque ad tenebras*

If I sleep, I say,
When will I wake up?
And then I will long
for *the* evening,

and be filled with sufferings
until *the* darkness.

7:5 *induta est caro mea putredine et sordibus pulveris cutis mea aruit et contracta est*

My flesh is covered
with infection
and powdery filth.
My skin withers
and is shrunken.

7:6 *dies mei velocius transierunt quam a texente tela succiditur et consumpti sunt absque ulla spe*

My days speed by faster
than *a* weaver's web
is cut down,
and they are consumed,
far from any hope.

7:7 *memento quia ventus est vita mea et non revertetur oculus meus ut videat bona*

Remember that
my life is *a* breath,
and my eye will not return
to see good *things*,

7:8 *nec aspiciet me visus hominis oculi tui in me et non subsistam*

nor will human vision
look at me.
Your eye *will be* on me,
and I will not exist.

7:9 *sicut consumitur nubes et pertransit sic qui descenderit ad inferos non ascendet*

As *a* cloud is consumed
and passes away,
so one who descends
to *the* dead
will not ascend again,

7:10 *nec revertetur ultra in domum suam neque cognoscet eum amplius locus eius*

nor come back again
to his house,
nor will his place
know him any more.

7:11 *quapropter et ego non parcam ori meo loquar in tribulatione spiritus mei confabulabor cum amaritudine animae meae*

For this reason also,
I will not restrain my speech!
I will speak
in *the* tribulation of my spirit!
I will discuss *the* bitterness
of my soul!

7:12 *numquid mare sum ego aut cetus quia circumdedisti me carcere*

Am I *a* sea *creature*,
or *a* dolphin,
that you shut me in *a* cage?

7:13 *si dixero consolabitur me lectulus meus et relevabor loquens mecum in strato meo*

If I say,
My bed will console me,
and I'll find relief,
talking to myself on my blanket,

7:14 *terrebis me per somnia et per visiones horrore concuties*

You terrify me with dreams,
and strike me with horror
by visions.

7:15 *quam ob rem elegit suspendium anima mea et mortem ossa mea*

Rather than this thing,
my soul would choose hanging,
and my bones death.

7:16 *desperavi nequaquam ultra iam vivam parce mihi nihil enim sunt dies mei*

I have given up hope!
I don't want to live anymore!
Spare me, for my days are nothing!

7:17 *quid est homo quia magnificas eum aut quia ponis erga eum cor tuum*

What is *a* man
that You magnify him,
or that You set Your heart toward him?

7:18 *visitas eum diluculo et subito probas illum*

You visit him at daybreak,
and quickly probe him.

7:19 *usquequo non parces mihi nec dimittis me ut gluttiam salivam meam*

How long will You
not spare me or let me go,
so I can swallow my *own* spit?

7:20 *peccavi quid faciam tibi o custos hominum quare posuisti me contrarium tibi et factus sum mihimet ipsi gravis*

Have I sinned?
What will I do to you,
O Keeper of men?

Why did You
set me against You,
and make me so painful
to myself?

7:21 *cur non tolles peccatum meum et quare non auferes iniquitatem meam ecce nunc in pulvere dormiam et si mane me quaesieris non subsistam*

Why not take away my sin,
and why not carry away
my treachery?
Look, now I'll go
to sleep in *the* dust,
and if You look for me
in the morning,
I will not be there!

Chapter 8

Baldad Speaks

8:1 *respondens autem Baldad Suites dixit*

But responding, Baldad the Shuhite said,

8:2 *usquequo loqueris talia et spiritus multiplex sermones oris tui*

How long will you talk
like this,
and *the* words of your mouth
be like *a* twisting wind?

8:3 *numquid Deus subplantat iudicium et Omnipotens subvertit quod iustum est*

Is it possible that God
subverts justice,
or that *the* Omnipotent
undermines what is right,

8:4 *etiam si filii tui peccaverunt ei et dimisit eos in manu iniquitatis suae*

even if your children sinned
against him,
and He left them
in *the* hand of your
iniquities?

8:5 *tu tamen si diluculo consurrexeris ad Deum et Omnipotentem fueris deprecatus*

Nevertheless, if you rise up
toward God at daybreak,
and make your plea
before the Omnipotent,

8:6 *si mundus et rectus incesseris statim evigilabit ad te et pacatum reddet habitaculum iustitiae tuae*

if you go forward,
clean and right,
He will see you at once,
and restore *the* peaceful
dwelling of your fairness,

8:7 *in tantum ut priora tua fuerint parva et novissima tua multiplicentur nimis*

so much so that what was
before will appear small,
and your legacy
will be greatly multiplied.

8:8 *interroga enim generationem pristinam et diligenter investiga patrum memoriam*

Ask, then, *the* former
generation,
and diligently search
the recollection
of *the* fathers.

8:9 *hesterni quippe sumus et ignoramus quoniam sicut umbra dies nostri sunt super terram*

(We are of yesterday,
of course,
and we do not know,
because our days on earth
are like *a* shadow)

8:10 *et ipsi docebunt te loquentur tibi et de corde suo proferent eloquia*

They will teach you.
They will speak to you,
and give eloquence
from their heart.

8:11 *numquid vivere potest scirpus absque humore aut crescet carectum sine aqua*

Can a marsh plant live
without liquid,
or *a* bullrush without water?

8:12 *cum adhuc sit in flore nec carpatur manu ante omnes herbas arescit*

Even if it is
already flowering,
it is hardly picked by hand

before all its leaves dry up.

8:13 *sic viae omnium qui obliviscuntur Deum et spes hypocritae peribit*

The ways of all
who forget God are like that,
and *the* hope of *a* hypocrite
will perish.

8:14 *non ei placebit vecordia sua et sicut tela aranearum fiducia eius*

His lack of self-control
will not please *God*,
and his faithfulness
is like *the* thread
of a spider's web.

8:15 *innitetur super domum suam et non stabit fulciet eam et non consurget*

He will lean on his house
and it will not stand.
He will prop it up
but it will not rise.

8:16 *humectus videtur antequam veniat sol et in horto suo germen eius egreditur*

He seems to be moist
before sunrise,
and in his garden
his seed will grow.

8:17 *super acervum petrarum radices eius densabuntur et inter lapides commorabitur*

Yet his roots will thicken
over *a* pile of stones,
and he will dwell
among *the* rocks.

8:18 *si absorbuerit eum de loco suo negabit eum et dicet non novi te*

If someone takes him
from his place,
he will deny it,
and will say,
I did not know you.

8:19 *haec est enim laetitia viae eius ut rursum de terra alii germinentur*

For this is
the consolation of his way,
that others will germinate
springing up from *the* earth.

8:20 *Deus non proiciet simplicem nec porriget manum malignis*

God will not reject
simplicity,
nor extend *His* hand

to *the* malignant,

8:21 *donec impleatur risu os tuum et labia tua iubilo*

until your mouth
is full of laughter,
and your lips with jubilation.

8:22 *qui oderunt te induentur confusione et tabernaculum impiorum non subsistet*

Those who hate you
will be dressed in confusion,
and *the* dwelling of *the*
lawless will not stand.

Chapter 9

Job Responds to Baldad
9:1 *et respondens Iob ait*

And responding, Job said,

9:2 *vere scio quod ita sit et quod non iustificetur homo conpositus Deo*

Of course I know it is so,
and that *a* man
cannot be justified
in comparison to God.

9:3 *si voluerit contendere cum eo non poterit ei respondere unum pro mille*

If someone wanted
to contend with Him,
he wouldn't be able
to answer Him
one *time* in *a* thousand.

9:4 *sapiens corde est et fortis robore quis restitit ei et pacem habuit*

He is wise in heart
and strong in power.
Who resisted Him
and had peace?

9:5 *qui transtulit montes et nescierunt hii quos subvertit in furore suo*

He is the One
who moved mountains,
and those whom
He overthrew in His fury
did not know;

9:6 *qui commovet terram de loco suo et columnae eius concutiuntur*

who moves *the* earth
from its place,
and its columns are shaken;

9:7 *qui praecipit soli et non oritur et stellas claudit quasi sub signaculo*

who commands *the* sun,
and it does not rise,
and dims *the* stars,
as if under *a* seal;

9:8 *qui extendit caelos solus et graditur super fluctus maris*

who alone stretched out
the heavens,
and walks over *the* waves
of *the* sea;

9:9 *qui facit Arcturum et Oriona et Hyadas et interiora austri*

who made Arcturus and
Orion,
and *the* Hyades,
and *the* inner south;[37]

9:10 *qui facit magna et inconprehensibilia et mirabilia quorum non est numerus*

who does great, unknowable,
and marvellous *things,*
without number

9:11 *si venerit ad me non videbo si abierit non intellegam eum*

If He were to come to me,
I would not see.
If He were to leave,
I would not understand it.

9:12 *si repente interroget quis respondebit ei vel quis dicere potest cur facis*

If He suddenly questions,
who could respond to Him,
or who can say,
What are you doing?

9:13 *Deus cuius resistere irae nemo potest et sub quo curvantur qui portant orbem*

God, whose wrath

---

[37] These are constellations in the night sky.

no one can resist,
and beneath whom
those who carry *the* world
bend down.

9:14 *quantus ergo sum ego qui respondeam ei et loquar verbis meis cum eo*

How much, then, am I,
that I should respond to him,
and I speak my words
with Him;

9:15 *qui etiam si habuero quippiam iustum non respondebo sed meum iudicem deprecabor*

whom, even if I had
a measure of right,
I would not answer,
but *instead* would beg mercy
from my Judge?

9:16 *et cum invocantem exaudierit me non credo quod audierit vocem meam*

And when He hears me
calling on Him?
I do not believe
He would hear my voice.

9:17 *in turbine enim conteret me et multiplicabit vulnera mea etiam sine causa*

For He will contend with me
from *a* tornado,
and He will multiply
my wounds,
even without reason.

9:18 *non concedit requiescere spiritum meum et implet me amaritudinibus*

He will not give
my spirit rest,
and He fills me
with bitterness.

9:19 *si fortitudo quaeritur robustissimus est si aequitas iudicii nemo pro me audet testimonium dicere*

If you ask about strength,
He is *the* mightiest.
If *you ask about*
fairness in judgment,
no one will hear testimony
spoken on my behalf.

9:20 *si iustificare me voluero os meum condemnabit me si innocentem ostendere pravum me conprobabit*

If I wanted to justify myself,
my mouth will condemn me.
If I show myself innocent,
He will prove me twisted.

9:21 *etiam si simplex fuero hoc ipsum ignorabit anima mea et taedebit me vitae meae*

Even if I were simple,
my soul wouldn't know it,
and I will get tired of my life.

9:22 *unum est quod locutus sum et innocentem et impium ipse consumit*

I have said one *thing*:
He will consume both
the innocent and *the* lawless.

9:23 *si flagellat occidat semel et non de poenis innocentum rideat*

If He strikes, let Him kill
at once,
and not laugh at
the punishment
of *the* innocent.

9:24 *terra data est in manu impii vultum iudicum eius operit quod si non ille est quis ergo est*

Earth is given into
a lawless hand.

9:25 *dies mei velociores fuerunt cursore fugerunt et non viderunt bonum*

My days flew
faster than runners.
They fled, and have not seen
the good.

9:26 *pertransierunt quasi naves poma portantes sicut aquila volans ad escam*

They passed away
like ships carrying fruit,
like *an* eagle flying to prey.

9:27 *cum dixero nequaquam ita loquar commuto faciem meam et dolore torqueor*

When I say,
I will no longer talk this way,
I change my mind,
and am twisted by pain.

9:28 *verebar omnia opera mea sciens quod non parceres delinquenti*

I fear all my works,
knowing that You
will not spare *the* wrongdoer.

9:29 *si autem et sic impius sum quare frustra laboravi*

But if even so I am lawless,
why did I work for nothing?

9:30 *si lotus fuero quasi aquis nivis et fulserint velut* *mundissimae manus meae*

If I were washed
as if with snow-melt,[38]
and my hands were cleaned
most purely,

9:31 *tamen sordibus intingues me et abominabuntur me vestimenta mea*

still You would stain me
with filth,
and my garments
would detest me.

9:32 *neque enim viro qui similis mei est respondebo nec qui mecum in iudicio ex aequo possit audiri*

For I would not be
responding
to *a* man like me,
nor someone who can be
heard in court,
the same as me.

9:33 *non est qui utrumque valeat arguere et ponere manum suam in ambobus*

There isn't another
who is strong enough
to argue with both *of us*,
and put his hand
on both of us.

9:34 *auferat a me virgam suam et pavor eius non me terreat*

Let him take His rod
away from me,
and His fear not terrorize me.

9:35 *loquar et non timebo eum neque enim possum metuens respondere*

Then I will speak
and not fear Him,
yet I can't respond,
because I fear *Him*!

---

[38] Snow melt here represents the cleanest of water.

Chapter 10

10:1 *taedet animam meam*
vitae meae dimittam
adversum me eloquium meum
loquar in amaritudine
animae meae

He wearies
my soul of my life.[39]
I will give up
my eloquence against myself.
I will speak in *the* bitterness
of my soul.

10:2 *dicam Deo noli me*
condemnare indica mihi cur
me ita iudices

I will say to God,
Don't condemn me!
Tell me why you judge me
so!

10:3 *numquid bonum tibi*
videtur si calumnieris et
opprimas me opus manuum
tuarum et consilium
impiorum adiuves

Does it seem good to You
if You abuse and oppress me,
the work of Your hands,
and aid *the* counsel
of *the* lawless?

10:4 *numquid oculi carnei*
tibi sunt aut sicut videt homo
et tu videbis

Do You have eyes of flesh,
or do You also see
as *a* man sees?

10:5 *numquid sicut dies*
hominis dies tui et anni tui
sicut humana sunt tempora

Are Your days
like man's days,
or Your years
like human times,

10:6 *ut quaeras iniquitatem*
meam et peccatum meum
scruteris

that You inquire
about my treachery,
and scrutinize my sin?

10:7 *et scias quia nihil*
impium fecerim cum sit nemo
qui de manu tua possit eruere

And You should know
that I have done
nothing lawless,
when *there* is no one who
can deliver from Your hand!

10:8 *manus tuae*
plasmaverunt me et fecerunt
me totum in circuitu et sic

---

[39] Compare to Job 10:1, RSV: *I loathe my life.*

repente praecipitas me

Your hands molded me
and made me, all in order,
and thus, suddenly,
You throw me down!

10:9 *memento quaeso quod sicut lutum feceris me et in pulverem reduces me*

Remember, I pray,
that You have made me
like dirt,
and You reduce me to dust.

10:10 *nonne sicut lac mulsisti me et sicut caseum me coagulasti*

You have squeezed me out
like milk,
and congealed me
like cheese.

10:11 *pelle et carnibus vestisti me et ossibus et nervis conpegisti me*

You dressed me
in skin and flesh,
and made me
of bones and sinews.

10:12 *vitam et misericordiam tribuisti mihi et visitatio tua custodivit spiritum meum*

You gave me life and mercy,
and your visitation
kept my spirit.

10:13 *licet haec celes in corde tuo tamen scio quia universorum memineris*

It is permitted
that You hide *these*
in Your heart,
yet I know that
You remember everything.

10:14 *si peccavi et ad horam pepercisti mihi cur ab iniquitate mea mundum me esse non pateris*

If I sinned,
and You held back from me
at that time,
why don't You let me
be cleansed from my
iniquity?

10:15 *et si impius fuero vae mihi est et si iustus non levabo caput saturatus adflictione et miseria*

And if I were lawless,
the fault is mine!
Yet if I am fair,
I will not lift up my head,
full *as it is* of affliction
and misery.

10:16 *et propter superbiam quasi leaenam capies me reversusque mirabiliter me crucias*

And because of pride,
You seize me like a lioness,
and, turning back,
torture me unbelievably!

10:17 *instauras testes tuos contra me et multiplicas iram tuam adversum me et poenae militant in me*

You strengthen Your own
witnesses against me,
and multiply Your anger
against me,
and *Your* punishments
make war against me!

10:18 *quare de vulva eduxisti me qui utinam consumptus essem ne oculus me videret*

Why did You lead me
out of *the* vulva?
If only I had been consumed!
If no eye *could* see me,

10:19 *fuissem quasi qui non essem de utero translatus ad tumulum*

I might have been
like someone who didn't
exist,
taken from *the* womb
to *the* grave.

10:20 *numquid non paucitas dierum meorum finietur brevi dimitte ergo me ut plangam paululum dolorem meum*

Aren't my few days
almost finished?
Therefore, let me go quickly,
so I can lament my pain
a little,

10:21 *antequam vadam et non revertar ad terram tenebrosam et opertam mortis caligine*

before I go,
and do not return,
to *the* land of shadows,
and *the* hidden gloom
of death,

10:22 *terram miseriae et tenebrarum ubi umbra mortis et nullus ordo et sempiternus horror inhabitans*

a land of misery
and darkness,
where is *the* shadow of death,
and *there is* no order,
and its inhabitant *is* enduring
horror.

Chapter 11

Sophar Speaks
11:1 *respondens autem Sophar Naamathites dixit*

But Sophar *the* Naamathite,
responding, said,

11:2 *numquid qui multa loquitur non et audiet aut vir verbosus iustificabitur*

Will someone
who speaks much
but doesn't listen,
or *a* long-winded man
be justified?

11:3 *tibi soli tacebunt homines et cum ceteros inriseris a nullo confutaberis*

Are men silent to you only,
and when you mock others,
will no one dispute you?

11:4 *dixisti enim purus est sermo meus et mundus sum in conspectu tuo*

For you said, My word
is pure,
and I am clean in Your sight.

11:5 *atque utinam Deus loqueretur tecum et aperiret labia sua tibi*

And, If only God
would talk with you,
and would open His lips
to you,

11:6 *ut ostenderet tibi secreta sapientiae et quod multiplex esset lex eius et intellegeres quod multo minora exigaris a Deo quam meretur iniquitas tua*

that He might show you
secret wisdom,
and that His law
is complicated,
and you would know
that you have finished
much less from God
than your treachery merits.

11:7 *forsitan vestigia Dei conprehendes et usque ad perfectum Omnipotentem repperies*

Maybe you understand
God's footsteps,
and you will discover
the Omnipotent
even to *the point of*
perfection.

11:8 *excelsior caelo est et quid facies profundior inferno et unde cognosces*

It is higher than *the* sky!

What will you do?
It is deeper than *the* inferno!
How will you know
about that?

11:9 *longior terrae mensura eius et latior mari*

His measure is longer
than *the* earth,
and wider than *the* sea.

11:10 *si subverterit omnia vel in unum coartaverit quis contradicet ei*

If He were
to overturn everything,
or press *everything*
together in one,
who could contradict Him?

11:11 *ipse enim novit hominum vanitatem et videns iniquitatem nonne considerat*

For He knows human vanity,
and, seeing treachery,
doesn't He consider it?

11:12 *vir vanus in superbiam erigitur et tamquam pullum onagri se liberum natum putat*

A vain man is raised in pride,
and like *the* colt
of *a* wild ass,
he believes himself born free.

11:13 *tu autem firmasti cor tuum et expandisti ad eum manus tuas*

But you hardened your heart,
and stretched out your hands
to Him.

11:14 *si iniquitatem quod est in manu tua abstuleris a te et non manserit in tabernaculo tuo iniustitia*

If you put behind you
the treachery that is
in your hand,
and lawlessness
does not remain in your tent,

11:15 *tum levare poteris faciem tuam absque macula et eris stabilis et non timebis*

then you will be able
to lift your face, without spot,
and will be stable,
and will not fear.

11:16 *miseriae quoque oblivisceris et quasi aquarum quae praeterierint recordaberis*

You also will forget misery,
and will remember it
like waters which pass.

11:17 *et quasi meridianus fulgor consurget tibi ad vesperam et cum te consumptum putaveris orieris ut lucifer*

And brightness like *the* noonday,
will rise up to you at evening,
and where you considered yourself consumed,
you will be born again
to bring light.

11:18 *et habebis fiduciam proposita tibi spe et defossus securus dormies*

And you will have faith,
His promise to you
being hope,
and, embedded securely,
you will sleep.

11:19 *requiesces et non erit qui te exterreat et deprecabuntur faciem tuam plurimi*

You will rest,
and *there* will be no one
who terrorizes you,
and they will beg mercy
to your face often.

11:20 *oculi autem impiorum deficient et effugium peribit ab eis et spes eorum abominatio animae*

But *the* eyes of *the* lawless
will be troubled,
and escape will perish
for them,
and their hope *will be*
a soul's abomination.

Chapter 12

Job Responds to Sophar

12:1 *respondens autem Iob dixit*

But responding, Job said,

12:2 *ergo vos estis soli homines et vobiscum morietur sapientia*

Then you are *the* only men
and wisdom will die with you.

12:3 *et mihi est cor sicut et vobis nec inferior vestri sum quis enim haec quae nostis ignorat*

A heart is in me also,
just like in you,
nor am I inferior to you,
for who doesn't know
what you know?

12:4 *qui deridetur ab amico suo sicut ego invocabit Deum et exaudiet eum deridetur enim iusti simplicitas*

Who is mocked
by his friend as I *am?*
He will invoke God
and He will hear him,
for *the* simplicity
of *the* fair is mocked.

12:5 *lampas contempta apud cogitationes divitum parata ad tempus statutum*

A lamp despised
in *the* thoughts of *the* rich
is prepared for *the* decided time.

12:6 *abundant tabernacula praedonum et audacter provocant Deum cum ipse dederit omnia in manibus eorum*

The tents of thieves overflow,
yet they audaciously
provoke God,
when He has given
all *the things* in their hands.

12:7 *nimirum interroga iumenta et docebunt te et volatilia caeli et indicabunt tibi*

Why don't you
question cattle,
and they will teach you,
and *the* birds of *the* sky,
and they will show it to you?

12:8 *loquere terrae et*

respondebit tibi et narrabunt pisces maris

Talk to *the* earth
and it will respond to you,
and *the* fish of *the* sea
will tell.

12:9 *quis ignorat quod omnia haec manus Domini fecerit*

Who doesn't know
that *the* hand of *the* Lord
made all these *things*,

12:10 *in cuius manu anima omnis viventis et spiritus universae carnis hominis*

in whose hand is *the* soul
of every living *being*,
and *the* spirit
of all human flesh?

12:11 *nonne auris verba diiudicat et fauces comedentis saporem*

Doesn't *the* ear
judge between words,
and *the* palate of one eating
judge flavor?

12:12 *in antiquis est sapientia et in multo tempore prudentia*

Wisdom is in *the* old,
and prudence in many
seasons.

12:13 *apud ipsum est sapientia et fortitudo ipse habet consilium et intellegentiam*

With Him is wisdom
and strength;
He has counsel and
intelligence.

12:14 *si destruxerit nemo est qui aedificet et si incluserit hominem nullus est qui aperiat*

If He destroys *there* is no one
who will build,
and if He shuts *a* man in,
there is no one who will
open.

12:15 *si continuerit aquas omnia siccabuntur et si emiserit eas subvertent terram*

If He holds fast *the* waters
all *things* will dry up,
and if He sends them,
they will undermine *the* land.

12:16 *apud ipsum est fortitudo et sapientia ipse novit et decipientem et eum qui decipitur*

Strength is with Him
and wisdom.
He knows both *the* deceiver
and *the* one who is deceived.

12:17 *adducit consiliarios in stultum finem et iudices in stuporem*

He leads counselors
to *a* foolish end,
and judges into stupor

12:18 *balteum regum dissolvit et praecingit fune renes eorum*

He loosens a king's belt,
and encircles his kidneys
with *a* rope.

12:19 *ducit sacerdotes inglorios et optimates subplantat*

He leads away priests
without distinctions,
and overthrows aristocrats,

12:20 *commutans labium veracium et doctrinam senum auferens*

changing *a* truthful lip
and taking away
the doctrine of *the* old.

12:21 *effundit despectionem super principes et eos qui oppressi fuerant relevans*

He pours out disdain
on princes,
and relieves those
who had been mistreated,

12:22 *qui revelat profunda de tenebris et producit in lucem umbram mortis*

who reveals profound *truths*
from darkness,
and produces *the* shadow
of death in light;[40]

12:23 *qui multiplicat gentes et perdet eas et subversas in integrum restituet*

who multiplies peoples
and destroys them,
and restores *the* undermined
to wholeness;

---

[40] Compare to Psalm 23, concerning the *shadow of death.*

12:24 *qui inmutat cor principum populi terrae et decipit eos ut frustra incedant per invium*

who changes *the* heart
of *the* princes
of *the* people of earth,
and deceives them,
so that for no reason
they march through
impassable *country.*

12:25 *palpabunt quasi in tenebris et non in luce et errare eos faciet quasi ebrios*

They will blink
as if in darkness
and not in light,
and *He* will make them
stagger, as if drunk.

Chapter 13

13:1 *ecce omnia et vidit oculus meus et audivit auris mea et intellexi singula*

Look, my eye has seen
everything *you've seen.*
My ear has heard,
and I understood *it* all *too.*

13:2 *secundum scientiam vestram et ego novi nec inferior vestri sum*

By your own standard,
I have known *these things*,
nor am I inferior to you.

13:3 *sed tamen ad Omnipotentem loquar et disputare cum Deo cupio*

It doesn't matter!
I want to speak
to *the* Omnipotent.
I want to dispute with God!

13:4 *prius vos ostendens fabricatores mendacii et cultores perversorum dogmatum*

First, *by* showing you
to be fabricators of lies,
and keepers of perverse

dogmas!

13:5 *atque utinam taceretis ut putaremini esse sapientes*

And if you would
just shut up,
you might convince
yourselves that you are wise!

13:6 *audite ergo correptiones meas et iudicium labiorum meorum adtendite*

So, listen to my rebukes.
Pay attention to
the judgments of my lips.

13:7 *numquid Deus indiget vestro mendacio ut pro illo loquamini dolos*

Does God need your lie,
that you should speak
deceit on His behalf?

13:8 *numquid faciem eius accipitis et pro Deo iudicare nitimini*

Will you favor His face,
and struggle to judge
on God's behalf?

13:9 *aut placebit ei quem celare nihil potest aut decipietur ut homo vestris fraudulentiis*

Will *that* please Him,
from whom nothing
can be hidden?
Will He be deceived
like *a* man, by your deceits?

13:10 *ipse vos arguet quoniam in abscondito faciem eius accipitis*

He Himself will dispute you,
because you have
favored His face in secret.

13:11 *statim ut se commoverit turbabit vos et terror eius inruet super vos*

As soon as He is moved,
He will disturb you
and His terror will rush in
over you.

13:12 *memoria vestra conparabitur cineri et redigentur in lutum cervices vestrae*

Your memory will be
like ashes,
and your necks will be
driven back in grief.

13:13 *tacete paulisper ut loquar quodcumque mihi mens suggesserit*

Shut up a little,
while I speak whatever my mind will suggest to me.

13:14 *quare lacero carnes meas dentibus meis et animam meam porto in manibus meis*

Why do I tear my flesh
with my teeth,
and carry my soul in my hands?

13:15 *etiam si occiderit me in ipso sperabo verumtamen vias meas in conspectu eius arguam*

Even if He kills me,
I will hope in Him.
Even so, I will defend
my ways in His sight.

13:16 *et ipse erit salvator meus non enim veniet in conspectu eius omnis hypocrita*

And He will be my savior,
for when He comes,
not all will be hypocrites
in His sight.

13:17 *audite sermonem meum et enigmata percipite auribus vestris*

Hear my word,
and perceive with your ears
my mysteries.[41]

13:18 *si fuero iudicatus scio quod iustus inveniar*

If I am judged, I know that
I will be found fair.

13:19 *quis est qui iudicetur mecum veniat quare tacens consumor*

Who is the one
who will judge me?
Let Him come!
Why am I consumed silently?

13:20 *duo tantum ne facias mihi et tunc a facie tua non abscondar*

Spare me two things.
Then I will not hide
from Your face:

---

[41] The Latin *enigmata* may be translated as riddles, mysteries, or enigmas.

13:21 *manum tuam longe fac a me et formido tua non me terreat*

Keep your hand off me,
and don't terrorize me
by your dread.

13:22 *et voca me et respondebo tibi aut certe loquar et tu responde mihi*

Call me and I will
respond to you,
Have no doubt
I will speak *to you,*
and you can respond to me.

13:23 *quantas habeo iniquitates et peccata scelera mea et delicta ostende mihi*

How many treacheries
and sins do I have?
Show me my crimes
and offenses!

13:24 *cur faciem tuam abscondis et arbitraris me inimicum tuum*

Why do You hide Your face,
and consider me Your
enemy?

13:25 *contra folium quod vento rapitur ostendis potentiam tuam et stipulam siccam persequeris*

You demonstrate Your power
against *a* leaf
which *the* wind takes away.
You hunt down dry stubble.

13:26 *scribis enim contra me amaritudines et consumere me vis peccatis adulescentiae meae*

For You write
bitter *judgments* against me,
Do you want to consume me
for the *sins* of my youth?

13:27 *posuisti in nervo pedem meum et observasti omnes semitas meas et vestigia pedum meorum considerasti*

You put my foot in *a* fetter.
You watched all my ways.
You judged *the* tracks
of my steps.

13:28 *qui quasi putredo consumendus sum et quasi vestimentum quod comeditur a tinea*

I, who *am* like something

which will be consumed
by rot.
I will be like *a* garment
which is eaten by moths.

Chapter 14

14:1 *homo natus de muliere brevi vivens tempore repletus multis miseriis*

Man born of woman
living *a* brief moment,
is full of many miseries.

14:2 *quasi flos egreditur et conteritur et fugit velut umbra et numquam in eodem statu permanet*

He comes forth like *a* flower
and is destroyed.
He vanishes like *a* shadow.
He will never endure
in his place.

14:3 *et dignum ducis super huiuscemodi aperire oculos tuos et adducere eum tecum in iudicium*

And do You consider *it* fair
to open your eyes over
one like him,
and bring him to you
in judgment?

14:4 *quis potest facere mundum de inmundo conceptum semine nonne tu* *qui solus es*

Who can make *him* clean,
conceived of unclean seed?
Isn't it You, who are unique?

14:5 *breves dies hominis
sunt numerus mensuum eius
apud te est constituisti
terminos eius qui praeterire
non poterunt*

Man only has *a* few days.
You Yourself placed *an* end
to *the* number of his months.
You have established
his limits,
which cannot be passed.

14:6 *recede paululum ab eo
ut quiescat donec optata
veniat sicut mercennarii dies
eius*

Turn away from him *a* little.
Let him rest until
his desire should come.
His days are like
a hired soldier's.

14:7 *lignum habet spem si
praecisum fuerit rursum
virescit et rami eius pullulant*

A tree has hope.
If it is cut down,
it will grow green again.
Its branches will bud.

14:8 *si senuerit in terra
radix eius et in pulvere
emortuus fuerit truncus illius*

If its roots
grow old in *the* soil
and its trunk decays into dust,

14:9 *ad odorem aquae
germinabit et faciet comam
quasi cum primum plantatum
est*

at *the* scent of water
it will germinate
and bear fruit,
like when it was first planted.

14:10 *homo vero cum
mortuus fuerit et nudatus
atque consumptus ubi quaeso
est*

But, truly,
when *a* man dies,
and *is* laid out
and eaten up,
where, I ask, is he?

14:11 *quomodo si recedant
aquae de mari et fluvius
vacuefactus arescat*

In *the* same way
the waters of *the* sea
ebb away,
and empty rivers dry up,

14:12 *sic homo cum dormierit non resurget donec adteratur caelum non evigilabit nec consurget de somno suo*

so man when he falls asleep
will not wake back up
until *the* sky grinds away.
He will not awaken
or get up from his sleep.

14:13 *quis mihi hoc tribuat ut in inferno protegas me ut abscondas me donec pertranseat furor tuus et constituas mihi tempus in quo recorderis mei*

Who can give this to me,
that You may protect me
in *the* inferno,
that You may hide me
until your fury passes over,
that You give me *a* time
when You will remember
me?

14:14 *putasne mortuus homo rursum vivet cunctis diebus quibus nunc milito expecto donec veniat inmutatio mea*

You don't believe
a dead man
can rise up again and live,
do you?
All of my days now
I campaign on.
I am waiting until
my release comes.

14:15 *vocabis et ego respondebo tibi operi manuum tuarum porriges dexteram*

You will call
and I will respond to you.
You will stretch out
your right hand
to *the* work of your hands.

14:16 *tu quidem gressus meos dinumerasti sed parces peccatis meis*

You indeed have
numbered my steps,
but You spare my sins.

14:17 *signasti quasi in sacculo delicta mea sed curasti iniquitatem meam*

You sealed my offenses
as if in *a* small sack,

yet have been concerned
with my treachery.

14:18 *mons cadens defluet et saxum transfertur de loco suo*

A mountain, falling,
will fade away,
and *a* rock is moved
from its place.

14:19 *lapides excavant aquae et adluvione paulatim terra consumitur et homines ergo similiter perdes*

Waters wear away stones
and earth is consumed
little by little by flood,
and You, therefore,
destroy men in *the* same way.

14:20 *roborasti eum paululum ut in perpetuum pertransiret inmutabis faciem eius et emittes eum*

You have strengthened him
a little,
that his face may
pass away forever,
and you will drive him out.

14:21 *sive nobiles fuerint filii eius sive ignobiles non intelleget*

Whether his children
will be noble or ignoble,
he does not know.

14:22 *attamen caro eius dum vivet dolebit et anima illius super semet ipso lugebit*

Yet his flesh,
while he still lives will ache,
and his soul will mourn
over him.

Chapter 15

Eliphaz Responds Again

15:1 *respondens autem Eliphaz Themanites dixit*

But Eliphaz *the* Themanite, responding, said,

15:2 *numquid sapiens respondebit quasi in ventum loquens et implebit ardore stomachum suum*

Will *the* wise ever respond
like someone talking
into *the* wind,
and *will he* fill his stomach
with fire?

15:3 *arguis verbis eum qui non est aequalis tui et loqueris quod tibi non expedit*

You contest by words
One who is not your equal,
and you say what is not
helpful to you.

15:4 *quantum in te est evacuasti timorem et tulisti preces coram Deo*

How much is in you!
You have removed fear
and taken away your prayers
before God.

15:5 *docuit enim iniquitas tua os tuum et imitaris linguam blasphemantium*

For your mouth has shown
your treachery,
and you have imitated
the tongue of blasphemers.

15:6 *condemnabit te os tuum et non ego et labia tua respondebunt tibi*

Your mouth will condemn
you and not me,
and your lips will answer
you.

15:7 *numquid primus homo tu natus es et ante colles formatus*

Were you *the* first man born,
and formed before *the* hills?

15:8 *numquid consilium Dei audisti et inferior te erit eius sapientia*

Have you heard God's
counsel
and is His wisdom
inferior to yours?

15:9 *quid nosti quod ignoremus quid intellegis quod nesciamus*

What have you known
that we are ignorant of?
What do you understand
that we do not know?

15:10 *et senes et antiqui sunt in nobis multo vetustiores quam patres tui*

Old men and elders
are among us,
much older than your parents.

15:11 *numquid grande est ut consoletur te Deus sed verba tua prava hoc prohibent*

Isn't *it* great that
God would console you,
but your twisted words
prevent this!

15:12 *quid te elevat cor tuum et quasi magna cogitans adtonitos habes oculos*

Why does your heart
lift you up,
and *why* do you have
astonished eyes,
as if from great thoughts?

15:13 *quid tumet contra Deum spiritus tuus ut proferas de ore huiuscemodi sermones*

Why does your spirit
swell against God,
that you offer such words
from your mouth?

15:14 *quid est homo ut inmaculatus sit et ut iustus appareat natus de muliere*

What is man
that he be spotless,
and that he seem fair,
born of woman?

15:15 *ecce inter sanctos eius nemo inmutabilis et caeli non sunt mundi in conspectu eius*

Look, among *God's* holy
ones no one is unchanging,[42]
and *the* heavens
are not clean in His sight.

15:16 *quanto magis abominabilis et inutilis homo qui bibit quasi aquas iniquitatem*

---

[42] As in much ancient thought, the author associates change with imperfection.

How much more detestable
and useless is man,
who drinks treachery
like waters?

15:17 *ostendam tibi audi me quod vidi narrabo tibi*

I will show you!
Listen to me,
because I have seen.
I will tell you.

15:18 *sapientes confitentur et non abscondunt patres suos*

The wise acknowledge,
and do not hide their fathers,

15:19 *quibus solis data est terra et non transibit alienus per eos*

to whom only *the* land
is given.
And *a* stranger will not pass
through them.

15:20 *cunctis diebus suis impius superbit et numerus annorum incertus est tyrannidis eius*

All his days
the lawless is proud,
yet *the* number of years
of his tyranny is uncertain.

15:21 *sonitus terroris semper in auribus illius et cum pax sit ille insidias suspicatur*

The sound of terror
is always in his ears,
and when *there* is peace,
he suspects plots.

15:22 *non credit quod reverti possit de tenebris circumspectans undique gladium*

He does not believe
that he can come back
from darkness,
watching for *the* sword
everywhere.

15:23 *cum se moverit ad quaerendum panem novit quod paratus sit in manu eius tenebrarum dies*

When he is moved
to look for bread,
he already knows that
a day of shadow
is prepared in his hand.

15:24 *terrebit eum tribulatio*

et angustia vallabit eum sicut regem qui praeparatur ad proelium

Tribulation will terrify him,
and anguish
will surround him,
like *a* king who prepares
for battle.

15:25 *tetendit enim adversus Deum manum suam et contra Omnipotentem roboratus est*

For his hand
has aimed against God,
and he has flexed his muscles
against *the* Omnipotent.

15:26 *cucurrit adversus eum erecto collo et pingui cervice armatus est*

He has run against him
with head upright,
and is armed with *a* fat neck.

15:27 *operuit faciem eius crassitudo et de lateribus eius arvina dependet*

Fatness has covered his face,
and fat hangs from his sides.

15:28 *habitavit in civitatibus desolatis et in domibus desertis quae in tumulos sunt redactae*

He has lived
in destroyed cities,
and in deserted houses,
which are reduced to rubble.

15:29 *non ditabitur nec perseverabit substantia eius nec mittet in terra radicem suam*

He will not grow rich,
nor will his substance last,
nor will he send his root
into *the* earth.

15:30 *non recedet de tenebris ramos eius arefaciet flamma et auferetur spiritu oris sui*

He will not step back
from shadows;
a flame will dry up
his branch,
and he will be carried away
by *the* spirit of his mouth.

15:31 *non credat frustra errore deceptus quod aliquo pretio redimendus sit*

Pointlessly deceived by error,
he will not believe

that he can be redeemed
even by something precious.

15:32 *antequam dies eius impleantur peribit et manus eius arescet*

Before his days are full,
he will perish,
and his hand will wither.

15:33 *laedetur quasi vinea in primo flore botrus eius et quasi oliva proiciens florem suum*

He will be struck
like *a* vineyard
whose grapes *are*
in first flower,
and like *an* olive tree
casting off its bloom.

15:34 *congregatio enim hypocritae sterilis et ignis devorabit tabernacula eorum qui munera libenter accipiunt*

For *a* gathering of hypocrites
is sterile,
and fire will devour
their tent,
who willingly take bribes.

15:35 *concepit dolorem et peperit iniquitatem et uterus eius praeparat dolos*

He has conceived pain
and given birth to treachery,
and his womb prepares
frauds.

Chapter 16

16:1 *respondens autem Iob dixit*

But Job, responding, said,

16:2 *audivi frequenter talia consolatores onerosi omnes vos estis*

I have heard
such things frequently.
All of you are lousy
comforters!

16:3 *numquid habebunt finem verba ventosa aut aliquid tibi molestum est si loquaris*

Will windy words
have no end,
or will something bother you
if you speak?

16:4 *poteram et ego similia vestri loqui atque utinam esset anima vestra pro anima mea*

I could also talk like you,
if only your soul
were for my soul.[43]

16:5 *consolarer et ego vos sermonibus et moverem caput meum super vos*

I might also
console you by words,
and shake my head over you.

16:6 *roborarem vos ore meo et moverem labia quasi parcens vobis*

I could build you up
by my mouth,
and move *my* lips
as if showing consideration
for you.

16:7 *sed quid agam si locutus fuero non quiescet dolor meus et si tacuero non recedet a me*

But what should I do?
If I spoke *that way*,
my pain would not ease.
Even if I were quiet,
it wouldn't recede from me.

16:8 *nunc autem oppressit me dolor meus et in nihili*

---

[43] ". . . if only you were in my place."

redacti sunt omnes artus mei

But now my pain
has oppressed me,
and all my limbs
are reduced to nothing.

16:9 *rugae meae*
testimonium dicunt contra me
et suscitatur falsiloquus
adversus faciem meam
contradicens mihi

My wrinkles speak
testimony against me,
and *a* liar rises up
against my face,
contradicting me.

16:10 *collegit furorem suum*
in me et comminans mihi
infremuit contra me dentibus
suis hostis meus terribilibus
oculis me intuitus est

He has brought together
his fury against me,
driving against me.
He has ground his teeth
at me.
My enemy has looked at me
with terrifying eyes.

16:11 *aperuerunt super me*
ora sua exprobrantes
percusserunt maxillam meam
satiati sunt poenis meis

They opened their mouths
over me, cursing.
They struck my jaw.
They are satisfied
by my punishments.

16:12 *conclusit me Deus*
apud iniquum et manibus
impiorum me tradidit

God included me
with *the* treacherous
and handed me over
into *the* hands of *the* lawless.

16:13 *ego ille quondam*
opulentus repente contritus
sum tenuit cervicem meam
confregit me et posuit sibi
quasi in signum

I, who was wealthy,
am suddenly penniless.
He had me by the neck.
He has broken me
and placed Himself
like *a* banner.

16:14 *circumdedit me*
lanceis suis convulneravit
lumbos meos non pepercit et
effudit in terra viscera mea

He has surrounded me

with his lances.
He wounded my manhood.
He has not spared *me*,
and has poured out
my guts on *the* ground.

16:15 *concidit me vulnere super vulnus inruit in me quasi gigans*

He struck me
with wound after wound.
He rushed in at me
like *a* giant.

16:16 *saccum consui super cutem meam et operui cinere cornu meum*

I have sown sackcloth
over my skin,
and covered my strength
with ashes.

16:17 *facies mea intumuit a fletu et palpebrae meae caligaverunt*

My face is swollen
with tears,
and my eyelids
have been darkened.

16:18 *haec passus sum absque iniquitate manus meae cum haberem mundas ad Deum preces*

I have suffered these *things*
without treachery
on my hands,
when I had pure prayers
to God!

16:19 *terra ne operias sanguinem meum neque inveniat locum in te latendi clamor meus*

Do not let *the* earth
cover up my blood,[44]
nor my cry find
a hidden place in you!

16:20 *ecce enim in caelo testis meus et conscius meus in excelsis*

Because, look,
my witness *is* in heaven,
and my confidante
is in *the* highest.

16:21 *verbosi mei amici mei ad Deum stillat oculus meus*

---

[44] Compare to Genesis 4:9-10: *Then the LORD said to Cain, "Where is Abel your brother?" He said, "I do not know; am I my brother's keeper?" And the LORD said, "What have you done? The voice of your brother's blood is crying to me from the ground.*

My friends are *just* talkers!
My eye pours out tears to
God!

16:22 *atque utinam sic iudicaretur vir cum Deo quomodo iudicatur filius hominis cum collega suo*

If only *a* man could be
judged *the* same way
against God,
as *a* human being is judged
against his companion!

16:23 *ecce enim breves anni transeunt et semitam per quam non revertar ambulo*

Because, look,
a few brief years pass
and I walk *a* path
from which I will not return.

Chapter 17

17:1 *spiritus meus adtenuabitur dies mei breviabuntur et solum mihi superest sepulchrum*

My spirit will be diminished.
My days will be shortened,
and only *the* grave is left
to me.

17:2 *non peccavi et in amaritudinibus moratur oculus meus*

I have not sinned,
yet my eye will stay
in bitterness.

17:3 *libera me et pone iuxta te et cuiusvis manus pugnet contra me*

Free me and put *me*
beside You,
and *then* let anyone's hand
fight against me!

17:4 *cor eorum longe fecisti a disciplina et propterea non exaltabuntur*

You made their heart
far from discipline,
and, as a result,

they will not be lifted up.

17:5 *praedam pollicetur sociis et oculi filiorum eius deficient*

He promises plunder
to partners,
yet *the* eyes of his children
will be lacking.

17:6 *posuit me quasi in proverbium vulgi et exemplum sum coram eis*

He placed me like *someone*
in *a* common proverb,
and I am *an* example
before them.

17:7 *caligavit ab indignatione oculus meus et membra mea quasi in nihili redacta sunt*

My eye is darkened
by trauma,
and my members are reduced
as if to nothing.

17:8 *stupebunt iusti super hoc et innocens contra hypocritam suscitabitur*

The fair will be
astounded by this,
and *the* innocent
will be stirred up
against *the* hypocrite.

17:9 *et tenebit iustus viam suam et mundis manibus addet fortitudinem*

And *the* fair will have
his way,
and by clean hands
he will add strength.

17:10 *igitur vos omnes convertimini et venite et non inveniam in vobis ullum sapientem*

Therefore, all of you
are turned upside down,
and you come,
and I will not find anyone
who is wise among you.

17:11 *dies mei transierunt cogitationes meae dissipatae sunt torquentes cor meum*

My days have passed by.
My ideas have been
scattered,
twisting my heart.

17:12 *noctem verterunt in diem et rursum post tenebras spero lucem*

They have turned
night to day,
and after darkness, in turn,
I hope for light.

17:13 *si sustinuero infernus domus mea est in tenebris stravi lectulum meum*

Even if I hold out,
my house is in hell![45]
I have strawed
my bed in darkness.

17:14 *putredini dixi pater meus es mater mea et soror mea vermibus*

I said to rot,
You are my father;
to worms, *you are* my mother
and my sister!

17:15 *ubi est ergo nunc praestolatio mea et patientiam meam quis considerat*

So, where is my reward now?
Who considers my patience?

17:16 *in profundissimum infernum descendent omnia mea putasne saltim ibi erit requies mihi*

All mine will descend
into *the* deepest hell!
You don't believe
rest will be there for me,
do you?

---

[45] House in this context means family, loved ones, and the totality of his domestic life.

Chapter 18

Baldad Responds
18:1 *respondens autem Baldad Suites dixit*

But Baldad *the* Shuhite,
responding, said,

18:2 *usque ad quem finem verba iactabitis intellegite prius et sic loquamur*

Why are you
throwing around words?
Understand first,
and so we may speak.

18:3 *quare reputati sumus ut iumenta et sorduimus coram vobis*

Why are we considered
like dumb animals,
and seem unworthy
before you?[46]

18:4 *qui perdis animam tuam in furore tuo numquid propter te derelinquetur terra et transferentur rupes de loco suo*

You, who are ruining
your soul in your fury,
should earth be abandoned
because of you,
and rocks be moved
from their place?

18:5 *nonne lux impii extinguetur nec splendebit flamma ignis eius*

Won't *the* light
of *the* lawless
be extinguished,
and *the* flame of his fire
not shine forth?

18:6 *lux obtenebrescet in tabernaculo illius et lucerna quae super eum est extinguetur*

The light will be darkened
in his tent,
and *the* lamp which is
over him will be put out.

18:7 *artabuntur gressus virtutis eius et praecipitabit eum consilium suum*

The step of his power
will be closed in,
and his counsel
will throw him down.

---

[46] The "you" in the sentence is plural.

18:8 *inmisit enim in rete pedes suos et in maculis eius ambulat*

For he has put his feet
in *a* trap,
and he tries to walk
in its mesh.

18:9 *tenebitur planta illius laqueo et exardescet contra eum sitis*

His sole *of his foot*
will be caught in *a* trap,
and thirst will burn in him.[47]

18:10 *abscondita est in terra pedica eius et decipula illius super semitam*

His trap is hidden
in *the* ground,
and his snare on *the* path.

18:11 *undique terrebunt eum formidines et involvent pedes eius*

Therefore, *the* hunter's traps
will terrify him,
and will wrap around his feet.

[47] The image is of someone caught in a trap in the desert, dying of thirst.

18:12 *adtenuetur fame robur eius et inedia invadat costas illius*

May his strength
be reduced by hunger,
and starvation invade his
sides.

18:13 *devoret pulchritudinem cutis eius consumat brachia illius primogenita mors*

May it devour
the beauty of his skin.
May death consume
the arms of his firstborn.

18:14 *avellatur de tabernaculo suo fiducia eius et calcet super eum quasi rex interitus*

May his confidence
be wrenched away
from his tent,
and destruction trample him,
like *a* king.

18:15 *habitent in tabernaculo illius socii eius qui non est aspergatur in tabernaculo eius sulphur*

May his companions

live in his tent,
because he no longer exists!
May sulphur be scattered
in his dwelling.

18:16 *deorsum radices eius siccentur sursum autem adteratur messis eius*

May his roots dry up below,
and his harvest diminish
above.

18:17 *memoria illius pereat de terra et non celebretur nomen eius in plateis*

May his memory perish
from *the* earth,
and his name not be
celebrated in public places.

18:18 *expellet eum de luce in tenebras et de orbe transferet eum*

He will expel him
from light into darkness,
and will take him out
of *the* world.

18:19 *non erit semen eius neque progenies in populo suo nec ullae reliquiae in regionibus eius*

His seed will not be found,
nor his offspring
among his people,
nor *any* other reminders
in his region.

18:20 *in die eius stupebunt novissimi et primos invadet horror*

In his day they will be
astounded at *his* end,
and horror will break through
to *the* important.

18:21 *haec sunt ergo tabernacula iniqui et iste locus eius qui ignorat Deum*

Therefore, these are
the tents of *the* treacherous,
and this *is the* place,
of *one* who does not know
God.

Chapter 19

Job Responds

19:1 *respondens autem Iob dixit*

But Job, responding, said,

19:2 *usquequo adfligitis animam meam et adteritis me sermonibus*

How long will you
afflict my soul,
and grind me down
with words?

19:3 *en decies confunditis me et non erubescitis opprimentes me*

Ten times you confound me,
and you aren't ashamed
to push me down.

19:4 *nempe et si ignoravi mecum erit ignorantia mea*

Of course, if I am ignorant,
my ignorance will be
with me.

19:5 *at vos contra me erigimini et arguitis me obprobriis meis*

But you build against me
and argue with me
by taunting me.

19:6 *saltim nunc intellegite quia Deus non aequo iudicio adflixerit me et flagellis suis me cinxerit*

At least know this:
that God has not afflicted me
with *a* fair judgment.
He has surrounded me
by His blows.

19:7 *ecce clamabo vim patiens et nemo audiet vociferabor et non est qui iudicet*

Look *at my* suffering!
I will shout violence,
and no one will hear!
I protest fiercely,
yet *there* is no one
who will judge!

19:8 *semitam meam circumsepsit et transire non possum et in calle meo tenebras posuit*

He has hedged my path,
and I cannot go across,
and has placed darkness
in my way.

19:9 *spoliavit me gloria mea et abstulit coronam de capite meo*

He robbed me of my glory,
and took away *the* crown
from my head.

19:10 *destruxit me undique et pereo et quasi evulsae arbori abstulit spem meam*

He destroyed me completely
and I perish,
and, like *an* uprooted tree,
He took away my hope.

19:11 *iratus est contra me furor eius et sic me habuit quasi hostem suum*

His fury is aroused
against me,
and so He considered me
His enemy.

19:12 *simul venerunt latrones eius et fecerunt sibi viam per me et obsederunt in gyro tabernaculum meum*

At the same time,
His bandits came
and made themselves
a road through me,
and besieged my tent
all around.

19:13 *fratres meos longe fecit a me et noti mei quasi alieni recesserunt a me*

He made my brothers
far from me,
and my acquaintances
pull back from me like
strangers.

19:14 *dereliquerunt me propinqui mei et qui me noverant obliti sunt mei*

My neighbors abandoned me,
and those who knew me
have forgotten me.

19:15 *inquilini domus meae et ancillae meae sicut alienum habuerunt me et quasi peregrinus fui in oculis eorum*

The inhabitants of my house
and my slave women
treat me like *a* stranger,
and I am like *a* homeless *man*
in their eyes.

19:16 *servum meum vocavi et non respondit ore proprio deprecabar illum*

I called my slave
and he didn't answer.
I pleaded with him
by *my* own mouth.

19:17 *halitum meum*
exhorruit uxor mea et
orabam filios uteri mei

My wife shuddered
at my breath,
and I begged from
the children of my womb.

19:18 *stulti quoque*
despiciebant me et cum ab
eis recessissem detrahebant
mihi

Even fools despised me.
When I passed by them,
they ridiculed me.

19:19 *abominati sunt me*
quondam consiliarii mei et
quem maxime diligebam
aversatus est me

Those who once counseled
me have detested me.
The one whom I loved most
has turned away from me.

19:20 *pelli meae consumptis*
carnibus adhesit os meum et
derelicta sunt tantummodo
labia circa dentes meos

My flesh *is* eaten up.
My bone clings to my skin.
and only lips are left
near my teeth.

19:21 *miseremini mei*
miseremini mei saltim vos
amici mei quia manus
Domini tetigit me

Have mercy on me!
At least you have mercy
on me, my friends,
because *the* Lord's hand
has touched me!

19:22 *quare persequimini*
me sicut Deus et carnibus
meis saturamini

Why do you persecute me
like God,
and fill *yourselves*
with my flesh?

19:23 *quis mihi tribuat ut*
scribantur sermones mei quis
mihi det ut exarentur in libro

Who will grant me that my
words be written down?
Who will give me
that they be noted in *a* book,

19:24 *stilo ferreo et plumbi lammina vel certe sculpantur in silice*

by *an* iron pen
and *a* lead plate,
even carved firmly in stone!

19:25 *scio enim quod redemptor meus vivat et in novissimo de terra surrecturus sim*

For I know
that my redeemer may live,
and in *the* end,
I may be raised up
from *the* earth.

19:26 *et rursum circumdabor pelle mea et in carne mea videbo Deum*

and I will be surrounded
once more by my skin,
and in my flesh I will see
God,

19:27 *quem visurus sum ego ipse et oculi mei conspecturi sunt et non alius reposita est haec spes mea in sinu meo*

whom I myself will see,
and my eyes catch sight of,
and not another.
My hope is laid up in this,
in my heart.

19:28 *quare ergo nunc dicitis persequamur eum et radicem verbi inveniamus contra eum*

Why, therefore,
are you now saying,
Let us pursue him,
and find *the* root of words
against him?

19:29 *fugite ergo a facie gladii quoniam ultor iniquitatum gladius est et scitote esse iudicium*

Flee, then,
from *the* face of *the* sword,
because *the* sword
is *the* avenger of treachery,
and understand that
a judgment will take place!

Chapter 20

Sophar the Naamathite Responds

20:1 *respondens autem Sophar Naamathites dixit*

But Sophar the Naamathite,
responding, said,

20:2 *idcirco cogitationes meae variae succedunt sibi et mens in diversa rapitur*

Because of that,
my various thoughts
follow themselves,
and *my* mind is taken away
by different *ideas*.

20:3 *doctrinam qua me arguis audiam et spiritus intellegentiae meae respondebit mihi*

The doctrine
which you advocate to me,
I will hear,
and the spirit of my
intelligence
will respond to me.

20:24 *hoc scio a principio ex quo positus est homo super terram*

This I know from *the*
beginning,
since man was placed on
earth,

20:5 *quod laus impiorum brevis sit et gaudium hypocritae ad instar puncti*

that *the* praise of *the* lawless
may be brief,
and *the* hypocrite's joy
punctured in *an* instant.

20:6 *si ascenderit usque ad caelum superbia eius et caput eius nubes tetigerit*

If his pride should mount
to *the* sky,
and his head should touch
the clouds,

20:7 *quasi sterquilinium in fine perdetur et qui eum viderant dicent ubi est*

in the end he will be lost
like *a* pile of dung,
and those who saw him
will say, Where is he?

20:8 *velut somnium avolans non invenietur transiet sicut visio nocturna*

Like *a* vanishing dream
he will not be found.
He will pass away
like *a* nightmare.

20:9 *oculus qui eum viderat non videbit neque ultra intuebitur eum locus suus*

The eye which saw him
will not see him,
nor will his place
consider him further.

20:10 *filii eius adterentur egestate et manus illius reddent ei dolorem suum*

His children will be ground
down by poverty,
and his hands will pay him
back his pain.

20:11 *ossa eius implebuntur vitiis adulescentiae eius et cum eo in pulverem dormient*

His bones will be filled
by *the* vices of his youth,
and they will sleep
with him in dust.

20:12 *cum enim dulce fuerit in ore eius malum abscondet illud sub lingua sua*

For when evil seems sweet
in his mouth,
he will hide it under his
tongue.

20:13 *parcet illi et non derelinquet illud et celabit in gutture suo*

He will spare it,
and not leave it behind,
and he will hide it
in his throat.

20:14 *panis eius in utero illius vertetur in fel aspidum intrinsecus*

His bread in his stomach
will turn into *an* asp's poison
inside.[48]

20:15 *divitias quas devoravit evomet et de ventre illius extrahet eas Deus*

The riches which
he has devoured
he will vomit,
and God will extract them
from his gut.

20:16 *caput aspidum suget*

---

[48] An asp is a deadly snake from northern Africa.

occidet eum lingua viperae

He will suck *the* asp's head.
The viper's tongue will kill him.

20:17 *non videat rivulos fluminis torrentes mellis et butyri*

May he not see
even rivulets of streams,
flowing with honey and butter.[49]

20:18 *luet quae fecit omnia nec tamen consumetur iuxta multitudinem adinventionum suarum sic et sustinebit*

He will pay
for all that he did,
nor yet be consumed
alongside the multitude
of his accomplishment.
Thus also he will be held back.

20:19 *quoniam confringens nudavit pauperes domum rapuit et non aedificavit eam*

Because, breaking in,
he stripped *the* house
of *the* poor.
He tore down
and did not build,

20:20 *nec est satiatus venter eius et cum habuerit quae cupierat possidere non poterit*

nor was his belly satisfied.
When he has what he wants,
he won't be able to keep it.

20:21 *non remansit de cibo eius et propterea nihil permanebit de bonis eius*

Nothing remains
from his *own* food,
and, because of this
nothing will endure
from his goods.

20:22 *cum satiatus fuerit artabitur aestuabit et omnis dolor inruet in eum*

When he reaches satisfaction
he will be hemmed in.
He will boil, and every pain
will rush in on him.

20:23 *utinam impleatur venter eius ut emittat in eum*

---

[49] Compare to RSV Exodus 3:8 *I have come down to deliver them out of the hand of the Egyptians, and to bring them up out of that land to a good and broad land, a land flowing with milk and honey . . .*

*iram furoris sui et pluat
super illum bellum suum*

If only his belly
might be filled,
that *God* may drive out on
him *the* anger of *His* fury,
and rain his conflict
down on him!

20:24 *fugiet arma ferrea et
inruet in arcum aereum*

He will flee iron weapons,
and throw *himself*
under *a* bronze arrow.

20:25 *eductus et egrediens
de vagina sua et fulgurans in
amaritudine sua vadent et
venient super eum horribiles*

Drawn out and coming forth
from their sheaths,
and shining in their bitterness
they will advance,
and horrible *things*
will come upon him.

20:26 *omnes tenebrae
absconditae sunt in occultis
eius devorabit eum ignis qui
non succenditur adfligetur
relictus in tabernaculo suo*

All shadows are hidden
in his darkness
Fire which is not burned
will devour him,
The one left in his tent
will be afflicted.

20:27 *revelabunt caeli
iniquitatem eius et terra
consurget adversus eum*

The skies will reveal
his treachery,
and earth will rise up
against him.

20:28 *apertum erit germen
domus illius detrahetur in die
furoris Dei*

The offspring of his house
will be exposed.
He will be taken away
in *the* day of God's fury.

20:29 *haec est pars hominis
impii a Deo et hereditas
verborum eius a Domino*

This is *a* lawless man's
portion from God,
and *the* legacy of his actions
from *the* Lord.

Chapter 21

21:1 *respondens autem Iob dixit*

But Job, responding, said

21:2 *audite quaeso sermones meos et agetis paenitentiam*

Hear my words, I pray,
and you will feel regret.

21:3 *sustinete me ut et ego loquar et post mea si videbitur verba ridete*

Put up with me,
and I will speak,
and after my words
it will be seen if you laugh.

21:4 *numquid contra hominem disputatio mea est ut merito non debeam contristari*

Is my dispute against *a* man,
that rightly I shouldn't
be depressed?

21:5 *adtendite me et obstupescite et superponite digitum ori vestro*

Pay attention to me
and be astounded,
and put your finger
over your mouth!

21:6 *et ego quando recordatus fuero pertimesco et concutit carnem meam tremor*

Even I, when I am reminded,
am terrified,
and shaking rocks my flesh.

21:7 *quare ergo impii vivunt sublevati sunt confortatique divitiis*

Why, then, do *the* lawless
go on living?
They are lifted up,
and comforted by riches.

21:8 *semen eorum permanet coram eis propinquorum turba et nepotum in conspectu eorum*

Their seed endures
before them,
uproar of their neighbors,
and grandchildren in their
sight.

21:9 *domus eorum securae sunt et pacatae et non est virga Dei super illos*

Their homes
are secure and peaceful,
and God's correction
is not over them.

21:10 *bos eorum concepit et non abortit vacca peperit et non est privata fetu suo*

Their ox has conceived
and doesn't abort.
Their cow has given birth
and is not deprived of her calf.

21:11 *egrediuntur quasi greges parvuli eorum et infantes eorum exultant lusibus*

Their little ones
go out like flocks,
and their infants
exult in luxuries.

21:12 *tenent tympanum et citharam et gaudent ad sonitum organi*

They have tympanies[50]
and harps,
and rejoice to *the* sound
of organs.

21:13 *ducunt in bonis dies suos et in puncto ad inferna descendunt*

They lead their days
in good *things*,
and descend to *the* inferno.
in an instant,

21:14 *qui dixerunt Deo recede a nobis et scientiam viarum tuarum nolumus*

who say to God,
Leave us alone,
and, We don't want
knowledge of Your ways.

21:15 *quid est Omnipotens ut serviamus ei et quid nobis prodest si oraverimus illum*

What is *the* Omnipotent,
that we should serve Him,
and what good is *it* to us
if we pray to Him?

21:16 *verumtamen quia non sunt in manu eorum bona sua consilium impiorum longe sit a me*

Nevertheless,
because their good
is not in their hands,
let *the* counsel

---

[50] A tympani is an musical instrument, resembling a small drum.

of *the* lawless be
far from me.

21:17 *quotiens lucerna impiorum extinguetur et superveniet eis inundatio et dolores dividet furoris sui*

How often
the lamp of *the* wicked
will be extinguished,
and *a* flood come over them,
and He will divide
the pains of His fury.

21:18 *erunt sicut paleae ante faciem venti et sicut favilla quam turbo dispergit*

They will be like chaff
before *the* face of *the* wind,
and like ash
when *the* wind stirs *it*.

21:19 *Deus servabit filiis illius dolorem patris et cum reddiderit tunc sciet*

God will store up
the father's pain for his children,
and when He repays,
then he will understand.

21:20 *videbunt oculi eius interfectionem suam et de furore Omnipotentis bibet*

His eyes will watch
his destruction,
and he will drink
from *the* fury
of *the* Omnipotent.

21:21 *quid enim ad eum pertinet de domo sua post se et si numerus mensuum eius dimidietur*

For what will belong to him
from his house after him,
if *the* number of his months
is cut in half?

21:22 *numquid Deum quispiam docebit scientiam qui excelsos iudicat*

Will someone
teach God knowledge,
who judges *the* highest?

21:23 *iste moritur robustus et sanus dives et felix*

One *person* dies
strong and healthy,
rich and happy.

21:24 *viscera eius plena sunt adipe et medullis ossa illius inrigantur*

His insides are full of fat,
and *the* marrow of his bones
is nourished.

21:25 *alius vero moritur in amaritudine animae absque ullis opibus*

Someone else truly
dies in bitterness of spirit,
apart from any resources.

21:26 *et tamen simul in pulverem dormient et vermes operient eos*

and yet, at *the* same time,
they will sleep in dust,
and worms will cover them.

21:27 *certe novi cogitationes vestras et sententias contra me iniquas*

Of course I knew
your twisted thoughts
and sentences against me.

21:28 *dicitis enim ubi est domus principis et ubi tabernacula impiorum*

For you said,
Where is *the* house
of *the* princes,
and Where *are*
the tents of *the* lawless?

21:29 *interrogate quemlibet de viatoribus et haec eadem eum intellegere cognoscetis*

Question whoever you please
from passersby,
and you will recognize *that*
he understands these *things*
too.

21:30 *quia in diem perditionis servabitur malus et ad diem furoris ducitur*

Because an evil *man*
will be guarded
on *the* day of judgment,
and led to *the* day of fury.

21:31 *quis arguet coram eo viam eius et quae fecit quis reddet illi*

Who will argue
his way before *God*,
and who will repay *God*
what He does?

21:32 *ipse ad sepulchra ducetur et in congerie mortuorum vigilabit*

He will be led to *the* grave,
and he will keep vigil

in *a* heap of *the* dead.

21:33 *dulcis fuit glareis Cocyti et post se omnem hominem trahet et ante se innumerabiles*

He has been sweet
to *the* gravel of Cocyti,[51]
and he will bring
every man after him,
and before him
they are numberless.

21:34 *quomodo igitur consolamini me frustra cum responsio vestra repugnare ostensa sit veritati*

How, then,
will you console me vainly,
when your response
is shown to be
repugnant to truth?

[51] Compare to RSV: *The clods of the valley are sweet to him.*

Chapter 22

22:1 *respondens autem Eliphaz Themanites dixit*

But Eliphaz *the* Themanite,
responding, said,

22:2 *numquid Deo conparari potest homo etiam cum perfectae fuerit scientiae*

Man can't be compared
to God, can he,
even if his knowledge
were perfect?

22:3 *quid prodest Deo si iustus fueris aut quid ei confers si inmaculata fuerit via tua*

What benefit is *it* to God
if you are fair,
or what do you confer
on Him
if your way is spotless?

22:4 *numquid timens arguet te et veniet tecum in iudicium*

Aren't you afraid
He will dispute you
and bring you with Him
into judgment,

22:5 *et non propter malitiam tuam plurimam et infinitas iniquitates tuas*

and not on account of
your many evil *deeds*
and your infinite treacheries?

22:6 *abstulisti enim pignus fratrum tuorum sine causa et nudos spoliasti vestibus*

For you have taken away
your brothers' pledge[52]
without cause,
and stripped them naked
of clothes.

22:7 *aquam lasso non dedisti et esurienti subtraxisti panem*

You have not given water
to *the* weary,
and have taken bread
away from *the* hungry.

22:8 *in fortitudine brachii tui possidebas terram et potentissimus obtinebas eam*

You possessed *the* land
in *the* strength of your arm,
and, *being the* most powerful,
you took it.

22:9 *viduas dimisisti vacuas et lacertos pupillorum comminuisti*

You have sent
widows away empty,
and have broken
the strength of orphans.

22:10 *propterea circumdatus es laqueis et conturbat te formido subita*

This is why
you are captured by snares,
and *a* hunter's trap
disturbs you suddenly!

22:11 *et putabas te tenebras non visurum et impetu aquarum inundantium non oppressurum*

And you supposed
you wouldn't see shadows,
and *the* force of flood-waters
wouldn't oppress you.

22:12 *an cogitas quod Deus excelsior caelo et super stellarum vertices sublimetur*

---

[52] A pledge is an item given as collateral, to secure a debt or promise. In this case, the pledge is a garment.

Or did you think
that God is higher
than *the* sky
and over *the* stars?

22:13 *et dicis quid enim novit Deus et quasi per caliginem iudicat*

And you said,
For what did God know,
and, He judges as if in gloom.

22:14 *nubes latibulum eius nec nostra considerat et circa cardines caeli perambulat*

His hiding place
is the clouds,
nor does He consider us,
and He walks near
the corners of *the* sky.

22:15 *numquid semitam saeculorum custodire cupis quam calcaverunt viri iniqui*

Do you want to keep
the path of *the* ages,
which treacherous men
have trampled?

22:16 *qui sublati sunt ante tempus suum et fluvius subvertit fundamentum eorum*

They are taken away
before their time,
and *a* river has undermined
their foundation.

22:17 *qui dicebant Deo recede a nobis et quasi nihil possit facere Omnipotens aestimabant eum*

They say to God,
Turn away from us,
and considered Him
as if *the* Omnipotent
could do nothing,

22:18 *cum ille implesset domos eorum bonis quorum sententia procul sit a me*

when He filled their homes
with good *things*,
May their opinions
be far from me!

22:19 *videbunt iusti et laetabuntur et innocens subsannabit eos*

The fair will see and rejoice,
and *the* innocent will mock
them.

22:20 *nonne succisa est erectio eorum et reliquias eorum devoravit ignis*

Wasn't their building
cut down,
and their remnants
devoured by fire?

22:21 *adquiesce igitur ei et habeto pacem et per haec habebis fructus optimos*

Rest, therefore, in Him,
and have peace,
and through this
you will have *the* best results.

22:22 *suscipe ex ore illius legem et pone sermones eius in corde tuo*

Receive *the* law
from His mouth,
and put His teachings
in your heart.

22:23 *si reversus fueris ad Omnipotentem aedificaberis et longe facies iniquitatem a tabernaculo tuo*

If you return yourself
to *the* Omnipotent,
you will be built up,
and you will put treachery
far from your tent.

22:24 *dabit pro terra silicem et pro silice torrentes aureos*

He will give you stones for
dirt,
and for stones torrents of
gold.

22:25 *eritque Omnipotens contra hostes tuos et argentum coacervabitur tibi*

And *the* Omnipotent
will be against your enemies,
and will pile up silver for
you.

22:26 *tunc super Omnipotentem deliciis afflues et elevabis ad Deum faciem tuam*

Then you will enjoy delights
from *the* Omnipotent,
and will lift up your face to
God.

22:27 *rogabis eum et exaudiet te et vota tua reddes*

You will pray to Him
and He will hear you,
and you will repay your
promise.

22:28 *decernes rem et veniet tibi et in viis tuis splendebit lumen*

You will discern *a* thing
and it will come to you,
and in your strength,
light will shine .

22:29 *qui enim humiliatus fuerit erit in gloria et qui inclinaverit oculos suos ipse salvabitur*

For one who was humbled
will be in glory,
and one who lowered his
eyes, he will be saved.

22:30 *salvabitur innocens salvabitur autem munditia manuum suarum*

The innocent will be saved,
but he will be saved
by *the* cleanness of his hands.

Chapter 23

23:1 *respondens autem Iob dixit*

But Job, responding, said,

23:2 *nunc quoque in amaritudine est sermo meus et manus plagae meae adgravata est super gemitum meum*

Now, also, my speech
is in bitterness,
and *the* hand of my affliction
is made worse than my
moaning.

23:3 *quis mihi tribuat ut cognoscam et inveniam illum et veniam usque ad solium eius*

Who will grant me
that I might know
how to find Him,
and come even to His throne?

23:4 *ponam coram eo iudicium et os meum replebo increpationibus*

I would place *my* cause
before Him,
and my mouth will be filled

with reproaches,

23:5 *ut sciam verba quae mihi respondeat et intellegam quid loquatur mihi*

so I could know
the words with which
He would respond to me,
and understand what
He would say to me.

23:6 *nolo multa fortitudine contendat mecum nec magnitudinis suae mole me premat*

I don't want
His tremendous strength
to contend with me,
or *the* immensity
of His greatness
to crush me.

23:7 *proponat aequitatem contra me et perveniat ad victoriam iudicium meum*

Let Him propose fairness
against me,
and my cause
may come to victory.

23:8 *si ad orientem iero non apparet si ad occidentem non intellegam eum*

If I walk to *the* east,
He doesn't appear.
If *I walk* to *the* west,
I will not understand Him.

23:9 *si ad sinistram quid agat non adprehendam eum si me vertam ad dextram non videbo illum*

If to *the* left,
what can be done?
I will not find Him.
If I turn to *the* right,
I will not see Him.

23:10 *ipse vero scit viam meam et probavit me quasi aurum quod per ignem transit*

Truly, He knows my way,
and has proved me like gold
that passed through fire.

23:11 *vestigia eius secutus est pes meus viam eius custodivi et non declinavi ex ea*

My foot has followed
His steps.
I have kept His way
and not turned aside from it.

23:12 *a mandatis labiorum*

eius non recessi et in sinu
meo abscondi verba oris eius

I have not turned back
from *the* commands
of His lips,
and I have hidden
the words of His mouth
in my being.

23:13 *ipse enim solus est et*
nemo avertere potest
cogitationem eius et anima
eius quodcumque voluerit
hoc facit

For He is unique,
and no one can hide
from His awareness,
and whatever His soul has
wished, this He does.

23:14 *cum expleverit in me*
voluntatem suam et alia
multa similia praesto sunt ei

When He has completed
His will in me,
many other similar *things*
also are ready for Him.

23:15 *et idcirco a facie eius*
turbatus sum et considerans
eum timore sollicitor

Therefore, I am agitated
by His face,
and disturbed by fear
considering Him.

23:16 *Deus mollivit cor*
meum et Omnipotens
conturbavit me

God has melted my heart,
and *the* Omnipotent
has disquieted me.

23:17 *non enim perii propter*
inminentes tenebras nec
faciem meam operuit caligo

For I have not perished
on account of impending
darkness,
nor has He covered
my face in gloom.

Chapter 24

24:1 *ab Omnipotente non sunt abscondita tempora qui autem noverunt eum ignorant dies illius*

Times are not hidden
from *the* Omnipotent,
but those who know Him
do not know His days.

24:2 *alii terminos transtulerunt diripuerunt greges et paverunt eos*

Some have taken away
boundary posts.
They have torn apart flocks
and eaten them.

24:3 *asinum pupillorum abigerunt et abstulerunt pro pignore bovem viduae*

They have driven away
the orphan's donkey,
and taken *the* widow's ox
for *a* pledge.

24:4 *subverterunt pauperum viam et oppresserunt pariter mansuetos terrae*

They have undermined
the poor man's way,
and oppressed together
the humble of earth.

24:5 *alii quasi onagri in deserto egrediuntur ad opus suum vigilantesque ad praedam praeparant panem liberis*

Others, like wild asses
in *the* desert,
go toward their work,
and watching for prey,
prepare *their* children's
bread.

24:6 *agrum non suum demetunt et vineam eius quem vi oppresserunt vindemiant*

They don't work
their own field,
and they harvest *the* vineyard
of one whom they oppress
by force.

24:7 *nudos dimittunt homines indumenta tollentes quibus non est operimentum in frigore*

They have sent men out
stripped, taking their coats,
leaving them uncovered
in winter,

24:8 *quos imbres montium rigant et non habentes velamen amplexantur lapides*

whom mountain rains drench,
and, having no *a* covering,
they embrace stones.

24:9 *vim fecerunt depraedantes pupillos et vulgum pauperem spoliaverunt*

Plundering orphans
has made them strong,
and they have robbed
the common poor,

24:10 *nudis et incedentibus absque vestitu et esurientibus tulerunt spicas*

leaving him stripped
and walking without
clothing.
And they have taken away
the grain of *the* hungry.

24:11 *inter acervos eorum meridiati sunt qui calcatis torcularibus sitiunt*

They have napped
amidst *the* treasures
of those who,
having trampled *the* wine
press, *still* thirst.

24:12 *de civitatibus fecerunt viros gemere et anima vulneratorum clamavit et Deus inultum abire non patitur*

They made *the* men
of the city groan,
and *the* soul
of *the* wounded cried out,
and God did not allow them
to go unpunished.

24:13 *ipsi fuerunt rebelles luminis nescierunt vias eius nec reversi sunt per semitas illius*

They were rebels
to *the* light.
They have not known
His ways,
nor have they turned back
from His path.

24:14 *mane primo consurgit homicida interficit egenum et pauperem per noctem vero erit quasi fur*

Early in the morning
the murderer gets up.
He destroys *the* needy
and *the* poor.

Truly, at night he will be
like *a* robber.

24:15 *oculus adulteri observat caliginem dicens non me videbit oculus et operiet vultum suum*

The adulterer's eye
watches *the* gloom, saying,
Eye will not see me,
and he will cover his face.

24:16 *perfodit in tenebris domos sicut in die condixerant sibi et ignoraverunt lucem*

He breaks through homes
in darkness,
as in day they had agreed
among themselves,
and they have not known
the light.

24:17 *si subito apparuerit aurora arbitrantur umbram mortis et sic in tenebris quasi in luce ambulant*

If dawn should arise
suddenly,
they are observed by
the shadow of death,
and they carry on in darkness,
as if in *the* light.

24:18 *levis est super faciem aquae maledicta sit pars eius in terra nec ambulet per viam vinearum*

He is slippery
over *the* face of waters.
May cursing be
his portion on earth,
nor may he walk
by *the* way of *the* vineyards.

24:19 *ad nimium calorem transeat ab aquis nivium et usque ad inferos peccatum illius*

Let him pass from snow melt
to too much heat,
and his sin even to *the* dead.

24:20 *obliviscatur eius misericordia dulcedo illius vermes non sit in recordatione sed conteratur quasi lignum infructuosum*

May mercy forget him,
his sweetness *be* for worms.
May he not be remembered,
but be destroyed
like *an* unfruitful tree.

24:21 *pavit enim sterilem et quae non parit et viduae bene non fecit*

For he has struck
the childless,
and she who has not
given birth,
and he has not done right
by *the* widow.

24:22 *detraxit fortes in fortitudine sua et cum steterit non credet vitae suae*

He has torn down *the* strong
in his strength,
and when he stands,
he will not trust his life
to others.

24:23 *dedit ei Deus locum paenitentiae et ille abutitur eo in superbiam oculi autem eius sunt in viis illius*

God gave him room
for regret,
and he misused it
in *his* pride.
But God's eyes are on his
ways.

24:24 *elevati sunt ad modicum et non subsistent et humiliabuntur sicut omnia et auferentur et sicut summitates spicarum conterentur*

They were lifted up
a short while,
yet will not remain.
And they will be humiliated,
like all *things*, and taken
away,
and like heads of grain
they will be crushed.

24:25 *quod si non est ita quis me potest arguere esse mentitum et ponere ante Deum verba mea*

For if this isn't so,
who can show me
to be *a* liar,
and put my words
before God?

Chapter 25

Baldad Responds[53]

25:1 *respondens autem Baldad Suites dixit*

But Baldad *the* Shuhite,
responding, said,

25:2 *potestas et terror apud eum est qui facit concordiam in sublimibus suis*

Power and terror
are with Him,
who makes concord
in His highest places.

25:3 *numquid est numerus militum eius et super quem non surget lumen illius*

Is there *a* number
of his soldiers?
Over whom does His light
not rise?

25:4 *numquid iustificari potest homo conparatus Deo aut apparere mundus natus de muliere*

Can man be justified
compared to God,
or appear clean,
born of woman?

25:5 *ecce etiam luna non splendet et stellae non sunt mundae in conspectu eius*

Look, even *the* moon
does not shine
and *the* stars
are not pure in His sight.

25:6 *quanto magis homo putredo et filius hominis vermis*

How much more
man *who* rots,
and *a* son of man
eaten by worms!

---

[53] Chapter 25 is fragmentary in the most reliable sources.

Chapter 26

Job Responds
26:1 *respondens autem Iob dixit*

But Job, responding, said,

26:2 *cuius adiutor es numquid inbecilli et sustentas brachium eius qui non est fortis*

Who are you helping?
One who *is* feeble?
And are you sustaining His arm, who isn't strong?

26:3 *cui dedisti consilium forsitan illi qui non habet sapientiam et prudentiam tuam ostendisti plurimam*

To whom have you
given counsel?
Perhaps to one who isn't wise?
Have you shown
your great prudence?

26:4 *quem docere voluisti nonne eum qui fecit spiramen tuum*

Whom do you want to teach?
Isn't it Him who made
your breath?

26:5 *ecce gigantes gemunt sub aquis et qui habitant cum eis*

Look, giant *beasts*
groan beneath *the* waters,
and those that live with them.

26:6 *nudus est inferus coram illo et nullum est operimentum perditioni*

The dead is stripped open
before Him,
and *the* covering of
destruction is nothing;

26:7 *qui extendit aquilonem super vacuum et adpendit terram super nihili*

Who extends *the* north wind
over *the* void,
and hangs *the* earth over
nothing;

26:8 *qui ligat aquas in nubibus suis ut non erumpant pariter deorsum*

Who binds waters
in His clouds,
that they not erupt
together downward;

26:9 *qui tenet vultum solii sui et expandit super illud nebulam suam*

Who holds *the* face
of his throne,
and spreads out
his cloud over it.[54]

26:10 *terminum circumdedit aquis usque dum finiantur lux et tenebrae*

He prescribed *the* limit
of *the* waters,
up to *the* point where
light and darkness are ended.

26:11 *columnae caeli contremescunt et pavent ad nutum eius*

The columns of *the* sky
tremble together,
and are terrified at His nod.

26:12 *in fortitudine illius repente maria congregata sunt et prudentia eius percussit superbum*

In His strength,
the seas are gathered
at once,
and His prudence
pounds *the* proud.

26:13 *spiritus eius ornavit caelos et obsetricante manu eius eductus est coluber tortuosus*

His Spirit
has adorned *the* skies,
and by *the* midwifery
of His hand,
the twisting serpent
is led forth.

26:14 *ecce haec ex parte dicta sunt viarum eius et cum vix parvam stillam sermonis eius audierimus quis poterit tonitruum magnitudinis illius intueri*

Look, these *things*
are said about
a portion of His ways!
When we have heard
hardly *a* tiny drop
of His word,
who can consider
the thunders of His
immensity?

---

[54] Compare to RSV: *He covers the face of the moon, and spreads over it his cloud.*

Chapter 27

27:1 *addidit quoque Iob adsumens parabolam suam et dixit*

And Job also added,
resuming his parable,
and said,

27:2 *vivit Deus qui abstulit iudicium meum et Omnipotens qui ad amaritudinem adduxit animam meam*

God lives,
who has taken away
my cause,
and *the* Omnipotent,
who has brought me
to bitterness.

27:3 *quia donec superest halitus in me et spiritus Dei in naribus meis*

Because, as long as
breath remains in me
and *the* Spirit of God
in my nostrils,

27:4 *non loquentur labia mea iniquitatem nec lingua mea meditabitur mendacium*

my lips will not
speak treachery,
nor will my tongue
meditate on lies.

27:5 *absit a me ut iustos vos esse iudicem donec deficiam non recedam ab innocentia mea*

Far be it from me,
that I judge you to be fair!
Until I die I will not
turn away from my
innocence.

27:6 *iustificationem meam quam coepi tenere non deseram nec enim reprehendit me cor meum in omni vita mea*

My justification,
which I began to have,
I have not deserted,
for my heart has not
reproached me
in all my life.

27:7 *sit ut impius inimicus meus et adversarius meus quasi iniquus*

May my enemy be
like *the* lawless,
and my adversary

like *the* treacherous.

27:8 *quae enim spes est hypocritae si avare rapiat et non liberet Deus animam eius*

For what hope is there
for *the* hypocrite
if he plunders greedily?
God will not free his soul.

27:9 *numquid clamorem eius Deus audiet cum venerit super illum angustia*

Will God hear his cry
when anguish comes over him?

27:10 *aut poterit in Omnipotente delectari et invocare Deum in omni tempore*

Nor will he
be able to delight
in *the* Omnipotent,
or invoke God at all times.

27:11 *docebo vos per manum Dei quae Omnipotens habeat nec abscondam*

I will teach you
by *the* hand of God,
what *the* Omnipotent has,
nor will I hide *it*.

27:12 *ecce vos omnes nostis et quid sine causa vana loquimini*

Look, you all know *it*,
so why do you speak
vainly, without cause?

27:13 *haec est pars hominis impii apud Deum et hereditas violentorum quam ab Omnipotente suscipient*

This is *the* portion
of *a* lawless man with God,
and *the* inheritance
of *the* violent,
which he will receive
from *the* Omnipotent.

27:14 *si multiplicati fuerint filii eius in gladio erunt et nepotes eius non saturabuntur pane*

If his children are multiplied,
they will go to *the* sword,
and his grandchildren
will not be filled with bread.

27:15 *qui reliqui fuerint ex eo sepelientur in interitu et viduae illius non plorabunt*

Those who are left from him
will be buried in destruction,
and their widows will not
weep.

27:16 *si conportaverit quasi terram argentum et sicut lutum praeparaverit vestimenta*

If he amasses silver like dirt,
and prepares garments like
clay,

27:17 *praeparabit quidem sed iustus vestietur illis et argentum innocens dividet*

he will prepare, indeed,
but *the* fair will wear them,
and *the* innocent
will divide *his* silver.

27:18 *aedificavit sicut tinea domum suam et sicut custos fecit umbraculum*

He has built his house
like *a* moth,
and made his keepers *a*
shelter.

27:19 *dives cum dormierit nihil secum auferet aperit oculos suos et nihil inveniet*

Yet a rich man,
when he sleeps,
will carry nothing
away with him.
He will open his eyes
and will find nothing.

27:20 *adprehendit eum quasi aqua inopia nocte opprimet eum tempestas*

Poverty will
wash over him like water.
A storm will oppress him
by night.

27:21 *tollet eum ventus urens et auferet et velut turbo rapiet eum de loco suo*

A burning wind
will take him,
and carry *him* away,
and, like *a* tornado,
will rip him from his place.

27:22 *et mittet super eum et non parcet de manu eius fugiens fugiet*

And He will send *it* over him,
and not spare from His hand.
In great haste, he will flee.

27:23 *stringet super eum manus suas et sibilabit super* *illum intuens locum eius*

God will draw
his hands tight over him,
and will hiss at him,
considering his position.

Chapter 28

28:1 *habet argentum venarum suarum principia et auro locus est in quo conflatur*

Silver has beginnings
of its veins,
and gold is found,
which is purified.[55]

28:2 *ferrum de terra tollitur et lapis solutus calore in aes vertitur*

Iron is taken from *the* earth,
and stone melted by heat
becomes bronze.

28:3 *tempus posuit tenebris et universorum finem ipse considerat lapidem quoque caliginis et umbram mortis*

He set *a* time
for darkness,
and *an* end of all *things*.
He considers stones,

---

[55] This chapter compares ancient mining practices to the search for wisdom. See Peake's Commentary on the Bible, Matthew Black, editor, Thomas Nelson, Nashville, 1962, pg. 403 (Hereafter cited as Peake's Commentary). As a hymn to wisdom, it is probably a separate poem integrated into the book.

and also gloom
and *the* shadow of death.

28:4 *dividit torrens a populo peregrinante eos quos oblitus est pes egentis hominum et invios*

A rushing stream divides
a traveling people,
those whom
the foot of needy men
have forgotten,
unreachable.[56]

28:5 *terra de qua oriebatur panis in loco suo igne subversa est*

The land
from which bread arises
is undone by fire
in its place.

28:6 *locus sapphyri lapides eius et glebae illius aurum*

Its stones *are*
the place of sapphires,
and its clods are gold.

[56] Compare to RSV: *They open shafts in a valley away from where men live; they are forgotten by travelers, they hang afar from men, they swing to and fro.*

28:7 *semitam ignoravit avis nec intuitus est oculus vulturis*

The bird has not known
its path,
nor has *the* vulture's eye
seen it.

28:8 *non calcaverunt eam filii institorum nec pertransivit per eam leaena*

The merchants' children
have not walked over it,
nor has *the* lioness
passed through it.[57]

28:9 *ad silicem extendit manum suam subvertit a radicibus montes*

He stretches out his hand
to stone.
He overturns *the* roots
of mountains.

28:10 *in petris rivos excidit et omne pretiosum vidit oculus eius*

He cuts streams into rocks,

[57] Compare to RSV: *The proud beasts have not trodden it; the lion has not passed over it.*

and his eye sees
everything precious.

28:11 *profunda quoque fluviorum scrutatus est et abscondita produxit in lucem*

Even *the* depth of rivers
is examined,
and he has brought
hidden *things* to light.

28:12 *sapientia vero ubi invenitur et quis est locus intellegentiae*

But truly,
where can wisdom
be found,
and who is *the* place
of understanding?[58]

28:13 *nescit homo pretium eius nec invenitur in terra suaviter viventium*

Man does not know
its price,
nor it is found
among those living
at ease on earth.

[58] The "place of understanding" is a person, denoted by *quis*, rather than a thing, denoted by *quid*.

28:14 *abyssus dicit non est in me et mare loquitur non est mecum*

The abyss said,
It is not in me,
and *the* sea says,
It is not with me.

28:15 *non dabitur aurum obrizum pro ea nec adpendetur argentum in commutatione eius*

Fine gold
will not be given
for it,
nor will silver
be weighed out
in its exchange.

28:16 *non conferetur tinctis Indiae coloribus nec lapidi sardonico pretiosissimo vel sapphyro*

Dyes of *the* colors of India
will not be traded *for it*,
nor most precious stones
of sardonyx or sapphire.

28:17 *non adaequabitur ei aurum vel vitrum nec commutabuntur pro ea vasa auri*

Gold will not adequate for it,
nor blue dye,
neither can golden vases
be exchanged for it.

28:18 *excelsa et eminentia non memorabuntur conparatione eius trahitur autem sapientia de occultis*

The most exalted
and eminent
will not be remembered
in comparison to it.
But wisdom is derived
from hiddenness.

28:19 *non adaequabitur ei topazium de Aethiopia nec tincturae mundissimae conponetur*

Topaz from Ethiopia
will not be equal to it,
nor will it be constructed
from *the* purest inks.

28:20 *unde ergo sapientia veniet et quis est locus intellegentiae*

Where, then,
will wisdom come from,
and who is *the* place
of understanding?

28:21 *abscondita est ab oculis omnium viventium volucres quoque caeli latet*

Wisdom is hidden
from *the* eyes
of all *the* living
and unseen by
the birds of *the* sky.

28:22 *perditio et mors dixerunt auribus nostris audivimus famam eius*

Destruction and death said,
Our ears have heard its fame.

28:23 *Deus intellegit viam eius et ipse novit locum illius*

God knows its way,
and He has known its place.

28:24 *ipse enim fines mundi intuetur et omnia quae sub caelo sunt respicit*

For He looks upon
the limits of *the* world,
and sees all *things*
that are under *the* sky.

28:25 *qui fecit ventis pondus et aquas adpendit mensura*

The One who made *a* weight

for *the* winds,
and weighed out
the waters by measure,

28:26 *quando ponebat pluviis legem et viam procellis sonantibus*

when he placed *a* law
on *the* rains,
and on *the* way
of thundering storms.

28:27 *tunc vidit illam et enarravit et praeparavit et investigavit*

Then He saw it,
and has told *of it*,
and prepared,
and investigated.

28:28 *et dixit homini ecce timor Domini ipsa est sapientia et recedere a malo intellegentia*

And He said to man,
Look, fear of *the* Lord,
this is wisdom,
and to turn away from evil
is intelligence.

Chapter 29

29:1 *addidit quoque Iob adsumens parabolam suam et dixit*

And Job also added,
resuming his parable,
and said,

29:2 *quis mihi tribuat ut sim iuxta menses pristinos secundum dies quibus Deus custodiebat me*

Who will grant me
that I may be like
I was in former months,
like *the* days in which
God guarded me;

29:3 *quando splendebat lucerna eius super caput meum et ad lumen eius ambulabam in tenebris*

when His lamp shone
over my head,
and I walked to His light
in darkness?

29:4 *sicut fui in diebus adulescentiae meae quando secreto Deus erat in tabernaculo meo*

As I was
in *the* days of my youth,
when God was in
the secret *place*
of my tent,

29:5 *quando erat Omnipotens mecum et in circuitu meo pueri mei*

when *the* Omnipotent
was with me,
and my servants
around me;

29:6 *quando lavabam pedes meos butyro et petra fundebat mihi rivos olei*

when I washed my feet
with butter,
when a rock
poured out to me
streams of oil;

29:7 *quando procedebam ad portam civitatis et in platea parabant cathedram mihi*

when I went
to *the* city's gate,
and in *the* streets
they prepared *a* seat
for me.

29:8 *videbant me iuvenes et absconsdebantur et senes adsurgentes stabant*

Young people saw me
and hid themselves,
and the old, rising up,
stood.

29:9 *principes cessabant loqui et digitum superponebant ori suo*

Princes ceased talking
and put their finger
over their mouth.

29:10 *vocem suam cohibebant duces et lingua eorum gutturi suo adherebat*

Leaders restrained
their voice,
and their tongue stuck
in their throat.

29:11 *auris audiens beatificabat me et oculus videns testimonium reddebat mihi*

The ear, hearing,
blessed me,
and *the* eye, seeing,
returned testimony to me,

29:12 *quod liberassem*

pauperem vociferantem et pupillum cui non esset adiutor

because I liberated
the poor man crying out,
and *the* orphan,
who had no helper.

29:13 *benedictio perituri super me veniebat et cor viduae consolatus sum*

The blessing
of those about to perish
came over me,
and I was consolation
to *the* widow's heart.

29:14 *iustitia indutus sum et vestivit me sicut vestimento et diademate iudicio meo*

I was dressed in fairness,
and I dressed myself
by *the* garment and crown
of my judgment.

29:15 *oculus fui caeco et pes claudo*

I was *an* eye to *the* blind
and *a* foot to *the* lame.

29:16 *pater eram pauperum et causam quam nesciebam diligentissime investigabam*

I was *a* father to *the* poor
and *the* cause I did not know,
I investigated diligently.

29:17 *conterebam molas iniqui et de dentibus illius auferebam praedam*

I broke *the* jaws
of *the* lawless,
and took away *the* prey
from their teeth.

29:18 *dicebamque in nidulo meo moriar et sicut palma multiplicabo dies*

And I said,
I will die
in my little nest,
and like *a* palm tree,
I will multiply *my* days.

29:19 *radix mea aperta est secus aquas et ros morabitur in messione mea*

My root is open
beside waters,
and *the* dew
will stay in my harvest.

29:20 *gloria mea semper innovabitur et arcus meus in*

manu mea instaurabitur

My glory
will always be renewed,
and my bow in my hand
will be restored.

29:21 *qui me audiebant expectabant sententiam et intenti tacebant ad consilium meum*

Those who heard me
expected *a wise* opinion,
and were silent,
eager for my counsel.

29:22 *verbis meis addere nihil audebant et super illos stillabat eloquium meum*

Nothing was heard
to add to my words,
and my eloquence
dripped down over them.

29:23 *expectabant me sicut pluviam et os suum aperiebant quasi ad imbrem serotinum*

They waited for me
like rain,
and they opened
their mouth
as if to *a* late rain shower.

29:24 *si quando ridebam ad eos non credebant et lux vultus mei non cadebat in terram*

If at any time
I laughed at them,
they did not believe *it*,
and *the* light of my face
did not sink to *the* ground.

29:25 *si voluissem ire ad eos sedebam primus cumque sederem quasi rex circumstante exercitu eram tamen maerentium consolator*

If I wanted
to go to them,
I sat as *the* leader,
and when I sat down,
I was like *a* king
surrounded by an army.
Yet I consoled *the* grieving.

Chapter 30

30:1 *nunc autem derident me iuniores tempore quorum non dignabar patres ponere cum canibus gregis mei*

But now, those junior
to me in age
mock me,
whose fathers
I did not consider worthy
to put with *the* dogs
of my flocks,

30:2 *quorum virtus manuum erat mihi pro nihilo et vita ipsa putabantur indigni*

whose strength of hand
was nothing to me,
and they were considered
unworthy of life itself,

30:3 *egestate et fame steriles qui rodebant in solitudine squalentes calamitate et miseria*

sterile from poverty
and hunger,
who gnawed away
in solitude,
made filthy
by calamity and misery.

30:4 *et mandebant herbas et arborum cortices et radix iuniperorum erat cibus eorum*

And they chewed grass
and tree bark,
and *a* juniper's root
was their food;

30:5 *qui de convallibus ista rapientes cum singula repperissent ad ea cum clamore currebant*

who stole these *things*
from valleys.
When they found one,
they ran to it shouting.

30:6 *in desertis habitabant torrentium et in cavernis terrae vel super glaream*

They lived in dried up rivers
and in caves of *the* earth,
or on gravel;

30:7 *qui inter huiuscemodi laetabantur et esse sub sentibus delicias conputabant*

who were happy
among themselves
and considered it
to be delightful

to be under thorn bushes.

30:8 *filii stultorum et ignobilium et in terra penitus non parentes*

They are the children
of fools and *the* worthless,
not standing out
even in *the* depths
of *the* earth.

30:9 *nunc in eorum canticum versus sum et factus sum eis proverbium*

Now I am sung about
in their songs,
and I have become
a proverb to them

30:10 *abominantur me et longe fugiunt a me et faciem meam conspuere non verentur*

They detest me
and flee far from me,
and aren't afraid
to spit in my face.

30:11 *faretram enim suam aperuit et adflixit me et frenum posuit in os meum*

For He opened *a* quiver
and shot me,
and put *a* bit in my mouth.

30:12 *ad dexteram orientis calamitatis meae ilico surrexerunt pedes meos subverterunt et oppresserunt quasi fluctibus semitis suis*

To *the* right of dawn
my calamities arose quickly.
They undermined my feet
and overwhelmed my paths
like waves.

30:13 *dissipaverunt itinera mea insidiati sunt mihi et praevaluerunt et non fuit qui ferret auxilium*

They have weakened
my way.
They are plotting against me,
and they have prevailed.
And *there* was no one
who brought help.

30:14 *quasi rupto muro et aperta ianua inruerunt super me et ad meas miserias devoluti sunt*

As if through *a* broken wall
or *an* opened door,
they rushed in at me,
and tumbled down

into my miseries.

30:15 *redactus sum in nihili abstulisti quasi ventus desiderium meum et velut nubes pertransiit salus mea*

I am reduced to nothing.
You have taken away
my desire like the wind,
and my health has vanished
like clouds.

30:16 *nunc autem in memet ipso marcescit anima mea et possident me dies adflictionis*

But now my soul
shrivels up within me,
and days of affliction
possess me.

30:17 *nocte os meum perforatur doloribus et qui me comedunt non dormiunt*

By night my bone
is pierced by pains,
and those who
are eating me
do not sleep.

30:18 *in multitudine eorum consumitur vestimentum meum et quasi capitio tunicae sic cinxerunt me*

My garment is consumed
by *the* number of them,
and like *the* collar of *a* shirt,
they enclose me.

30:19 *conparatus sum luto et adsimilatus favillae et cineri*

I am like dirt,
and similar to
embers and ashes.

30:20 *clamo ad te et non exaudis me sto et non respicis me*

I cry out to You
and You don't hear me.
I stand still
and You don't look at me.

30:21 *mutatus es mihi in crudelem et in duritia manus tuae adversaris mihi*

You have changed
toward me in cruelty
and in *the* hardness
of Your hand against me.

30:22 *elevasti me et quasi super ventum ponens elisisti me valide*

You have lifted me up,
and, as if throwing *me*

on the wind,
have struck me powerfully.

30:23 *scio quia morti tradas me ubi constituta domus est omni viventi*

I know that
you will hand me over
to death,
where *a* house
is established
for all *the* living.

30:24 *verumtamen non ad consumptionem eorum emittis manum tuam et si corruerint ipse salvabis*

Nevertheless,
You do not stretch out
Your hand
to their consumption,
and if they have fallen,
You Yourself will save.

30:25 *flebam quondam super eum qui adflictus erat et conpatiebatur anima mea pauperi*

I used to weep for him
who was afflicted,
and my soul suffered
with *the* poor.

30:26 *expectabam bona et venerunt mihi mala praestolabar lucem et eruperunt tenebrae*

I expected good,
and evil came over me.
I waited for light
and darkness erupted.

30:27 *interiora mea efferbuerunt absque ulla requie praevenerunt me dies adflictionis*

My insides
have boiled up,
without any peace.
Days of affliction
have come over me.

30:28 *maerens incedebam sine furore consurgens in turba clamavi*

I walked along grieving,
without anger.
Rising up in *a* crowd
I have cried out.

30:29 *frater fui draconum et socius strutionum*

I was *a* brother
of dragons,
and *a* companion

of ostriches,

30:30 *cutis mea denigrata est super me et ossa mea aruerunt prae caumate*

My skin
is blackened
over me,
and my bones
have dried out
before *the* heat.

30:31 *versa est in luctum cithara mea et organum meum in vocem flentium*

My guitar is turned
to mourning,
and my organ
to *the* voice of weeping.

Chapter 31

31:1 *pepigi foedus cum oculis meis ut ne cogitarem quidem de virgine*

I have made *an* agreement
with my eyes,
that I wouldn't think about
a young woman,

31:2 *quam enim partem haberet Deus in me desuper et hereditatem Omnipotens de excelsis*

for what portion
did God have in me above,
and *what* inheritance
the Omnipotent
from on high?

31:3 *numquid non perditio est iniquo et alienatio operantibus iniustitiam*

Is not destruction
to *the* lawless,
and alienation to
workers of unfairness?

31:4 *nonne ipse considerat vias meas et cunctos gressus meos dinumerat*

Does He not

consider my ways,
and number all my steps?

31:5 *si ambulavi in vanitate et festinavit in dolo pes meus*

If I have walked
in vanity
and my foot
hurried into deceit,

31:6 *adpendat me in statera iusta et sciat Deus simplicitatem meam*

let Him put me
in *a* just scale,
and let God know
my simplicity.

31:7 *si declinavit gressus meus de via et si secutum est oculos meos cor meum et in manibus meis adhesit macula*

If my step
has turned
from *the* way,
and my heart
has followed my eyes,
and *a* stain sticks
to my hands,

31:8 *seram et alius comedat et progenies mea eradicetur*

I will sow
and another eat,
and my offspring
will be wiped out.

31:9 *si deceptum est cor meum super mulierem et si ad ostium amici mei insidiatus sum*

If my heart
has been deceived
over *a* woman,
and if I have plotted
against *the* doorway
of my friend,

31:10 *scortum sit alteri uxor mea et super illam incurventur alii*

may my wife
be *a* whore
to another,
and may others
bend down to her.

31:11 *hoc enim nefas est et iniquitas maxima*

For this is sin
and *the* greatest treachery.

31:12 *ignis est usque ad perditionem devorans et omnia eradicans genimina*

It is fire devouring
to *the* point of destruction,
and eradicating
all offspring.

31:13 *si contempsi subire iudicium cum servo meo et ancillae meae cum disceptarent adversum me*

If I have disdained
dealing fairly
with my servant
and my slave women,
when they disputed
against me,

31:14 *quid enim faciam cum surrexerit ad iudicandum Deus et cum quaesierit quid respondebo illi*

what, then, will I do,
when God rises up to judge
me?
When He demands,
what will I say to Him?

31:15 *numquid non in utero fecit me qui et illum operatus est et formavit in vulva unus*

Didn't He who made me
in *the* uterus,
also make him,
and hasn't One
formed *us* both
in *the* vulva?

31:16 *si negavi quod volebant pauperibus et oculos viduae expectare feci*

If I have denied
what *the* poor desired,
and made *the* widow's eyes
wait;

31:17 *si comedi buccellam meam solus et non comedit pupillus ex ea*

if I ate my morsel alone
and *the* orphan
did not eat from it;

31:18 *quia ab infantia mea crevit mecum miseratio et de utero matris meae egressa est mecum*

(because from my infancy
compassion has grown
with me,
and came out with me
from my mother's uterus)

31:19 *si despexi pereuntem eo quod non habuerit indumentum et absque operimento pauperem*

if I have despised
the one perishing
because he did not
have clothing,
and *the* poor
for having no covering;

31:20 *si non benedixerunt mihi latera eius et de velleribus ovium mearum calefactus est*

if his sides
have not blessed me,
and he was not warmed
by *the* fleece of my sheep;

31:21 *si levavi super pupillum manum meam etiam cum viderem me in porta superiorem*

if I have raised my hand
over the orphan,
even when I saw myself
as superior in *the* gate;

31:22 *umerus meus a iunctura sua cadat et brachium meum cum suis ossibus confringatur*

may my shoulder
fall from its socket,
and my arm be broken
with its bones!

31:23 *semper enim quasi tumentes super me fluctus timui Deum et pondus eius ferre non potui*

For I always feared God,
like *a* flood swelling over
me!
I could not bear His weight.

31:24 *si putavi aurum robur meum et obrizae dixi fiducia mea*

If I considered
gold my strength,
or said to fine gold,
You are my confidence;

31:25 *si laetatus sum super multis divitiis meis et quia plurima repperit manus mea*

if I have rejoiced
over my many riches,
and because my hand
received much;

31:26 *si vidi solem cum fulgeret et lunam incedentem clare*

if I saw *the* sun
when it shines,
and *the* moon
glowing clearly;

31:27 *et lactatum est in abscondito cor meum et osculatus sum manum meam ore meo*

and my heart
was led on in secret,
and I kissed my hand
with my mouth;

31:28 *quae est iniquitas maxima et negatio contra Deum altissimum*

which is the greatest
treachery
and *a* denial
against God most high;

31:29 *si gavisus sum ad ruinam eius qui me oderat et exultavi quod invenisset eum malum*

if I have rejoiced
at *the* ruin
of one who hates me,
and have been thrilled
when evil found him;

31:30 *non enim dedi ad peccandum guttur meum ut expeterem maledicens animam eius*

(For I have not given
my throat to sinning,
that I not aspire
to cursing his soul!)

31:31 *si non dixerunt viri tabernaculi mei quis det de carnibus eius ut saturemur*

if *the* men
of my tent
did not say,
Who will give us
some of his meat,
that we might be full . . .

31:32 *foris non mansit peregrinus ostium meum viatori patuit*

The stranger did not stay
outside my doorway.
It opened to *the* traveler!

31:33 *si abscondi quasi homo peccatum meum et celavi in sinu meo iniquitatem meam*

If I hid my sin
like *a* man,
and buried my treachery
in my chest;

31:34 *si expavi ad multitudinem nimiam et despectio propinquorum* *terruit me et non magis tacui nec egressus sum ostium*

If I have been too frightened
at *a* crowd,
and *the* disdain of neighbors
terrorized me,
and I was silent too much,
and did not go out *my* door . . .

31:35 *quis mihi tribuat auditorem ut desiderium meum Omnipotens audiat et librum scribat ipse qui iudicat*

Who will give me *a* hearing,
that *the* Omnipotent
may hear my desire,
and He who judges
write *a* book,

31:36 *ut in umero meo portem illum et circumdem illum quasi coronam mihi*

so I may carry it
in my arm,
and hold on to it
like my crown.

31:37 *per singulos gradus meos pronuntiabo illum et quasi principi offeram eum*

I will describe to Him
each one of my steps,
and offer it like *a* prince.

31:28 *si adversum me terra mea clamat et cum ipsa sulci eius deflent*

If my land
cries out against me,
when its furrows weep,

31:29 *si fructus eius comedi absque pecunia et animam agricolarum eius adflixi*

if I have eaten its fruit
without paying,
or afflicted *the* soul
of its laborers,

31:40 *pro frumento oriatur mihi tribulus et pro hordeo spina finita sunt verba Iob*

let briars spring up for me
instead of grain,
and thorns for barley!

Job's words are ended.

Chapter 32

Heliu Answers Job

32:1 *omiserunt autem tres viri isti respondere Iob eo quod iustus sibi videretur*

But these three men
declined to answer Job,
because he considered
himself just.

32:2 *et iratus indignatusque Heliu filius Barachel Buzites de cognatione Ram iratus est autem adversus Iob eo quod iustum se esse diceret coram Deo*

And Heliu,
son of Barachel Buzites,
of *the* family of Ram,[59]
angry and indignant,
was furious at Job
because he was saying
he was just before God.

32:3 *porro adversum amicos eius indignatus est eo quod non invenissent responsionem rationabilem sed tantummodo condemnassent Iob*

He was also angry
with his friends,
because they had not found
a rational response,
but had only condemned Job.

32:4 *igitur Heliu expectavit Iob loquentem eo quod seniores se essent qui loquebantur*

Therefore, Heliu had waited
while Job spoke,
because those who were
speaking
were older than him.

32:5 *cum autem vidisset quod tres respondere non potuissent iratus est vehementer*

But when he saw that
the three could not respond,
he was very angry.

32:6 *respondensque Heliu*

---

[59]Heliu is identified as a Buzite, a member of a clan descended from Abraham's nephew, Buz, second son of Nahor. See Genesis 27:22. He is thus a relative of Job and the only character in the book with a distinctly Israelite name. The identity of "the family of Ram" is unknown. Ram is the name of an ancestor of David in Ruth 4:19-22: *Hezron of Ram, Ram of Amminadab, [20] Amminadab of Nahshon, Nahshon of Salmon, [21] Salmon of Boaz, Boaz of Obed, [22] Obed of Jesse, and Jesse of David.*

filius Barachel Buzites dixit iunior sum tempore vos autem antiquiores idcirco dimisso capite veritus sum indicare vobis meam sententiam

And Heliu,
son of Barachel Buzites, said,
I am younger in age,
and you are older.
For this reason
I gave *you* place.
I was afraid to show you
my opinion.

32:7 *sperabam enim quod aetas prolixior loqueretur et annorum multitudo doceret sapientiam*

For I hoped that age
might speak better,
and many years
might teach wisdom.

32:8 *sed ut video spiritus est in hominibus et inspiratio Omnipotentis dat intellegentiam*

But as I see,
a spirit is in men,
and *the* inspiration
of *the* Omnipotent
gives understanding.

32:9 *non sunt longevi sapientes nec senes intellegunt iudicium*

The long-lived
are not wise,
nor do old men
understand judgment.

32:10 *ideo dicam audite me ostendam vobis etiam ego meam scientiam*

Therefore I will speak.
Listen to me.
Even I will show you
my knowledge.

32:11 *expectavi enim sermones vestros audivi prudentiam vestram donec disceptaremini sermonibus*

For I waited through
your speeches.
I heard your prudence
while you debated words.

32:12 *et donec putabam vos aliquid dicere considerabam sed ut video non est qui arguere possit Iob et respondere ex vobis sermonibus eius*

And as long as I thought

you would say something
I considered.
But now I see
that *it* is not possible
to argue with Job
or for you to respond
to his words.

32:13 *ne forte dicatis
invenimus sapientiam Deus
proiecit eum non homo*

Unless perhaps you say,
We found wisdom.
God threw him down,
not man.

32:14 *nihil locutus est mihi
et ego non secundum vestros
sermones respondebo illi*

Nothing is said to me,
and I will not respond to him
according to what you said.

32:15 *extimuerunt non
responderunt ultra
abstuleruntque a se eloquia*

They were afraid.
They haven't responded
further
and they put an end
to their eloquence.

32:16 *quoniam igitur
expectavi et non sunt locuti
steterunt nec responderunt
ultra*

Because, therefore,
I have waited
and they have not spoken,
they stood and
did not respond further,

32:17 *respondebo et ego
partem meam et ostendam
scientiam meam*

I will even respond
on my part,
and will show
my knowledge.

32:18 *plenus sum enim
sermonibus et coartat me
spiritus uteri mei*

For I am full of words,
and *the* spirit of my insides
crowds me.

32:19 *en venter meus quasi
mustum absque spiraculo
quod lagunculas novas
disrumpit*

They are in my gut,
like new wine
without *a* vent,
which bursts new containers.

32:20 *loquar et respirabo paululum aperiam labia mea et respondebo*

I will speak
and breathe *a* little.
I will open my lips
and will respond.

32:21 *non accipiam personam viri et Deum homini non aequabo*

I will not favor
the person of *a* man,
and I will not equate
God with man.

32:22 *nescio enim quamdiu subsistam et si post modicum tollat me factor meus*

For I do not know
how long I will stand,
and if my Maker
will take me away
after awhile.

Chapter 33

Heliu Continues

33:1 *audi igitur Iob eloquia mea et omnes sermones meos ausculta*

So listen, Job,
to my eloquence,
and understand all my words.

33:2 *ecce aperui os meum loquatur lingua mea in faucibus meis*

Look, I have opened
my mouth.
My tongue will speak
in my jaws.

33:3 *simplici corde meo sermones mei et sententiam labia mea puram loquentur*

My words *come from*
the simplicity of my heart,
and my lips will speak
a pure sentence.

33:4 *spiritus Dei fecit me et spiraculum Omnipotentis vivificavit me*

The Spirit of God made me,
and *the* Omnipotent's breath
has given me life.

33:5 *si potes responde mihi et adversus faciem meam consiste*

If you can, respond to me,
and stand up before my face.

33:6 *ecce et me sicut et te fecit Deus et de eodem luto ego quoque formatus sum*

Look, God made
both me and you,
and from *the* same dirt,
I too was formed.

33:7 *verumtamen miraculum meum non te terreat et eloquentia mea non sit tibi gravis*

Nevertheless, may my
wonder not frighten you,
and my eloquence not be
heavy to you.

33:8 *dixisti ergo in auribus meis et vocem verborum audivi*

You have spoken, therefore,
in my ears,
and I have heard
the sound of your words.

33:9 *mundus sum ego absque delicto inmaculatus et non est iniquitas in me*

'I am clean,
without fault, spotless,
and *there* is no treachery
in me.

33:10 *quia querellas in me repperit ideo arbitratus est me inimicum sibi*

'Because He finds faults
in me,
therefore, He has counted me
as His enemy.

33:11 *posuit in nervo pedes meos custodivit omnes semitas meas*

'He placed my feet in *a*
fetter.
He watched over all my
ways.'

33:12 *hoc est ergo in quo non es iustificatus respondebo tibi quia maior sit Deus homine*

This is *the thing*, therefore,
in which you are not
justified!
I will respond to you,
because God is greater

than man!

33:13 *adversum eum contendis quod non ad omnia verba responderit tibi*

You contend against Him,
because He did not respond
to you in all your words.

33:14 *semel loquitur Deus et secundo id ipsum non repetit*

God spoke it once
and doesn't repeat it
a second *time.*

33:15 *per somnium in visione nocturna quando inruit sopor super homines et dormiunt in lectulo*

In sleep, in *a* vision at night,
when drowsiness rushes in
over men
and they sleep in bed,

33:16 *tunc aperit aures virorum et erudiens eos instruit disciplinam*

then, He opens the ears
of *the* living
and, teaching them,
He instructs discipline.

33:17 *ut avertat hominem ab his quae facit et liberet eum de superbia*

that He might turn man away
from *the* things he is doing,
and free him from pride,

33:18 *eruens animam eius a corruptione et vitam illius ut non transeat in gladium*

snatching his soul away
from corruption,
and his life,
that he not cross over
to *the* sword.[60]

33:19 *increpat quoque per dolorem in lectulo et omnia ossa eius marcescere facit*

He rebukes him also by pain,
in *his* bed,
and makes all his bones
dry up,

33:20 *abominabilis ei fit in vita sua panis et animae illius cibus ante desiderabilis*

that bread may become
detestable to him in life,

---

[60] The last sentence intends to say, ." . . that he not die by violence."

and food which before
was desirable to his soul.

33:21 *tabescet caro eius et ossa quae tecta fuerant nudabuntur*

His flesh will be consumed,
and *the* bones
which were touched,
will be stripped bare.

33:22 *adpropinquabit corruptioni anima eius et vita illius mortiferis*

His soul will come close
to corruption,
and his life deadly.

33:23 *si fuerit pro eo angelus loquens unum de milibus ut adnuntiet hominis aequitatem*

If *an* angel
were speaking on his behalf,
one from a thousand,
that he may announce
a man's equity,

33:24 *miserebitur eius et dicet libera eum et non descendat in corruptionem inveni in quo ei propitier*

he will have mercy on him,
and say, Free him,
and may he not descend
to corruption.
I have found in him
that which may warrant
pardon.

33:25 *consumpta est caro eius a suppliciis revertatur ad dies adulescentiae suae*

His flesh is eaten by
sufferings.
Let him revert
to *the* days of his youth.

33:26 *deprecabitur Deum et placabilis ei erit et videbit faciem eius in iubilo et reddet homini iustitiam suam*

He will plead with God,
and *God* will be pleased
with him,
and he will see his face
in jubilation,
and repay *a* man his fairness.

33:27 *respiciet homines et dicet peccavi et vere deliqui et ut eram dignus non recepi*

He will regard men,
and *a man* will say
Truly I have abandoned *God*.

I have sinned,
and was not worthy.
I have not received
what I deserved.

33:28 *liberavit animam suam ne pergeret in interitum sed vivens lucem videret*

He has freed his soul,
that he not continue
to destruction,
but, living, will see light.

33:29 *ecce haec omnia operatur Deus tribus vicibus per singulos*

Look, God does all these
three times for each one,

33:30 *ut revocet animas eorum a corruptione et inluminet luce viventium*

that He may call back
their souls from corruption,
and enlighten *them*
by *the* light of *the* living.

33:31 *adtende Iob et audi me et tace dum ego loquar*

Listen, Job, and hear me,
and be quiet while I speak.

33:32 *si autem habes quod loquaris responde mihi loquere volo enim te apparere iustum*

But if you have
something to say,
answer me.
Speak, for I want you
to appear fair,

33:32 *quod si non habes audi me tace et docebo te sapientiam*

which, if you don't have *it*,
listen to me.
Be quiet
and I will teach you wisdom.

Chapter 34

Heliu Speaks Further

34:1 *pronuntians itaque Heliu etiam haec locutus est*

And so Heliu,
pronouncing even this,
spoke.

34:2 *audite sapientes verba mea et eruditi auscultate me*

Hear my words, wise *men*,
and you will learn.
Pay attention to me.

34:3 *auris enim verba probat et guttur escas gustu diiudicat*

For *the* ear proves words
by hearing
and *the* throat judges foods
by tasting.

34:4 *iudicium eligamus nobis et inter nos videamus quid sit melius*

Let us choose judgment
by ourselves,
and see among ourselves
what is best.

34:5 *quia dixit Iob iustus sum et Deus subvertit iudicium meum*

Because Job has said,
'I am fair,'
and 'God has undermined
my judgment,'

34:6 *in iudicando enim me mendacium est violenta sagitta mea absque ullo peccato*

For in judging me
there is a lie.
My arrow is violent,
apart from any sin.

34:7 *quis est vir ut est Iob qui bibit subsannationem quasi aquam*

Who is *a* man
like Job is,
who drinks mockery
like water,

34:8 *qui graditur cum operantibus iniquitatem et ambulat cum viris impiis*

who goes with those
who work treachery
and walks with
lawless men.

34:9 *dixit enim non placebit vir Deo etiam si cucurrerit cum eo*

For he said,
'Man will not please God,
even if he has run
with Him.'

34:10 *ideo viri cordati audite me absit a Deo impietas et ab Omnipotente iniquitas*

Therefore, prudent men,
hear me!
May lawlessness
be far from God,
and treachery
far from *the* Omnipotent.

34:11 *opus enim hominis reddet ei et iuxta vias singulorum restituet*

For *God* repays
a man's work to him,
and *He* restores
according to each one's
ways.

34:12 *vere enim Deus non condemnabit frustra nec Omnipotens subvertet iudicium*

For truly
God will not condemn
without reason,
nor will *the* Omnipotent
subvert judgment.

34:13 *quem constituit alium super terram aut quem posuit super orbem quem fabricatus est*

What other is appointed
over *the* earth,
or who is placed
over *the* world,
which is made?

34:14 *si direxerit ad eum cor suum spiritum illius et flatum ad se trahet*

If He directs His heart
to Himself,
and He brings
His Spirit and breath
to Himself,

34:15 *deficiet omnis caro simul et homo in cinerem revertetur*

all flesh would die at once,
and man would return to
dust.

34:16 *si habes ergo*

intellectum audi quod dicitur
et ausculta vocem eloquii mei

Therefore,
if you have intelligence,
hear what is said,
and pay attention
to *the* voice of my eloquence.

34:17 *numquid qui non amat iudicium sanare potest et quomodo tu eum qui iustus est in tantum condemnas*

Can one who
does not love fairness
be healed?
And how can you
condemn One
who is fair in so much?

34:18 *qui dicit regi apostata qui vocat duces impios*

How can you condemn One
who says to kings, Apostate,
and calls leaders lawless;

34:19 *qui non accipit personas principum nec cognovit tyrannum cum disceptaret contra pauperem opus enim manuum eius sunt universi*

who does not favor
the persons of princes,
or approve of *the* tyrant
when he disputes
against *the* poor,
for all are works
of His hands!

34:20 *subito morientur et in media nocte turbabuntur populi et pertransibunt et auferent violentum absque manu*

They will die suddenly,
and peoples will be disturbed
at midnight
and will pass away,
and they will take away
the violent,
without *a* hand.

34:21 *oculi enim eius super vias hominum et omnes gressus eorum considerat*

For His eyes
are on *the* ways of men,
and He considers
all their steps.

34:22 *non sunt tenebrae et non est umbra mortis ut abscondantur ibi qui operantur iniquitatem*

There is no darkness

and *there* is no
shadow of death,
that one who works treachery
may hide there.

34:23 *neque enim ultra in hominis potestate est ut veniat ad Deum in iudicium*

For neither is *there*
further power in men
that he may come
into judgment with God.

34:24 *conteret multos innumerabiles et stare faciet alios pro eis*

He will destroy
uncountable multitudes,
and will cause others
to stand in their place.

34:25 *novit enim opera eorum et idcirco inducet noctem et conterentur*

For He knew their works,
and therefore
He will bring night
and they will be destroyed.

34:26 *quasi impios percussit eos in loco videntium*

He strikes them,
like *the* lawless,
in *the* place of *the* living,

34:27 *qui quasi de industria recesserunt ab eo et omnes vias eius intellegere noluerunt*

those who,
as if diligent
have backed away from him,
and do not want
to understand
all His ways,

34:28 *ut pervenire facerent ad eum clamorem egeni et audiret vocem pauperum*

that *the* cry of *the* needy
might be made
to come to Him,
and He might hear
the voice of *the* poor.

34:29 *ipso enim concedente pacem quis est qui condemnet ex quo absconderit vultum quis est qui contempletur eum et super gentem et super omnes homines*

For to One giving peace,
who is *he* who will condemn?
From where He

has hidden His face,
who is one who
will contemplate Him,
either over nations
or over all men,

34:30 *qui regnare facit hominem hypocritam propter peccata populi*

One who makes
a hypocritical man reign,
because of *the* people's sins.

34:31 *quia ergo ego locutus sum ad Deum te quoque non prohibeo*

Because, therefore,
I have spoken about God,
I will not keep you
from speaking.

34:32 *si erravi tu doce me si iniquitatem locutus sum ultra non addam*

If I have erred, you teach me!
If I have spoken treachery,
I will not add another *word.*

34:33 *numquid a te Deus expetit eam quia displicuit tibi tu enim coepisti loqui et non ego quod si quid nosti melius loquere*

Will God ask it of you,
because He has displeased
you?
For you began to speak
and not me.
If you knew
something better, say *it*!

34:34 *viri intellegentes loquantur mihi et vir sapiens audiat me*

Let intelligent men
speak to me,
and let *a* wise man hear me.

34:35 *Iob autem stulte locutus est et verba illius non sonant disciplinam*

But Job has spoken foolishly,
and his words
do not sound discipline.

34:36 *pater mi probetur Iob usque ad finem ne desinas in hominibus iniquitatis*

My father,
let Job be proved
to *the* end.
Do not break off
from treacherous men.

34:37 *quia addit super peccata sua blasphemiam*

inter nos interim constringatur et tunc ad iudicium provocet sermonibus suis Deum

Because he added blasphemy
on top of his sins,
let him be tied up among us,
and then let him provoke God
to judgment by his words.

Chapter 35

Heliu Goes On
35:1 *igitur Heliu haec rursum locutus est*

Therefore, Heliu

again spoke these *things*.

35:2 *numquid aequa tibi videtur tua cogitatio ut diceres iustior Deo sum*

Does your thought
seem fair to you,
that you say,
'I am fairer than God?'

35:3 *dixisti enim non tibi placet quod rectum est vel quid tibi proderit si ego peccavero*

For you said, 'What is right
does not please You,'
or, 'What benefit is *it*
to You if I sin?'

35:4 *itaque ego respondebo sermonibus tuis et amicis tuis tecum*

So I will respond
to your words,
and to your friends with you.

35:5 *suspice caelum et intuere et contemplare aethera quod altior te sit*

Look up at *the* sky
and consider.
Contemplate *the* ether,
because *it* is higher
than you.[61]

35:6 *si peccaveris quid ei nocebis et si multiplicatae fuerint iniquitates tuae quid facies contra eum*

If you sin,
how do you harm Him?
And if your treacheries
are multiplied,
what do you do
against Him?

35:7 *porro si iuste egeris quid donabis ei aut quid de manu tua accipiet*

Again, if you live fairly,
what will you give Him,
or what will He accept
from your hand?

35:8 *homini qui similis tui est nocebit impietas tua et filium hominis adiuvabit iustitia tua*

Your lawlessness will harm
a man who is like you,
and your fairness
will help *a* son of man.

35:9 *propter multitudinem calumniatorum clamabunt et heiulabunt propter vim brachii tyrannorum*

Because of *a* multitude
of oppressions,
they will cry out,
and will weep
because of *the* strength
of *the* tyrants' arm.

35:10 *et non dixit ubi est Deus qui fecit me qui dedit carmina in nocte*

Yet he has not said,
Where is God who made me,
who has given songs
in *the* night,

35:11 *qui docet nos super iumenta terrae et super volucres caeli erudit nos*

who shows us more
than *the* beasts of *the* earth,

[61] "Ether" is the fine fluid the ancients believed filled what we know of as outer space.

and teaches us more
than *the* birds of *the* sky?

35:12 *ibi clamabunt et non exaudiet propter superbiam malorum*

They will cry out there
and He will not hear,
because of *the* pride
of *the* harmful.

35:13 *non ergo frustra audiet Deus et Omnipotens singulorum causas intuebitur*

For God will not hear in vain,
and *the* Omnipotent
will consider *the* causes
of each person,

35:14 *etiam cum dixeris non considerat iudicare coram eo et expecta eum*

even when you have said,
He does not consider,
be judged before Him,
and wait for Him.

35:15 *nunc enim non infert furorem suum nec ulciscitur scelus valde*

For now, He is not
inflicting His fury,
nor is He punishing
crime overwhelmingly.

35:16 *ergo Iob frustra aperit os suum et absque scientia verba multiplicat*

Therefore, Job has
opened his mouth
for nothing,
and has multiplied words
without knowledge.

Chapter 36

Heliu Speaks More

36:1 *addens quoque Heliu haec locutus est*

Adding also this, Heliu said,

36:2 *sustine me paululum et indicabo tibi adhuc enim habeo quod pro Deo loquar*

Bear with me *a* little,
and I will show you.
For up to now
I have to speak
for God.

36:3 *repetam scientiam meam a principio et operatorem meum probabo iustum*

I will repeat my knowledge
from *the* beginning,
and I will prove
my Maker fair.

36:4 *vere enim absque mendacio sermones mei et perfecta scientia probabitur tibi*

For truly my words
are far from lying,
and perfect knowledge
will be proved to you.

36:5 *Deus potentes non abicit cum et ipse sit potens*

God does not
throw down *the* powerful
when He also is powerful.

36:6 *sed non salvat impios et iudicium pauperibus tribuit*

But He does not save
the lawless,
and gives judgment
to *the* poor.

36:7 *non aufert a iusto oculos suos et reges in solio conlocat in perpetuum et illi eriguntur*

He does not take
His eyes away
from *the* fair,
and He places kings
on thrones forever,
and they are built.

36:8 *et si fuerint in catenis et vinciantur funibus paupertatis*

And even if they
have been in chains,
and are bound

by *the* ropes of poverty,

36:9 *indicabit eis opera eorum et scelera eorum quia violenti fuerint*

He will show them
their acts and their crimes,
because they have been
violent.

36:10 *revelabit quoque aurem eorum ut corripiat et loquetur ut revertantur ab iniquitate*

And He will also open
their ear,
that He may rebuke,
and speak,
that they may turn back
from iniquity.

36:11 *si audierint et observaverint conplebunt dies suos in bono et annos suos in gloria*

If they will hear and see,
they will complete
their days in good,
and their years in glory.

36:12 *si autem non audierint transibunt per gladium et consumentur in stultitia*

But if they will not hear,
they will pass away
by *the* sword,
and be consumed
in foolishness.

36:13 *simulatores et callidi provocant iram Dei neque clamabunt cum vincti fuerint*

Liars and cheats
provoke God's anger,
nor will they cry out
when they have been
chained.

36:14 *morietur in tempestate anima eorum et vita eorum inter effeminatos*

Their soul will die
in *a* storm,
and their life
among *the* effeminate.

36:15 *eripiet pauperem de angustia sua et revelabit in tribulatione aurem eius*

He will snatch
the poor man away
from his anguish,
and He will open
his ear in tribulation.

36:16 *igitur salvabit te de*

ore angusto latissime et non habentis fundamentum subter se requies autem mensae tuae erit plena pinguedine

Therefore, He will
save you broadly
from *a* narrow mouth,
not having *a* foundation
beneath it.
But your table
will be peaceful,
full of prosperity.

36:17 *causa tua quasi impii iudicata est causam iudiciumque recipies*

Your cause,
like *the* lawless,
is judged.
You will recover
cause and judgment.

36:18 *non te ergo superet ira ut aliquem opprimas nec multitudo donorum inclinet te*

Therefore,
do not let anger
overcome you
so that you oppress another,
nor let *a* multitude of bribes
turn you away.

36:19 *depone magnitudinem tuam absque tribulatione et omnes robustos fortitudine*

Lay aside your greatness,
apart from tribulation,
and all *the* robust
their strength.

36:20 *ne protrahas noctem ut ascendant populi pro eis*

Do not draw out *the* night,
that people may climb up
before them.

36:21 *cave ne declines ad iniquitatem hanc enim coepisti sequi post miseriam*

Beware that you
do not turn away
toward iniquity,
for you have begun
to follow this *way*
after misery.

36:22 *ecce Deus excelsus in fortitudine sua et nullus ei similis in legislatoribus*

Look, God is *the* highest
in His strength,
and, among law-givers,
no one *is* like Him.

36:23 *quis poterit scrutari*

vias eius aut quis ei dicere operatus es iniquitatem

Who can scrutinize His ways,
or who can say to Him,
You have worked iniquity?

36:24 *memento quod ignores opus eius de quo cecinerunt viri*

Remember that
you do not know His work,
of which men have sung.

36:25 *omnes homines vident eum unusquisque intuetur procul*

All men see Him.
Each one watches
far away.

36:26 *ecce Deus magnus vincens scientiam nostram numerus annorum eius inaestimabilis*

Look, God is great,
conquering our knowledge!
The number of His years
cannot be guessed,

36:27 *qui aufert stillas pluviae et effundit imbres ad instar gurgitum*

who takes away
drops of rain,
and pours out storms
like *the* raging seas,

36:28 *qui de nubibus fluunt quae praetexunt cuncta desuper*

which flow from clouds,
that cloak all *things* above!

36:29 *si voluerit extendere nubes quasi tentorium suum*

If He wanted,
He would extend clouds
like His tent,

36:30 *et fulgurare lumine suo desuper cardines quoque maris operiet*

and flash His light
from above *the* poles,
and likewise cover *the* seas.

36:31 *per haec enim iudicat populos et dat escas multis mortalibus*

For through these
He judges peoples,
and gives food
to many mortal *creatures.*

36:32 *in manibus abscondit lucem et praecipit ei ut rursus adveniat*

He hides light
in His hands,
and takes it,
that again *light*
may come forth.

36:33 *adnuntiat de ea amico suo quod possessio eius sit et ad eam possit ascendere*

He tells His friend about it,
that *it* is His possession,
and he may climb up to it.

Chapter 37

Heliu's Speech Ends

37:1 *super hoc expavit cor meum et emotum est de loco suo*

My hear fears over this,
and is moved from its place.

37:2 *audite auditionem in terrore vocis eius et sonum de ore illius procedentem*

Listen to *the* report
of His voice in terror,
and *the* sound
proceeding from His mouth.

37:3 *subter omnes caelos ipse considerat et lumen illius super terminos terrae*

He considers all things
under *the* skies,
and His light *extends*
over *the* ends of *the* earth.

37:4 *post eum rugiet sonitus tonabit voce magnitudinis suae et non investigabitur cum audita fuerit vox eius*

The sound will roar
after Him.
He will thunder

in *the* voice of His greatness,
and will not be found
when His voice is heard.

37:5 *tonabit Deus in voce sua mirabiliter qui facit magna et inscrutabilia*

God will thunder awesomely
in His voice,
who makes great
and unsearchable *things;*

37:6 *qui praecipit nivi ut descendat in terram et hiemis pluviis et imbri fortitudinis suae*

who commands snow
that it may fall on earth,
and winter rains,
and storms of His greatness;

37:7 *qui in manu omnium hominum signat ut noverint singuli opera sua*

who seals every man
in *His* hand,
that each of their works
may be known.

37:8 *ingredietur bestia latibulum et in antro suo morabitur*

A beast will go in
to its den,
and will stay
in its cave.

37:9 *ab interioribus egreditur tempestas et ab Arcturo frigus*

Storms will rise
out of *the* interior *places*,
and cold from Arcturus.[62]

37:10 *flante Deo concrescit gelu et rursum latissimae funduntur aquae*

By God's breath,
frost forms,
and again waters
are poured out broadly.

37:11 *frumentum desiderat nubes et nubes spargunt lumen suum*

Grain desires *the* clouds,
and *the* clouds disperse
their light,

37:12 *quae lustrant per circuitum quocumque eas voluntas gubernantis duxerit*

---

[62] Arcturus is the constellation associated with the North Star.

ad omne quod praeceperit illis super faciem orbis terrarum

which processes by circuit
wherever *the* will
of *the One* governing
will lead,
to all that He has commanded
over *the* face of *the* world
of earth.

37:13 *sive in una tribu sive in terra sua sive in quocumque loco misericordiae suae eas iusserit inveniri*

Whether in one tribe,
or in His land,
or in whatever place
He has commanded
of His mercy
to be found.

37:14 *ausculta haec Iob sta et considera miracula Dei*

Hear these *things*, Job.
Stand and consider
God's miracles.

37:15 *numquid scis quando praeceperit Deus pluviis ut ostenderent lucem nubium eius*

You don't know
when God commands *the* rains,
that they show *the* light
of His clouds,
do you?

37:16 *numquid nosti semitas nubium magnas et perfectas scientias*

You haven't known
the great paths of *the* clouds,
and perfect knowledge,
have you?

37:17 *nonne vestimenta tua calida sunt cum perflata fuerit terra austro*

Isn't your clothing hot
when *the* south wind
blows over the earth?

37:18 *tu forsitan cum eo fabricatus es caelos qui solidissimi quasi aere fusi sunt*

Were you perhaps with Him?
Did you make the skies,
which were poured out
most solid, like bronze?

37:19 *ostende nobis quid dicamus illi nos quippe*

involvimur tenebris

Show us what
we may say to Him.
We, of course,
are wrapped up in darkness.

37:20 *quis narrabit ei quae loquor etiam si locutus fuerit homo devorabitur*

Who will tell Him
what I say?
If he even speaks,
man will be devoured!

37:21 *at nunc non vident lucem subito aer cogitur in nubes et ventus transiens fugabit eas*

But now they
do not see light.
Air is suddenly gathered
into clouds,
and *the* passing wind
will make them flee.

37:22 *ab aquilone aurum venit et ad Deum formidolosa laudatio*

Gold comes
from *the* north,
and fearful praise to God.

37:23 *digne eum invenire non possumus magnus fortitudine et iudicio et iustitia et enarrari non potest*

We are not worthy
to find Him.
So great in strength
and judgment and fairness,
it cannot be told.

37:24 *ideo timebunt eum viri et non audebunt contemplari omnes qui sibi videntur esse sapientes*

Therefore,
men will fear Him,
and they will not dare
to contemplate *Him*,
all who seem to be wise
to themselves.

Chapter 38

The Lord Responds to Job

38:1 *respondens autem Dominus Iob de turbine dixit*

But *the* Lord,
responding to Job
from *a* tornado,
said,

38:2 *quis est iste involvens sententias sermonibus inperitis*

Who is this
wrapping opinions
in ignorant words?

38:3 *accinge sicut vir lumbos tuos interrogabo te et responde mihi*

Cover your privates
like *a* man.
I will question you,
and you respond to me.

38:4 *ubi eras quando ponebam fundamenta terrae indica mihi si habes intellegentiam*

Where were you
when I laid *the* foundations
of *the* earth?
Tell me,
if you have understanding.

38:5 *quis posuit mensuras eius si nosti vel quis tetendit super eam lineam*

Who placed its measures,
if you know,
or who stretched out
a line over it?

38:6 *super quo bases illius solidatae sunt aut quis dimisit lapidem angularem eius*

Over what
were its bases solidified,
or who set down
its cornerstone,

38:7 *cum me laudarent simul astra matutina et iubilarent omnes filii Dei*

when *the* morning stars
praised Me together,
and all *the* sons of God
rejoiced?

38:9 *quis conclusit ostiis mare quando erumpebat quasi de vulva procedens*

Who closed

the doors of *the* sea,
when it erupted
like one proceeding
from *the* vulva,

38:10 *cum ponerem nubem vestimentum eius et caligine illud quasi pannis infantiae obvolverem*

when I made *a* cloud
its garment,
and wrapped it in gloom,
as if in *an* infant's diaper?

38:11 *circumdedi illud terminis meis et posui vectem et ostia*

I surrounded it
by My limits,
and established
bar and doors.

38:11 *et dixi usque huc venies et non procedes amplius et hic confringes tumentes fluctus tuos*

And I said,
You will come this far
and proceed no further,
and here you will shatter
the swells of your waves.

38:12 *numquid post ortum tuum praecepisti diluculo et ostendisti aurorae locum suum*

Did you command
the morning
from your birth,
or show *the* dawn
its place?

38:13 *et tenuisti concutiens extrema terrae et excussisti impios ex ea*

And have you struck
the ends of *the* earth
and driven *the* lawless
from it?

38:14 *restituetur ut lutum signaculum et stabit sicut vestimentum*

It will be restored
as *a* sign of payment,
and it will stand
like *a* garment.

38:15 *auferetur ab impiis lux sua et brachium excelsum confringetur*

Their light
will be taken away
from *the* lawless,
and *the* raised arm

will be broken.

38:16 *numquid ingressus es profunda maris et in novissimis abyssis deambulasti*

Have you gone into
the depths of *the* sea,
or walked around
the ends of *the* abyss?

38:17 *numquid apertae tibi sunt portae mortis et ostia tenebrosa vidisti*

Are *the* gates of death
aren't open to you,
or have you seen
the doorways of darkness?

38:18 *numquid considerasti latitudines terrae indica mihi si nosti omnia*

Have you considered
the breadth of *the* earth?
Tell me,
if you know all *things*.

38:19 *in qua via habitet lux et tenebrarum quis locus sit*

In what pathway
does light live,
and what is
the place of shadows,

38:20 *ut ducas unumquodque ad terminos suos et intellegas semitas domus eius*

that you may lead
each one to its limits,
and know *the* paths
to its house?

38:21 *sciebas tunc quod nasciturus esses et numerum dierum tuorum noveras*

You knew, then,
that you would be born,
and understood
the number of your days?

38:22 *numquid ingressus es thesauros nivis aut thesauros grandinis aspexisti*

Have you gone into
the storerooms of snow,
or seen *the* treasuries of hail,

38:23 *quae praeparavi in tempus hostis in diem pugnae et belli*

which I have prepared
for *the* time of *the* enemy,
in *the* day

of combat and war?

38:24 *per quam viam*
spargitur lux dividitur aestus
super terram

By what road
is light dispersed,
is heat divided
over earth?

38:25 *quis dedit*
vehementissimo imbri cursum
et viam sonantis tonitrui

Who gave
the fiercest storms
their course,
and *a* way
to *the* sounding thunder,

38:26 *ut plueret super*
terram absque homine in
deserto ubi nullus mortalium
commoratur

that it may rain
on *the* earth,
away from men
in *the* desert,
where no mortal *being* lives;

38:27 *ut impleret inviam et*
desolatam et produceret
herbas virentes

that it may fill up
the trackless and desolate,
and produce green grass?

38:28 *quis est pluviae pater*
vel quis genuit stillas roris

Who is *the* father
of rain,
or who gave birth
to drops of dew?

38:29 *de cuius utero egressa*
est glacies et gelu de caelo
quis genuit

From whose womb
has ice come forth,
and who birthed
the frost of *the* sky?

38:30 *in similitudinem*
lapidis aquae durantur et
superficies abyssi
constringitur

Waters stand
like rocks,
and *the* surface
of *the* abyss
is bound up.

39:31 *numquid coniungere*
valebis micantes stellas
Pliadis aut gyrum Arcturi
poteris dissipare

Will you be able
to join together *the* vibrations
of *the* stars of *the* Pliades,
or can you undo
the course of *the* Arcturi?

38:32 *numquid producis
luciferum in tempore suo et
vesperum super filios terrae
consurgere facis*

Have you produced
the morning star
in its time,
and made *the* evening
rise up over
the sons of earth?

38:33 *numquid nosti
ordinem caeli et pones
rationem eius in terra*

Have you known
the order of *the* sky,
and placed its reason
on earth?

38:34 *numquid elevabis in
nebula vocem tuam et
impetus aquarum operiet te*

Have you raised your voice
in *the* fog,
and will *the* force
of *the* waters hide you?

38:35 *numquid mittes
fulgura et ibunt et revertentia
dicent tibi adsumus*

Have you sent lightning
and it will go,
and returning,
it will say to you,
Here I am?[63]

38:36 *quis posuit in
visceribus hominis
sapientiam vel quis dedit
gallo intellegentiam*

Who put wisdom
in man's insides,
or who gave *the* rooster
its understanding?

38:37 *quis enarravit
caelorum rationem et
concentum caeli quis dormire
faciet*

Who told *the* reason
of *the* skies,
and who will make
the music of *the* sky
sleep?

38:38 *quando fundebatur*

---

[63] *Fulgura* is plural, meaning "lightnings." For the sake of correct English, I have rendered it singular, "lightning."

pulvis in terram et glebae conpingebantur

When was dust formed
on *the* earth,
and *when* was soil
joined together?

38:39 *numquid capies leaenae praedam et animam catulorum eius implebis*

Will you capture
the prey of *the* lioness,
and fill *the* soul
of her cubs,

38:40 *quando cubant in antris et in specubus insidiantur*

when they lie down
in *a* den,
and lie in wait
in caves?

38:41 *quis praeparat corvo escam suam quando pulli eius ad Deum clamant vagantes eo quod non habeant cibos*

Who prepares
for *the* crow
its meat,
when its chicks
cry out to God,
hungry because
they have no food?

Chapter 39

The Lord Continues

39:1 *numquid nosti tempus partus hibicum in petris vel parturientes cervas observasti*

No doubt you have known
the time of birth
of *the* wild goat among *the* rocks,
or have observed
deer giving birth.[64]

39:2 *dinumerasti menses conceptus earum et scisti tempus partus earum*

Have you numbered
the months of their conception,
and known *the* moment
of their birth?

39:3 *incurvantur ad fetum et pariunt et rugitus emittunt*

They are bent down
over *the* newborn,
and give birth,
and, bellowing, cry out.

[64] The question word *numquid* is used when the speaker assumes the answer will be no.

39:4 *separantur filii earum pergunt ad pastum egrediuntur et non revertuntur ad eas*

Their children are weaned.
They go on to pasture.
They go out
and do not return
to them.

39:4 *quis dimisit onagrum liberum et vincula eius quis solvit*

Who sets *the* wild ass free,
and loosens its chains,

39:6 *cui dedi in solitudine domum et tabernacula eius in terra salsuginis*

to whom I have given
a home in solitude,
and its tent *is*
in *a* salty wasteland?

39:7 *contemnit multitudinem civitatis clamorem exactoris non audit*

He scorns *a* crowded city.
He does not hear
the task-master's shout.

39:8 *circumspicit montes*

pascuae suae et virentia
quaeque perquirit

He looks around
over *the* mountains
of his pasture.
He searches
for green *grass*.

39:9 *numquid volet*
rinoceros servire tibi aut
morabitur ad praesepe tuum

Does *the* rhinoceros
want to serve you,
or stay by your hay stall?

39:10 *numquid alligabis*
rinocerota ad arandum loro
tuo aut confringet glebas
vallium post te

Will you tie
the rhinoceros
to your reins,
or will *she* break up
the clods of *the* valley
behind you?

39:11 *numquid fiduciam*
habebis in magna fortitudine
eius et derelinques ei labores
tuos

Will you have faith
in her great strength,
and relinquish your labors
to her?

39:12 *numquid credes ei*
quoniam reddat sementem
tibi et aream tuam congreget

Will you trust her
that she will return
seed to you,
and will she gather *it*
in your threshing floor?

39:13 *pinna strutionum*
similis est pinnis herodii et
accipitris

An ostrich feather
is like *the* feather
of *an* owl or *a* hawk.

39:14 *quando derelinquit in*
terra ova sua tu forsitan in
pulvere calefacis ea

When she leaves her eggs
on *the* ground,
is it you who warms them
in *the* sand?

39:15 *obliviscitur quod pes*
conculcet ea aut bestiae agri
conterant

She forgets that
a foot may step on them,

or that beasts of *the* field
may destroy them.

39:16 *duratur ad filios suos quasi non sint sui frustra laboravit nullo timore cogente*

She is hardened
toward her children
as if they weren't hers,
She labored for no reason,
not fearing to gather them up.

39:17 *privavit enim eam Deus sapientia nec dedit illi intellegentiam*

For God has deprived her
of wisdom,
nor given her intelligence.

39:18 *cum tempus fuerit in altum alas erigit deridet equitem et ascensorem eius*

When *the* time comes,
she raises her wings high.
She mocks *the* horse
and *the* one riding it.

39:19 *numquid praebebis equo fortitudinem aut circumdabis collo eius hinnitum*

Will you give strength
to *a* horse,
or capture *the* whinny
in its neck?

39:20 *numquid suscitabis eum quasi lucustas gloria narium eius terror*

Will you stir him up
like locusts?
The glory of his nostrils
is terror.

39:21 *terram ungula fodit exultat audacter in occursum pergit armatis*

He paws *the* ground
with his hoof.
He prances boldly
in running.
He goes out
against armed *men*.

39:22 *contemnit pavorem nec cedit gladio*

He disdains fear,
nor falls back
from *the* sword.

39:23 *super ipsum sonabit faretra vibrabit hasta et clypeus*

The quiver echoes above him.
The rider will brandish
spear and shield.[65]

39:24 *fervens et fremens sorbet terram nec reputat tubae sonare clangorem*

Impetuous and raging,
he drinks up *the* ground,
nor considers *the* blaring
trumpet.

39:25 *ubi audierit bucinam dicet va procul odoratur bellum exhortationem ducum et ululatum exercitus*

Where the bugle is heard,
he says, A-ha!
He smells *the* battle
far off,
the leaders' exhortation,
and *the* army's shouting.

39:26 *numquid per sapientiam tuam plumescit accipiter expandens alas suas ad austrum*

Does *the* hawk
grow feathers
according to your wisdom,
spreading its wings
to *the* south wind?

39:27 *aut ad praeceptum tuum elevabitur aquila et in arduis ponet nidum suum*

Or will *the* eagle fly up
at your command,
and put its nest
on *the* high *hill*?

39:28 *in petris manet et in praeruptis silicibus commoratur atque inaccessis rupibus*

It stays in *the* rocks
and lives in *the* steep stones
and inaccessible cliffs.

39:29 *inde contemplatur escam et de longe oculi eius prospiciunt*

From there
it looks for meat.
Its eyes watch
from far away.

39:30 *pulli eius lambent sanguinem et ubicumque cadaver fuerit statim adest*

Its chicks lap up blood,
and wherever *there* is *a* dead

[65] Literally, "*He* will brandish spear and shield."

body,
it is quickly there.

39:31 *et adiecit Dominus et locutus est ad Iob*

And *the* Lord added,
and spoke to Job,

39:32 *numquid qui contendit cum Deo tam facile conquiescit utique qui arguit Deum debet respondere ei*

Will one who contended
with God so easily be quiet?
Surely one who argued
against God
must respond to Him!

Job Responds to the Lord
39:33 *respondens autem Iob Domino dixit*

But Job,
responding to *the* Lord,
said,

39:34 *qui leviter locutus sum respondere quid possum manum meam ponam super os meum*

I have spoken lightly.
What can I answer?
I will put my hand
over my mouth.

39:35 *unum locutus sum quod utinam non dixissem et alterum quibus ultra non addam*

I have spoken once
what I wish I had not said,
and another time,
to which I will not add more.

Chapter 40

The Lord Questions Job Again

40:1 *respondens autem Dominus Iob de turbine ait*

But *the* Lord,
responding to Job
from *a* tornado, said,

40:2 *accinge sicut vir lumbos tuos interrogabo te et indica mihi*

Cover your privates
like *a* man.
I will question you,
and you answer me.

40:3 *numquid irritum facies iudicium meum et condemnabis me ut tu iustificeris*

Will you make
My judgment useless,
and condemn Me
that you may be justified?

40:4 *et si habes brachium sicut Deus et si voce simili tonas*

And if you have
an arm like God,
and if you *can* thunder
in a voice like *His*,

40:5 *circumda tibi decorem et in sublime erigere et esto gloriosus et speciosis induere vestibus*

surround yourself
with beauty,
and rise up on high,
and be glorious,
and dress yourself
spectacularly.

40:6 *disperge superbos furore tuo et respiciens omnem arrogantem humilia*

Disperse *the* proud
by your fury,
and, looking at
every arrogant *man,*
humble *all*.

40:7 *respice cunctos superbos et confunde eos et contere impios in loco suo*

Look down on all *the* proud
and confound them,
and destroy *the* lawless
in their place.

40:8 *absconde eos in pulvere simul et facies eorum*

demerge in foveam

Hide them in ashes at once,
and plunge their faces
in *a* pit.

40:9 *et ego confitebor quod salvare te possit dextera tua*

And I will confess
that your right arm
can save you.

40:10 *ecce Behemoth quem feci tecum faenum quasi bos comedet*

Look, Behemoth,
whom I made with you,
will eat hay like an ox.[66]

40:11 *fortitudo eius in lumbis eius et virtus illius in umbilicis ventris eius*

His strength
is in his hips,
and his power
in *the* cord of his belly.

40:12 *constringit caudam suam quasi cedrum nervi testiculorum eius perplexi sunt*

He binds up his tail
like cedar.
The sinew of his testicles
is wrapped tightly.

40:13 *ossa eius velut fistulae aeris cartilago illius quasi lamminae ferreae*

His bones *are* like
brass tubes,
his cartilage like
iron plates.

40:14 *ipse principium est viarum Dei qui fecit eum adplicabit gladium eius*

He is *the* beginning
of God's ways,
who made him.
He will apply his sword,

40:15 *huic montes herbas ferunt omnes bestiae agri ludent ibi*

by whom mountains bear
grass.
All *the* beasts of *the* field

---

[66] From Wikipedia: *"In Jewish belief, Behemoth is the primal unconquerable monster of the land, as Leviathan is the primal monster of the waters of the sea and Ziz the primordial monster of the sky."* See http://en.wikipedia.org/wiki/Behemoth.

will play there.

40:16 *sub umbra dormit in secreto calami et locis humentibus*

He sleeps in secret
beneath *the* shadow
of *a* reed,
and in wet places.

40:17 *protegunt umbrae umbram eius circumdabunt eum salices torrentis*

Shadows protect his shadow.
Willows of *the* rivers
will surround him.

40:18 *ecce absorbebit fluvium et non mirabitur habet fiduciam quod influat Iordanis in os eius*

Look, he swallows *a* river
and is not amazed.
He has confidence
that *the* Jordan[67] could flow
into his mouth.

40:19 *in oculis eius quasi hamo capiet eum et in sudibus perforabit nares eius*

He captures him
in his eyes
like *a* hook,
and will pierce
his nostrils like *a* stake.

40:20 *an extrahere poteris Leviathan hamo et fune ligabis linguam eius*

Or will you
take out Leviathan
with *a* hook,
and bind his tongue
with *a* rope?[68]

40:21 *numquid pones circulum in naribus eius et armilla perforabis maxillam eius*

Will you put *a* ring
in his nostrils,

---

[67] The Jordan River flows south from the Sea of Galilee into the Dead Sea, forming the boundary between present-day Israel and Jordan.

[68] From Wikipedia: *The word Leviathan is also mentioned in Rashi's commentary on Genesis 1:21: "God created the great sea monsters - Taninim." Jastrow translates the word "Taninim" as "sea monsters, crocodiles or large snakes". Rashi comments: "According to legend this refers to the Leviathan and its mate. God created a male and female Leviathan, then killed the female and salted it for the righteous, for if the Leviathans were to procreate the world could not stand before them."*
See http://en.wikipedia.org/wiki/Leviathan.

and pierce his jaw
with *a* buckle?

40:22 *numquid multiplicabit ad te preces aut loquetur tibi mollia*

Will he multiply prayers
to you,
or speak to you softly?

40:23 *numquid feriet tecum pactum et accipies eum servum sempiternum*

Will he make
a pact with you,
or will you accept him
as your eternal slave?

40:24 *numquid inludes ei quasi avi aut ligabis illum ancillis tuis*

Will you mock him
like *a* bird,
or bind him
for your slave girls?

40:25 *concident eum amici divident illum negotiatores*

Will friends kill him?
Will traders divide him.

40:26 *numquid implebis sagenas pelle eius et gurgustium piscium capite illius*

Will you fill *a* net
with his skin,
and baskets of fish
with his head?

40:27 *pone super eum manum tuam memento belli nec ultra addas loqui*

Put your hand on him.
Remember the fight,
nor will you have
anything further to say.

40:28 *ecce spes eius frustrabitur eum et videntibus cunctis praecipitabitur*

Look, his hope
will frustrate him,
and he will be thrown down
in *the* sight of all.

Chapter 41

41:1 *non quasi crudelis suscitabo eum quis enim resistere potest vultui meo*

I will not arouse him
like *the* cruel,
for who can resist
My face?

41:2 *quis ante dedit mihi ut reddam ei omnia quae sub caelo sunt mea sunt*

Who gave to Me before
that I should repay him?
All *things* under *the* sky
are mine.

41:3 *non parcam ei et verbis potentibus et ad deprecandum conpositis*

I will not spare him,
and *his* mighty words,
prepared for begging *mercy*.

41:4 *quis revelavit faciem indumenti eius et in medium oris eius quis intrabit*

Who has opened
the face of his garments,
and who will enter
the middle of *his* mouth?

41:5 *portas vultus eius quis aperiet per gyrum dentium eius formido*

Who will open
the gates of his face?
The circle of his teeth
is fearsome.

41:6 *corpus illius quasi scuta fusilia et conpactum squamis se prementibus*

His body *is* like
molded shields,
compacted like armor
pressed together.

41:7 *una uni coniungitur et ne spiraculum quidem incedit per eas*

One is joined to another
and not even *an* air-hole
passes through them.

41:8 *una alteri adherebunt et tenentes se nequaquam separabuntur*

One adheres to *the* other,
and, having each other,
by no means
will they be separated.

41:9 *sternutatio eius splendor ignis et oculi eius ut palpebrae diluculi*

His snort is
the splendor of fire,
and his eyes
like *the* eyelids
of morning.

41:10 *de ore eius lampades procedunt sicut taedae ignis accensae*

Flames proceed
from his mouth,
like kindled torches of fire.

41:11 *de naribus eius procedit fumus sicut ollae succensae atque ferventis*

Smoke pours
from his nostrils,
as if from *a* blazing pot,
inflamed.

41:12 *halitus eius prunas ardere facit et flamma de ore eius egreditur*

His breath makes
coals burn,
and flame comes out
from his mouth.

41:13 *in collo eius morabitur fortitudo et faciem eius praecedet egestas*

Strength will dwell
in his neck,
and poverty
will go before
his face.

41:14 *membra carnium eius coherentia sibi mittet contra eum fulmina et ad locum alium non ferentur*

The members
of his body
are connected
to each other.
He will hurl lightning
against him,
and they will not be carried
to another place.

41:15 *cor eius indurabitur quasi lapis et stringetur quasi malleatoris incus*

His heart
will be hardened
like *a* stone,
and drawn tight
like *a* blacksmith's anvil.

41:16 *cum sublatus fuerit timebunt angeli et territi*

purgabuntur

When he
is taken away,
the angels will fear,
and they
will be purged
by terror.

41:17 *cum adprehenderit eum gladius subsistere non poterit neque hasta neque torax*

When *the* sword finds him,
it won't be able to stop him,
nor *will a* spear,
or *a* breastplate.

41:18 *reputabit enim quasi paleas ferrum et quasi lignum putridum aes*

For he will consider
iron like straw,
and bronze like rotted wood.

41:19 *non fugabit eum vir sagittarius in stipulam versi sunt ei lapides fundae*

An archer will not
make him run away.
The stones of *a* slingshot
bounce off him like stubble.

41:20 *quasi stipulam aestimabit malleum et deridebit vibrantem hastam*

He will consider
a hammer
like stubble,
and will mock
the one brandishing
a spear.

41:21 *sub ipso erunt radii solis sternet sibi aurum quasi lutum*

The sun's rays
will be beneath him.
He will spread out
gold for himself
like dirt.

41:22 *fervescere faciet quasi ollam profundum mare ponet quasi cum unguenta bulliunt*

He will make
the deep sea boil
like *a* pot.
He will make it like
when ointments boil.

41:23 *post eum lucebit semita aestimabit abyssum quasi senescentem*

A path will shine after him.

He will esteem *the* abyss
like *an* aging *man*.

41:24 *non est super terram potestas quae conparetur ei qui factus est ut nullum timeret*

There is no power on earth
which compares to him,
who was made to fear
no one.

41:25 *omne sublime videt ipse est rex super universos filios superbiae*

He sees every thing lifted up.
He is king over
all *the* sons of pride.

Chapter 42

Job Responds Again to the Lord

42:1 *respondens autem Iob Domino dixit*

But Job, responding,
said to *the* Lord,

42:2 *scio quia omnia potes et nulla te latet cogitatio*

I know that You
can do all *things*,
and no thought
lies hidden from You.

42:3 *quis est iste qui celat consilium absque scientia ideo insipienter locutus sum et quae ultra modum excederent scientiam meam*

Who is he
who hides counsel
without knowledge?
Therefore I have spoken
foolishly,
and what exceeded
beyond *the* manner
of my understanding.

42:4 *audi et ego loquar interrogabo et ostende mihi*

Hear, and I will speak.
I will question
and you show me.

42:5 *auditu auris audivi te nunc autem oculus meus videt te*

I have heard you
with *the* hearing
of the ear,
but now my eye
sees you.

42:6 *idcirco ipse me reprehendo et ago paenitentiam in favilla et cinere*

Therefore I reproach myself
and do penance
in embers and ashes.

The Lord Addresses Job's Friends

42:7 *postquam autem locutus est Dominus verba haec ad Iob dixit ad Eliphaz Themaniten iratus est furor meus in te et in duos amicos tuos quoniam non estis locuti coram me rectum sicut servus meus Iob*

But after *the* Lord had spoken
these words to Job,
He said to Eliphaz
the Themanite,
My fury is enraged at you,
and at your two friends,
because you haven't spoken
rightly before me
like my slave Job.[69]

42:8 *sumite igitur vobis septem tauros et septem arietes et ite ad servum meum Iob et offerte holocaustum pro vobis Iob autem servus meus orabit pro vobis faciem eius suscipiam ut non vobis inputetur stultitia neque enim locuti estis ad me recta sicut servus meus Iob*

Therefore, bring up
for yourselves
seven bulls and seven rams.
Go to my slave, Job,
and offer *a* holocaust
for yourselves.
But Job, my slave,
will pray for you.
I will accept his face,
that your foolishness
not be charged against you,
for you have not
spoken rightly about Me,

[69] Notice that Heliu isn't mentioned.

like my slave, Job.

Job's Friends Obey the Lord

42:9 *abierunt ergo Eliphaz Themanites et Baldad Suites et Sophar Naamathites et fecerunt sicut locutus fuerat ad eos Dominus et suscepit Dominus faciem Iob*

Therefore, Eliphaz
the Themanite
and Baldad *the* Shuhite
and Sophar *the* Naamathite
went up and did
as *the* Lord had spoken
to them,
and *the* Lord accepted
Job's face.

The Lord Restores Job's Prosperity

42:10 *Dominus quoque conversus est ad paenitentiam Iob cum oraret ille pro amicis suis et addidit Dominus omnia quaecumque fuerant Iob duplicia*

The Lord was turned also
to Job's penitence,
when he had prayed
for his friends,
and *the* Lord added
all that Job had possessed
twice over.

42:11 *venerunt autem ad eum omnes fratres sui et universae sorores suae et cuncti qui noverant eum prius et comederunt cum eo panem in domo eius et moverunt super eum caput et consolati sunt eum super omni malo quod intulerat Dominus super eum et dederunt ei unusquisque ovem unam et inaurem auream unam*

But all his brothers
and all his sisters
and all who knew him before
came to him
and ate bread with him
in his house,
and grieved over him.
And they comforted him
over all *the* evil
which God had inflicted
on him.
And each one gave to him
one sheep and one gold
earring.

42:11 *Dominus autem benedixit novissimis Iob magis quam principio eius et facta sunt ei quattuordecim milia ovium et sex milia* *camelorum et mille iuga boum et mille asinae*

But *the* Lord blessed Job's end more than his beginning, and his possession was fourteen thousand sheep, and six thousand camels, and one thousand yoke of oxen, and one thousand female donkeys.

42:13 *et fuerunt ei septem filii et filiae tres*

And *there* were to him seven sons and three daughters.

42:14 *et vocavit nomen unius Diem et nomen secundae Cassia et nomen tertiae Cornu stibii*

And he called *the* name of one Dies, and *the* name of *the* second Cassia, and *the* name of *the* third Cornustibii.

42:15 *non sunt autem inventae mulieres speciosae sicut filiae Iob in universa terra deditque eis pater suus hereditatem inter fratres earum*

But women as spectacular as Job's daughters were not found in all *the* land. And their father gave them *an* inheritance among their brothers.

42:16 *vixit autem Iob post haec centum quadraginta annis et vidit filios suos et filios filiorum suorum usque ad quartam generationem et mortuus est senex et plenus dierum*

But Job lived after this one hundred forty years, and saw his children and *the* children of his children, up to *the* fourth generation. And old and full of days, he died.

About Solomon

King of Israel
in Jerusalem,
son of David.

Reigned: 971 B.C.E. (Before the Common Era, formerly B.C.) and 931 B.C.E.[70]

Tradition teaches that Solomon, king of Israel, wrote the Biblical books of "Proverbs," "Ecclesiastes," and "Song of Solomon."

- He wrote"Song of Solomon" as a young man.
- "Proverbs" was the work of his middle age, as he governed his kingdom and labored to raise his family.
- "Ecclesiastes" was the work of his old age, as he reflected on his earthly life.[71]

[70] The Ryrie Study Bible, New International Version, Charles Ryrie, ed, Moody Press, Chicago, 1986, pg. 891.

[71] Interpreter's Dictionary of the Bible, E-J, George Buttrick, ed, Abingdon Press, Nashville, 1962, pg. 7.

The Book of Proverbs

As the first verse of the Book of Proverbs makes clear, Jewish and Christian traditions both long assumed that King Solomon was its author.[72] The book itself acknowledges the contributions made by others to its composition. The collection of proverbs from chapters 25 through 29 are presented as, *proverbs of Solomon which the men of Hezekiah king of Judah copied.* Chapter 30 is presented as "*The words of Agur son of Jakeh of Massa*," though Jerome translates the names more colorfully. Chapter 31 is ascribed to King Lemuel. Neither Agur nor Lemuel appear elsewhere in the Bible.

The book is divided into the following sections:

Chapters 1-9, contains the intertwining of several similar themes: exhortations to youth; hymns praising Wisdom, and

[72] See Proverbs 1:1, RSV: *The proverbs of Solomon, son of David, king of Israel.*

speeches by Wisdom herself.[73]

Chapters 10-22:16, offers us the largest collection of Solomon's proverbs.

Chapters 22:17-25, presents further instructions on living wisely, differing in format from the two-line couplets of the previous section.

Chapters 25 through 29 shares further Solomonic proverbs, as described above.

Chapters 30 and 31 gives the appended words of Agur and Lemuel.

The book contains religious poetry, a form that is more or less familiar to us. It contains exhortations, a scholarly term many of us are not familiar with. An exhortation urges us to behave in a certain way. Parents often exhort their children, in more or less colorful language, to clean up their rooms or do their homework. We may not know the word "exhortation," but all of us know what it means to be exhorted.

It also contains the proverbs themselves. Proverbs are brief, episodic lessons in applied wisdom. Proverbs are written in such a way that, when we read them, our minds tend to fill in the blanks with real-life experiences. We find the proverbs relevant to our lives, however distant they may seem from us in space and time. In the words of Baba Ram Dass, they have "an intuitive validity."[74]

Proverbs have come down to us from many sources and traditions. Through them, teachers try to communicate to us the essence of what it means to live intelligently. Their teaching speaks to us, wherever we find ourselves in life. Quick to read, they are far from quick to understand fully, much less exhaust.

Solomon's life opens a window on what Wisdom seeks to accomplish.

[73] *Sapientia*, "Wisdom" in Latin, is a feminine noun, as is σοφία in Greek.

[74] See http://www.ramdasstapes.org/index.htm.

Solomon's childhood was marred by terrible events: the rape of a sister; the murder of a brother; the death in battle of another brother in terrible circumstances for the entire family. Solomon was determined to do his part to prevent such catastrophes in the future, through wise teaching.

Yet Solomon had a kingdom to govern, as well as a family to raise. As with many busy people, there was rarely time enough in the day to do all the things he needed to do. We may imagine him writing proverbs in his spare moments, as insight and inspiration came to him. Through his writing, he was able to teach people he might never have seen otherwise. Through his writing he teaches us, who read these words today.

Looking over his shoulder, we learn from him what Wisdom looks like. We cannot reduce Wisdom to a formula, or trap it in our words. Sometimes we don't recognize it, even when we see it. Yet under the right circumstances, Wisdom reveals itself to us in a flash of insight, when a masterful teacher makes it clear.

We also discover, as Solomon affirms and the rest of scripture echoes, that Wisdom is divine. It is God's active presence in the world, with which we are invited to live in harmony. Christians later understood Wisdom in light of Jesus Christ. Jesus Christ is *logos*, "Wisdom", incarnate.[75] And, as Jesus himself puts it in Luke 7:35, ". . . *wisdom is justified by all her children.*"

The spirit of Wisdom is the spirit of careful observation and thorough inquiry, wedded to an unsentimental determination to learn from experience. It is the same spirit that gives rise to the scientific method, and that continues to transform human life for the better. This spirit is never received without resistance, yet it is the key to our species' survival on the planet.

---

[75] See John 1:1.

The Wisdom which inspired Solomon and the Wisdom incarnate in Christ are one and the same. To understand the Wisdom of Proverbs is to understand the only wisdom that exists. It is to understand Christ. Whatever name we call that Wisdom, the reality of it abides forever

Chapter 1

The Purpose of the Book

1:1 *parabolae Salomonis filii David regis Israhel*[76]

Parables of Solomon,
son of David,
king of Israel,[77]

1:2 *ad sciendam sapientiam et disciplinam*

dedicated to knowing
wisdom and discipline;

1:3 *ad intellegenda verba prudentiae et suscipiendam eruditionem doctrinae iustitiam et iudicium et aequitatem*

to understanding prudent words;
to supporting *the* learning

---

[76] Latin was not the original language of "Proverbs." The book, written in Hebrew several centuries before Christ, was translated into Latin by St. Jerome, around the 4th Century of the Common Era. See http://en.wikipedia.org/wiki/Jerome.

[77] The biblical tradition teaches that Solomon, King David's son and heir, wrote this book. Solomon's story may be found in I Kings and II Chronicles. See: http://en.wikipedia.org/wiki/Solomon.

of doctrine;
to justice, judgment,
and fairness;

1:4 *ut detur parvulis astutia adulescenti scientia et intellectus*

that *the* young
might turn to cleverness,
youths to knowledge[78]
and intellect.

1:5 *audiens sapiens sapientior erit et intellegens gubernacula possidebit*

Hearing, *the* wise become wiser,
and *the* understanding will possess leadership.

1:6 *animadvertet parabolam et interpretationem verba sapientium et enigmata eorum*

He will pay attention
to parable and interpretation,
to wise words and their enigmas.

1:7 *timor Domini principium scientiae sapientiam atque doctrinam stulti despiciunt*

Fear of *the* Lord[79]
is the beginning of understanding.
Fools despise wisdom
and even teaching.

1:8 *audi fili mi disciplinam patris tui et ne dimittas legem matris tuae*

Understand *the* discipline
of your father, my son,
and do not renounce your
mother's legacy,

1:9 *ut addatur gratia capiti*

---

[78] I toyed with the idea of translating *scientia* literally, as "science." While it would be an anachronism to put the word "science" in the Book of Proverbs, that element of the human spirit which birthed the scientific impulse is certainly at work here. The knowledge Proverbs exhorts its reader to is systematic, reflective, and verified by experience. These qualities distinguish scientific understanding from mere opinion.

[79] "Fear of the Lord" is a a troubling phrase for many. This is not a superstitious fear, though. It is, rather, a healthy regard for the immensity of the real world in which we live, for what even insurance companies call "acts of God," and for One who is almost unimaginably greater than we are in all senses. This sense of awe, even fear, dawns in us as we realize how immense the universe is and how small we are within it. Once this sense of awe awakens, we begin to see ourselves as we are. Then, understanding becomes possible.

tuo et torques collo tuo

that grace
may be added to your head,
and strength to your neck.

Don't Let Others Entrap You

1:10 *fili mi si te lactaverint peccatores ne adquiescas*

My son,
if sinners lead you on,
do not give in.

1:11 *si dixerint veni nobiscum insidiemur sanguini abscondamus tendiculas contra insontem frustra*

If they say, 'Come with us!
Let us lie in wait for blood.
Let us hide traps
against *the* harmless,
without cause.'

1:12 *degluttiamus eum sicut infernus viventem et integrum quasi descendentem in lacum*

'Let us swallow them down
whole, as if into *the* inferno,
alive, descending into *a* pit.

1:13 *omnem pretiosam substantiam repperiemus implebimus domos nostras spoliis*

'Let us find
every precious substance!
Let us fill our houses with
spoils.

1:14 *sortem mitte nobiscum marsuppium unum sit omnium nostrum*

'Come out with us.
Let there be one money bag
for all of us.'

1:15 *fili mi ne ambules cum eis prohibe pedem tuum a semitis eorum*

My son, do not go with them!
Keep your feet
from walking their paths.

1:16 *pedes enim illorum ad malum currunt et festinant ut effundant sanguinem*

For their feet run to evil,
and hurry to *the* pouring out
of blood.

1:17 *frustra autem iacitur rete ante oculos pinnatorum*

But *a* net is cast pointlessly
before *the* eyes of *the* birds.

1:18 *ipsique contra sanguinem suum insidiantur et moliuntur fraudes contra animas suas*

In spite of that,
these fools lie in wait
against their own blood,
and plan frauds against
their own souls.[80]

1:19 *sic semitae omnis avari animas possidentium rapiunt*

So are *the* actions
of every greedy *heart*,
destroying *the* souls
of those possessing them.

Wisdom Calls Out

1:20 *sapientia foris praedicat in plateis dat vocem suam*

Wisdom proclaims outside;
in broad streets it gives its voice.

1:21 *in capite turbarum clamitat in foribus portarum urbis profert verba sua dicens*

At *the* head of *a* multitude,
it clamors;
at *the* entrance gates
to *the* city
it offers its words, saying,

1:22 *usquequo parvuli diligitis infantiam et stulti ea quae sibi sunt noxia cupiunt et inprudentes odibunt scientiam*

'How long, children,
will you delight in infancy,
How long will fools
be captured
by that which is toxic
to them,
and the imprudent despise
understanding?

1:23 *convertimini ad correptionem meam en proferam vobis spiritum meum et ostendam verba mea*

'Pay attention to my rebuke,
when I offer my spirit to you,
and I will show you my
teachings.

---

[80] The word "soul" translates the Latin *anima*, which can also be rendered as "life force." Anima refers to the entirety of a being's inner experience of life, as opposed to the outward perspective we have of the lives of others.

1:24 *quia vocavi et rennuistis extendi manum meam et non fuit qui aspiceret*

'Because I called
and you refused,
because I have
extended my hand,
and no one considered,

1:25 *despexistis omne consilium meum et increpationes meas neglexistis*

'you despised
my whole counsel,
and neglected my warnings.

1:26 *ego quoque in interitu vestro ridebo et subsannabo cum vobis quod timebatis advenerit*

'I, in turn, will laugh
at your destruction,
and will mock you
when what you fear
comes upon you.

1:27 *cum inruerit repentina calamitas et interitus quasi tempestas ingruerit quando venerit super vos tribulatio et angustia*

'When calamities
explode suddenly,
and destruction,
like a tempest, breaks in,
when trial and anguish
come to you,

1:29 *tunc invocabunt me et non exaudiam mane consurgent et non invenient me*

'then they will invoke me,
and I will not hear.
They will rise up early,
yet will not find me.'

1:30 *eo quod exosam habuerint disciplinam et timorem Domini non susceperint*

'Then, because they have
a distaste for discipline,
and did not accept
reverence of God,

1:31 *nec adquieverint consilio meo et detraxerint universae correptioni meae*

'*nor* assent to my counsel,
and will throw aside
all my rebukes,

1:32 *comedent igitur fructus*

viae suae suisque consiliis saturabuntur

'let them eat, therefore,
the fruit of their ways
themselves,
and let them be satisfied
by their own counsel.[81]

1:32 *aversio parvulorum interficiet eos et prosperitas stultorum perdet illos*

'*The* turning away
of *the* children kills them,
and *the* prosperity of fools
destroys them.

1:33 *qui autem me audierit absque terrore requiescet et abundantia perfruetur malorum timore sublato*

'But *one* who hears me
rests far away from terror,
and enjoys abundance,
fear of evil removed.'

[81] Compare to Romans 1:24-25 *Therefore God gave them up in the lusts of their hearts to impurity, to the dishonoring of their bodies among themselves, because they exchanged the truth about God for a lie and worshiped and served the creature rather than the Creator, who is blessed for ever! Amen.*

Chapter 2

A Father Exhorts His Son

2:1 *fili mi si susceperis sermones meos et mandata mea absconderis penes te*

My son, if you accept
my words
and hide my commandment
in your manhood,

2:2 *ut audiat sapientiam auris tua inclina cor tuum ad noscendam prudentiam*

that your ear
may hear wisdom,
incline your heart
to learning prudence.

2:3 *si enim sapientiam invocaveris et inclinaveris cor tuum prudentiae*

If you invoke wisdom
and incline your heart
to prudence,

2:4 *si quaesieris eam quasi pecuniam et sicut thesauros effoderis illam*

if you seek her like money
and dig for her like treasure,

2:5 *tunc intelleges timorem Domini et scientiam Dei invenies*

Then you will understand
the fear of *the* Lord,
and will find knowledge
of God,

2:6 *quia Dominus dat sapientiam et ex ore eius scientia et prudentia*

because *the* Lord
gives wisdom,
and, from his mouth,
knowledge and prudence.

2:7 *custodiet rectorum salutem et proteget gradientes simpliciter*

He guards
the well-being
of *the* fair,
and protects *the* steps
of *the* honest,

2:8 *servans semitas iustitiae et vias sanctorum custodiens*

saving fair-minded paths
and guarding holy ways.

2:9 *tunc intelleges iustitiam et iudicium et aequitatem et omnem semitam bonam*

Then, you will know
fairness and judgment,
equity and every good path.

2:10 *si intraverit sapientia cor tuum et scientia animae tuae placuerit*

If wisdom penetrates
your heart
and knowledge pleases
your soul,

2:11 *consilium custodiet te prudentia servabit te*

counsel will guard you,
prudence will save you,

2:12 *ut eruaris de via mala ab homine qui perversa loquitur*

that you may be rescued
from *the* evil way,
from *a* man
who speaks perversity,

2:13 *qui relinquunt iter rectum et ambulant per vias tenebrosas*

from *those* who relinquish
a fair-minded course

and walk in shady practices;

2:14 *qui laetantur cum malefecerint et exultant in rebus pessimis*

who are happy
when they are doing evil,
and exult in dismal affairs,

2:15 *quorum viae perversae et infames gressus eorum*

whose habits are perverse,
and their steps unsavory.

Warning Against Strange Women

2:16 *ut eruaris a muliere aliena et ab extranea quae mollit sermones suos*

I pray that you be delivered
from *the* foreign woman,
and *the* stranger
who softens her words,

2:17 *et relinquit ducem pubertatis suae*

and gives up
the direction of her youth,

2:18 *et pacti Dei sui oblita est inclinata est enim ad mortem domus eius et ad impios semitae ipsius*

and *the* pact of her God
is forgotten,
for her house is sliding
to death,
and her paths to *the* lawless.[82]

2:19 *omnes qui ingrediuntur ad eam non revertentur nec adprehendent semitas vitae*

All who go in to her
neither return,
nor learn *the* ways of life.

Walk in the Good Way

2:20 *ut ambules in via bona et calles iustorum custodias*

Walk *in* a good way,

---

[82] The Latin word *impietas* and its personal correlate, *impius*, means "lacking reverence or respect for the divine." It is often rendered as "impious" in English translation. The word "impious," though, is fuzzy for most modern hearers.

Since the God of Israel was a God of Law, before almost all else, I have translated *impietas* as lawlessness. The *impius* is one who disrespects or disobeys divine law. Divine law is perhaps best summarized in Micah 6:8.

We may not know what it means to be impious in this self-absorbed age of ours. We do know what being lawless is. Since Proverbs is, above all, a practical book, intended to help us live well, it is important to make its words as relevant as possible to contemporary readers.

and guard *the* stony tracks
of fairness,

2:21 *qui enim recti sunt habitabunt in terra et simplices permanebunt in ea*

for those who live
rightly in *the* land,
will remain in simplicity
upon it.

2:22 *impii vero de terra perdentur et qui inique agunt auferentur ex ea*

The lawless, truly,
will be destroyed
from *the* land,
and those who practice
treachery
will be swept away from it.

Chapter 3

Urging a Son to Pay Attention

3:1 *fili mi ne obliviscaris legis meae et praecepta mea custodiat cor tuum*

My son, do not forget
my laws,
and let your heart keep
my precepts,

3:2 *longitudinem enim dierum et annos vitae et pacem adponent tibi*

for they will set before you
length of days, years of life,
and peace.

3:3 *misericordia et veritas non te deserant circumda eas gutturi tuo et describe in tabulis cordis tui*

May mercy and truth
not desert you.
Place them around your neck,
and carve them on *the* tablets
of your heart,

3:4 *et invenies gratiam et disciplinam bonam coram Deo et hominibus*

and you will find grace
and good discipline,
before God and men.

3:5 *habe fiduciam in Domino ex toto corde tuo et ne innitaris prudentiae tuae*

Have faith in God
with all your heart,
and do not lean
on your prudence.

3:6 *in omnibus viis tuis cogita illum et ipse diriget gressus tuos*

In all your ways,
remember him,
and he will direct your steps.

3:7 *ne sis sapiens apud temet ipsum time Dominum et recede a malo*

Do not be wise
in your own eyes.
Fear God and turn back
from evil.

3:8 *sanitas quippe erit umbilico tuo et inrigatio ossuum tuorum*

Sanity, as you see,
will be your center,
and *will be* refreshment
to your bones.

3:9 *honora Dominum de tua substantia et de primitiis omnium frugum tuarum*

Honor *the* Lord
with your substance,
and from *the* first
of all your produce,

3:10 *et implebuntur horrea tua saturitate et vino torcularia redundabunt*

and your barns
will be full completely,
and *your* wine-presses
will overflow.

Understand Correction

3:11 *disciplinam Domini fili mi ne abicias nec deficias cum ab eo corriperis*

My son, do not throw aside
the Lord's discipline,
nor turn away from him
when you are corrected.

3:12 *quem enim diligit Dominus corripit et quasi pater in filio conplacet sibi*

for whom *the* Lord delights

in, he corrects,
and, like a father, He pleases
Himself in His son.

The Value of Wisdom

3:13 *beatus homo qui invenit sapientiam et qui affluit prudentia*

A man who finds wisdom
and who flows
toward prudence is blessed.

3:14 *melior est adquisitio eius negotiatione argenti et auro primo fructus eius*

It is better than
a business in silver,
and gold *is* its first fruit.

3:15 *pretiosior est cunctis opibus et omnia quae desiderantur huic non valent conparari*

It is more precious
than all works.
All *things* which are desired
cannot be compared to it.

3:16 *longitudo dierum in dextera eius in sinistra illius divitiae et gloria*

Length of days *is*
in its right *hand*,
riches and glory in its left.

3:17 *viae eius viae pulchrae et omnes semitae illius pacificae*

Its ways *are* beautiful ways,
and all its paths peaceful.

3:18 *lignum vitae est his qui adprehenderint eam et qui tenuerit eam beatus*

It is *a* tree of life
to those who lay hold of it,
and *one* who comprehends
is blessed.

God Created by Wisdom

3:19 *Dominus sapientia fundavit terram stabilivit caelos prudentia*

The Lord founded
the earth by wisdom.
He established
the skies by prudence.

3:20 *sapientia illius eruperunt abyssi et nubes rore concrescunt*

By His wisdom,
the depths burst forth,
and clouds condensed

from rain drops.

Keep Counsel

3:21 *fili mi ne effluant haec ab oculis tuis custodi legem atque consilium*

My son, may *these things*
not wash out of your eyes.
Keep *the* law and also
counsel,

3:22 *et erit vita animae tuae et gratia faucibus tuis*

and *it* will be life
to your soul,
and grace to your appearance.

3:23 *tunc ambulabis fiducialiter in via tua et pes tuus non inpinget*

Then, you will walk
faithfully in your way,
and your foot will not be
struck.

3:24 *si dormieris non timebis quiesces et suavis erit somnus tuus*

If you sleep,
you will not be afraid.
You will be at peace,
and your dreams
will be pleasant.

3:25 *ne paveas repentino terrore et inruentes tibi potentias impiorum*

Do not be terrified
by terrible circumstance,
or lawless powers suddenly
rushing upon you.

3:26 *Dominus enim erit in latere tuo et custodiet pedem tuum ne capiaris*

for *the* Lord will be
at your side,
and he will guard your step,
that you not be captured.

3:27 *noli prohibere benefacere eum qui potest si vales et ipse benefac*

Do not stop someone
who is able to do good.
If you are able,
you do good as well.

3:28 *ne dicas amico tuo vade et revertere et cras dabo tibi cum statim possis dare*

Do not say to your friend,
'Go, and come back later;

tomorrow I will
give you *something*,'
when *it* is possible
to give right now.

3:29 *ne moliaris amico tuo malum cum ille in te habeat fiduciam*

Do not plan evil
for your friend,
when he has faith in you.

3:30 *ne contendas adversus hominem frustra cum ipse tibi nihil mali fecerit*

Do not contend against *a* man, without cause,
when he has done
nothing bad to you.

3:31 *ne aemuleris hominem iniustum nec imiteris vias eius*

Do not copy *an* unfair man,
nor imitate his ways.

3:32 *quia abominatio Domini est omnis inlusor et cum simplicibus sermocinatio eius*

because *the* Lord detests
every scoffer,
and his careful conversation
is with *the* simple.

Consequence of Our Actions

3:33 *egestas a Domino in domo impii habitacula autem iustorum benedicentur*

Lack in *an* lawless house
is from *the* Lord;
but *the* dwelling of *the* fair
will be blessed.

3:34 *inlusores ipse deludet et mansuetis dabit gratiam*

He will deceive mockers,
but will give grace to *the* gentle.

3:35 *gloriam sapientes possidebunt stultorum exaltatio ignominia*

The wise will possess glory,
but glorifying *a* fool is shameful.

Chapter 4

A Mother's Teaching

4:1 *audite filii disciplinam patris et adtendite ut sciatis prudentiam*

Hear *the* discipline
of your father, my son,
and attend to *the* learning
of prudence.

4:2 *donum bonum tribuam vobis legem meam ne derelinquatis*

I will give you *a* good gift.
Do not abandon my law,

4:3 *nam et ego filius fui patris mei tenellus et unigenitus coram matre mea*

for I also was *a* son
of my father,
a tender and only child
before my mother,[83]

4:4 *et docebat me atque dicebat suscipiat verba mea cor tuum custodi praecepta mea et vives*

and she taught me,
and also said to me,
'Accept my words
and guard my precepts,
that you may live.

4:5 *posside sapientiam posside prudentiam ne obliviscaris neque declines a verbis oris mei*

'Possess wisdom,
possess prudence,
and neither forget
nor turn away
from *the* words of my mouth.

4:6 *ne dimittas eam et custodiet te dilige eam et servabit te*

'Do not dismiss it,
that *it* may guard you.
Delight in it,
and *it* will serve you.

The Beginning of Wisdom

4:7 *principium sapientiae posside sapientiam et in omni possessione tua adquire prudentiam*

The beginning of wisdom:
possess wisdom,
and in all your possessing,
buy prudence.

[83] See 2 Samuel 11 for the story of Solomon's mother, Bathsheba.

4:8 *arripe illam et exaltabit te glorificaberis ab ea cum eam fueris amplexatus*

Take hold of it,
and *it* will exalt you.
You will be glorified by it
when you embrace it.

4:9 *dabit capiti tuo augmenta gratiarum et corona inclita proteget te*

It will give your head
the increase of grace,
and *the* celebrated crown
will protect you.

4:10 *audi fili mi et suscipe verba mea ut multiplicentur tibi anni vitae*

Hear, my son,
and accept my words,
that years of life may be
multiplied to you.

4:11 *viam sapientiae monstravi tibi duxi te per semitas aequitatis*

I have shown you
the way of wisdom.
I have guided you by
paths of equity,

4:12 *quas cum ingressus fueris non artabuntur gressus tui et currens non habebis offendiculum*

which, when you walk
in them,
will not limit your path,
and, when you run,
you will not have *an*
obstacle.

4:13 *tene disciplinam ne dimittas eam custodi illam quia ipsa est vita tua*

Have discipline.
Do not dismiss it.
Keep them,
because it is your life.

Stay Off Lawless Ways

4:14 *ne delecteris semitis impiorum nec tibi placeat malorum via*

Do not delight
in lawless paths,
or let *an* evil way please you.

4:15 *fuge ab ea ne transeas per illam declina et desere eam*

Flee from it!
Do not cross it!

Turn away and desert it!

4:16 *non enim dormiunt nisi malefecerint et rapitur somnus ab eis nisi subplantaverint*

For *some* do not sleep
unless they are doing evil,
and sleep is robbed
from them
unless they are causing
others to fall.

4:17 *comedunt panem impietatis et vinum iniquitatis bibunt*

They eat bread
of lawlessness,
and drink wine of treachery,

4:18 *iustorum autem semita quasi lux splendens procedit et crescit usque ad perfectam diem*

but *the* path of *the* fair,
like light,
proceeds and grows
until *the* perfect day.

4:19 *via impiorum tenebrosa nesciunt ubi corruant*

The way of *the* lawless
is dark!
They do not know
where they are running!

Obey My Teaching

4:20 *fili mi ausculta sermones meos et ad eloquia mea inclina aurem tuam*

My son, obey my words,
and incline your ear
to my eloquence.

4:21 *ne recedant ab oculis tuis custodi ea in medio cordis tui*

Do not let them
recede from your eyes.
Keep them
in *the* middle of your heart!

4:22 *vita enim sunt invenientibus ea et universae carni sanitas*

For life is found in them,
and *the* health of all flesh.

4:23 *omni custodia serva cor tuum quia ex ipso vita procedit*

Keeping all, save your heart,
because life proceeds from it.

4:24 *remove a te os pravum et detrahentia labia sint procul a te*

Turn yourself away from
a perverse mouth,
and may scornful lips
be far from you.

4:25 *oculi tui recta videant et palpebrae tuae praecedant gressus tuos*

Let your eyes see right,
and let your eyelids watch
ahead of your steps.

4:26 *dirige semitam pedibus tuis et omnes viae tuae stabilientur*

Direct *the* path of your feet,
and all your ways
will be established.

4:27 *ne declines ad dexteram et ad sinistram averte pedem tuum a malo*

Do not turn away
to *the* right or to *the* left.
Turn your step, *rather*,
away from evil.

Chapter 5

Learn to Guard Your Thoughts

5:1 *fili mi adtende sapientiam meam et prudentiae meae inclina aurem tuam*

My son, pay attention
to my wisdom,
and incline your ear
to my prudence.

5:2 *ut custodias cogitationes et disciplinam labia tua conservent*

that you may guard
your thoughts,
and *the* discipline of your lips
will preserve *you*.

The Ways of a Whore

5:3 *favus enim stillans labia meretricis et nitidius oleo guttur eius*

For *the* lips of *a* whore are
a dripping honeycomb,
and *the* scent of her neck
fresh,

5:4 *novissima autem illius amara quasi absinthium et acuta quasi gladius biceps*

but her end *is* bitter,
like absinthe,
and sharp,
like *a* two-edged sword.

5:5 *pedes eius descendunt in mortem et ad inferos gressus illius penetrant*

Her feet descend to death,
and her steps penetrate to
the house of *the* dead.

5:6 *per semitam vitae non ambulat vagi sunt gressus eius et investigabiles*

She does not walk
by *the* path of life.
Her steps are wandering
and hidden.

5:7 *nunc ergo fili audi me et ne recedas a verbis oris mei*

Now, therefore, my son,
hear me,
and do not turn back
from *the* words of my mouth.

5:8 *longe fac ab ea viam tuam et ne adpropinques foribus domus eius*

Make your way far from her,
and do not even go near
the doors of her house,

Be Wary of Strangers

5:9 *ne des alienis honorem tuum et annos tuos crudeli*

lest you give your honor
to strangers,
and your years to *the* cruel,

5:10 *ne forte impleantur extranei viribus tuis et labores tui sint in domo aliena*

lest strangers be enriched
by your talents,
and your labors be
in *a* foreign house.

5:11 *et gemas in novissimis quando consumpseris carnes et corpus tuum et dicas*

And you will moan
in *the* end,
when you have consumed
even your own flesh
and body, and you say,

5:12 *cur detestatus sum disciplinam et increpationibus non adquievit cor meum*

'Why did I detest discipline,

and my heart not assent
to reproofs?

5:13 *nec audivi vocem docentium me et magistris non inclinavi aurem meam*

'I did not hear *the* voice
of those teaching me,
nor incline my ear
to 'authorities.'

5:14 *paene fui in omni malo in medio ecclesiae et synagogae*

'I was in nearly
all *the* mischief,
in *the* middle of *the* gathering
and of *the* synagogue.'

Enjoy What Is Yours

5:15 *bibe aquam de cisterna tua et fluenta putei tui*

Drink water
from your cistern,
and *the* flow of your well.

5:16 *deriventur fontes tui foras et in plateis aquas tuas divide*

Let your springs
be turned outside,
and in *the* streets
divide your waters.

5:17 *habeto eas solus nec sint alieni participes tui*

Let them be to you alone,
nor let strangers share yours.

Love Your Wife

5:18 *sit vena tua benedicta et laetare cum muliere adulescentiae tuae*

May your vein be blessed,
and be happy with
the wife of your youth.

5:19 *cerva carissima et gratissimus hinulus ubera eius inebrient te omni tempore in amore illius delectare iugiter*

A precious deer
and *a* gracious fawn,
her breasts inebriate you
all *the* time.
Delight in her love
continually.

5:20 *quare seduceris fili mi ab aliena et foveris sinu alterius*

Why be seduced
by *a* stranger, my son,

and be cherished
in another's embrace?

God Pays Attention to Human Actions

5:21 *respicit Dominus vias hominis et omnes gressus illius considerat*

The Lord pays attention
to *the* ways of men,
and considers all their steps.

5:22 *iniquitates suae capiunt impium et funibus peccatorum suorum constringitur*

His own treacheries
capture *the* lawless,
and *the* ropes of his *own* sin
bind him.

5:23 *ipse morietur quia non habuit disciplinam et multitudine stultitiae suae decipietur*

He will die because
he did not have discipline,
and will be deceived by
his own multitude of idiocies.

Chapter 6

Watch What You Promise

6:1 *fili mi si spoponderis pro amico tuo defixisti apud extraneum manum tuam*

My son, if you give
a pledge for your friend,
you are buried in
a stranger's hand.

6:2 *inlaqueatus es verbis oris tui et captus propriis sermonibus*

You are ensnared
by *the* words of your mouth,
and captured by
your own promises.

6:3 *fac ergo quod dico fili mi et temet ipsum libera quia incidisti in manu proximi tui discurre festina suscita amicum tuum*

Do, therefore, what I say, my
son, and free yourself,
because you have fallen
into *the* hand
of your neighbor.
Run away quickly!
Rouse your friend!

6:4 *ne dederis somnum*

oculis tuis nec dormitent palpebrae tuae

Do not give sleep
to your eyes,
nor let your eyelids rest!

6:5 *eruere quasi dammula de manu et quasi avis de insidiis aucupis*

Free yourself
like *a* deer from *the* hand,
and like *a* bird from
the bird-seller's trap!

Look to the Ant

6:6 *vade ad formicam o piger et considera vias eius et disce sapientiam*

Look to *the* ant, O lazy *one*,
consider its ways
and learn wisdom!

6:7 *quae cum non habeat ducem nec praeceptorem nec principem*

Because, having neither
leader, nor precept,
nor prince,

6:8 *parat aestate cibum sibi et congregat in messe quod comedat*

in summer it prepares food
for itself,
and gathers in harvest time,
that it might eat.

6:9 *usquequo piger dormis quando consurges ex somno tuo*

How long, lazy *one*,
will you sleep?
When will you rouse yourself
from your dream?

6:10 *paululum dormies paululum dormitabis paululum conseres manus ut dormias*

You will be idle *a* little,
you will be drowsy *a* little,
you will fold your hands *a*
little, that you may sleep;

6:11 *et veniet tibi quasi viator egestas et pauperies quasi vir armatus*

and need will come to you
like *a* thief,
poverty like *an* armed man.

A Useless Man

6:12 *homo apostata vir inutilis graditur ore perverso*

An apostate man,
a useless man,
goes along by perverse
mouth.

6:13 *annuit oculis terit pede digito loquitur*

He smiles with *the* eyes,
he wears out with *the* foot,
he talks with *the* finger.

6:14 *pravo corde machinatur malum et in omni tempore iurgia seminat*

With *a* crooked heart
he plots evil,
and at each opportunity
he starts quarrels.

6:15 *huic extemplo veniet perditio sua et subito conteretur nec habebit ultra medicinam*

By these his destruction
will come,
and soon he will be
ground to pieces,
nor will he have other
remedy.

Six Things the Lord Hates

6:16 *sex sunt quae odit Dominus et septimum detestatur anima eius*

There are six *things*
which *the* Lord hates,
and *a* seventh is detested
by His soul:

6:17 *oculos sublimes linguam mendacem manus effundentes innoxium sanguinem*

proud eyes, lying tongue,
hands shedding innocent
blood,

6:18 *cor machinans cogitationes pessimas pedes veloces ad currendum in malum*

a heart plotting
dismal schemes,
feet running swiftly to evil,

6:19 *proferentem mendacia testem fallacem et eum qui seminat inter fratres discordias*

a liar giving out
false testimony,
and those who spread
quarrels between brothers.

A True Conservative

6:20 *conserva fili mi praecepta patris tui et ne dimittas legem matris tuae*

Conserve, my son,
your father's precepts,
and do not dismiss
your mother's law.

6:21 *liga ea in corde tuo iugiter et circumda gutturi tuo*

Bind them in your heart
continually,
and tie them around your
neck.

6:22 *cum ambulaveris gradiantur tecum cum dormieris custodiant te et evigilans loquere cum eis*

When you walk,
they will go with you;
When you sleep,
they will keep you;
and, waking up, talk about
them,

6:23 *quia mandatum lucerna est et lex lux et via vitae increpatio disciplinae*

because *the* commandment
is *a* lamp,
and *the* law *a* light
and discipline's rebuke
is *the* way of life,

6:24 *ut custodiant te a muliere mala et a blanda lingua extraneae*

that they may keep you
from an evil woman,
and from *a* flattering,
foreign tongue.

6:25 *non concupiscat pulchritudinem eius cor tuum nec capiaris nutibus illius*

Do not let your heart
lust for her beauty,
nor be captured by her
charms;

6:26 *pretium enim scorti vix unius est panis mulier autem viri pretiosam animam capit*

for *the* price of *a* whore
is hardly loaf of bread,
yet *the* woman captures
the costly soul of *a* man.

A Warning Against Adultery

6:27 *numquid abscondere potest homo ignem in sinu*

suo ut vestimenta illius non ardeant

Can man hide *a* hot coal
against his chest,
and his clothes not burn,

6:28 *aut ambulare super prunas et non conburentur plantae eius*

or walk over glowing coals
and not burn *the* soles of his *feet*?

6:29 *sic qui ingreditur ad mulierem proximi sui non erit mundus cum tetigerit eam*

So one who goes in
to his neighbor's wife
will not be clean
when he touches her.

6:30 *non grandis est culpae cum quis furatus fuerit furatur enim ut esurientem impleat animam*

Guilt is not as great
when someone has stolen.
He stole out of hunger
that he might fill his soul.

6:31 *deprehensus quoque reddet septuplum et omnem substantiam domus suae tradet*

When seized, likewise,
he will pay back seven times
and hand over all
the substance of his house.

6:32 *qui autem adulter est propter cordis inopiam perdet animam suam*

Yet one who is *an* adulterer
will destroy his impoverished soul.

6:33 *turpitudinem et ignominiam congregat sibi et obprobrium illius non delebitur*

He gathers to himself
a bad reputation and shame,
and his disrepute
will not disappear.

6:34 *quia zelus et furor viri non parcet in die vindictae*

because *the* husband's
jealousy and fury,
will not spare *him*
in *the* day of vengeance,

6:35 *nec adquiescet cuiusquam precibus nec*

suscipiet pro redemptione dona plurima

nor will *he* be calmed
by any payment,
nor accept in settlement
many bribes.

Chapter 7

Serve My Commandment

7:1 *fili mi custodi sermones meos et praecepta mea reconde tibi*

My son, guard my teachings,
and hide my precepts with you.

7:2 *serva mandata mea et vives et legem meam quasi pupillam oculi tui*

Serve my commandment,
that you may live,
and my law, like the pupil
of your eye.

7:3 *liga eam in digitis tuis scribe illam in tabulis cordis tui*

Bind it to your fingers.
Write it on *the* tablets
of your heart.

7:4 *dic sapientiae soror mea es et prudentiam voca amicam tuam*

Say to wisdom,
'You are my sister,'
and call prudence your
friend.

7:5 *ut custodiat te a muliere extranea et ab aliena quae verba sua dulcia facit*

that she guard you
from *a* strange woman,
and from *a* foreigner
whose words make sweet.

A Strange Woman Entices

7:6 *de fenestra enim domus meae per cancellos prospexi*

For from *the* window
of my house,
I looked through *the* lattice,

7:7 *et video parvulos considero vecordem iuvenem*

and I see little ones.
I consider *a* wild youth,

7:8 *qui transit in platea iuxta angulum et propter viam domus illius graditur*

who crosses *the* street
near *the* corner,
and walks near *the* walkway
to her house.

7:9 *in obscuro advesperascente die in noctis tenebris et caligine*

Evening is coming on
with darkness.
Day is shadowed over
in night and gloom.

7:10 *et ecce mulier occurrit illi ornatu meretricio praeparata ad capiendas animas garrula et vaga*

And, look, *a* woman
hurries to him,
dressed like *a* whore,
prepared for capturing souls,
mindless and chattering.

7:11 *quietis inpatiens nec valens in domo consistere pedibus suis*

Impatient with quietness,
nor eager to keep her feet
in her house,

7:12 *nunc foris nunc in plateis nunc iuxta angulos insidians*

now outside, now in *the*
streets,
now near hidden corners,

7:13 *adprehensumque deosculatur iuvenem et procaci vultu blanditur dicens*

she seizes and kisses *the* youth,
and with *an* impudent face,
she allures him.

7:14 *victimas pro salute debui hodie reddidi vota mea*

'I owed sacrifices for health.
Today I repaid my promise.

7:15 *idcirco egressa sum in occursum tuum desiderans te videre et repperi*

'For this reason,
I have come to meet you,
wanting to see you
and get to know you.

7:16 *intexui funibus lectum meum stravi tapetibus pictis ex Aegypto*

'I covered my couch
with fine fabric.
I laid out painted tapestries
from Egypt.

7:17 *aspersi cubile meum murra et aloe et cinnamomo*

'I sprayed my bed with myrrh
and aloe and cinnamon.

7:18 *veni inebriemur uberibus donec inlucescat dies et fruamur cupitis amplexibus*

'Come! Let us get drunk
in *my* breasts
until day begins to dawn,
and let us enjoy
passion's embracing!

7:19 *non est enim vir in domo sua abiit via longissima*

'For *my* husband is not
in his house,
He went on *a* long trip.

7:20 *sacculum pecuniae secum tulit in die plenae lunae reversurus est domum suam*

'He took *a* bag of money
with him.
He will return to his house
at full moon.'

7:21 *inretivit eum multis sermonibus et blanditiis labiorum protraxit illum*

She has caught him
by many words,
and taken him
by *the* sweetness of *her* lips

7:22 *statim eam sequitur quasi bos ductus ad victimam et quasi agnus lasciviens et ignorans quod ad vincula stultus trahatur*

He follows her at once,
like *a* bull led to sacrifice,
and like *a* lamb,
horny and ignorant,
because *the* fool is led to chains,

7:23 *donec transfigat sagitta iecur eius velut si avis festinet ad laqueum et nescit quia de periculo animae illius agitur*

until *an* arrow
pierces his liver.
He is like *a* bird
that hurries to *the* net,
and does not know that *it*
is led in danger of its life.

Do Not Let Your Mind Be Dragged Away

7:24 *nunc ergo fili audi me et adtende verba oris mei*

Now, therefore, son, hear me,
and attend to *the* words
of my mouth.

7:25 *ne abstrahatur in viis illius mens tua neque decipiaris semitis eius*

Do not let your mind
be dragged away
by her methods,
nor be deceived
by her habits,

7:26 *multos enim vulneratos deiecit et fortissimi quique interfecti sunt ab ea*

for she has struck down
many wounded,
and how many
of *the* strongest
have been killed by her!

7:27 *viae inferi domus eius penetrantes interiora mortis*

Her house *is the* way
to *the* dead,
penetrating to *the* inner
reaches of death.

Chapter 8

Does Wisdom Not Cry Out

8:1 *numquid non sapientia clamitat et prudentia dat vocem suam*

Does wisdom not cry out,
and prudence give her voice?

8:2 *in summis excelsisque verticibus super viam in mediis semitis stans*

Standing in *the* highest
places and prominences
above *the* road,
in *the* middle of paths,

8:3 *iuxta portas civitatis in ipsis foribus loquitur dicens*

beside *the* gates of *a* city,
in *the* doors themselves,
she speaks, saying,

8:4 *o viri ad vos clamito et vox mea ad filios hominum*

'O men, I cry out to you,
and my voice *speaks*
to *the* children of men,

8:5 *intellegite parvuli astutiam et insipientes animadvertite*

'Understand cleverness,
little ones,
and pay attention,
you foolish!

8:6 *audite quoniam de rebus magnis locutura sum et aperientur labia mea ut recta praedicent*

'Hear, because I will speak
of great issues,
and my lips will open
to set forth what is right!

8:7 *veritatem meditabitur guttur meum et labia mea detestabuntur impium*

'My throat will meditate
on truth,
and my lips will detest
the lawless.

8:8 *iusti sunt omnes sermones mei non est in eis pravum quid neque perversum*

'All my words are fair.
There is no meanness in them
because *there* is nothing
dishonest.

8:9 *recti sunt intellegentibus et aequi invenientibus*

scientiam

'*They* are straightforward
to understanding,
and fair to *those*
finding knowledge.

8:10 *accipite disciplinam meam et non pecuniam doctrinam magis quam aurum eligite*

'Accept my discipline
and not money.
Choose learning
more than gold,

8:11 *melior est enim sapientia cunctis pretiosissimis et omne desiderabile ei non potest conparari*

'for wisdom is better than all
most precious *objects*,
and all *that is* desirable
cannot compare with it.

8:12 *ego sapientia habito in consilio et eruditis intersum cogitationibus*

'I, wisdom, dwell in counsel,
and am present
in *the* thoughts of *the* learned.

The Fear of the Lord Hates Arrogance

8:13 *timor Domini odit malum arrogantiam et superbiam et viam pravam et os bilingue detestor*

'*The* fear of *the* Lord hates
evil, arrogance, and pride,
I detest *a* vicious path
and *a* lying tongue.

8:14 *meum est consilium et aequitas mea prudentia mea est fortitudo*

'Counsel is mine, and equity;
prudence mine,
and strength is mine.

8:15 *per me reges regnant et legum conditores iusta decernunt*

'Kings reign by me,
and law-makers discern
fairly.

8:16 *per me principes imperant et potentes decernunt iustitiam*

Princes command by me,
and *the* powerful
discern fairness.

8:17 *ego diligentes me diligo et qui mane vigilant ad me invenient me*

'I delight in those
delighting in me,
and *those* who watch for me
early will find me.

8:18 *mecum sunt divitiae et gloria opes superbae et iustitia*

'Riches and glory
are with me,
works worthy of pride,
and fairness.

8:19 *melior est fructus meus auro et pretioso lapide et genimina mea argento electo*

'My fruit is better than gold
and precious stones,
and my progeny
are chosen over silver.

8:20 *in viis iustitiae ambulo in medio semitarum iudicii*

'I walk in ways of fairness,
in *the* middle of paths
of judgment,

8:21 *ut ditem diligentes me et thesauros eorum repleam*

'that I may enrich
those delighting in me,
and may fill their treasuries.

The Lord Possessed Me in the Beginning

8:22 *Dominus possedit me initium viarum suarum antequam quicquam faceret a principio*

'*The* Lord possessed me
at *the* start of all his ways,
in *the* beginning,
before He made anything.[84]

8:23 *ab aeterno ordita sum et ex antiquis antequam terra fieret*

'I was set up from eternity,
and from antiquity,
before earth was made.[85]

---

[84] Compare this passage to Colossians 1:15-17: *He [Christ] is the image of the invisible God, the first-born of all creation; for in him all things were created, in heaven and on earth, visible and invisible, whether thrones or dominions or principalities or authorities -- all things were created through him and for him. He is before all things, and in him all things hold together.*

[85] The preexistence of wisdom is echoed in John 1:1-3: *In the beginning was the Word, and the Word was with God, and the Word was God. 2 He was in the beginning with God; 3 all things were made*

8:24 *necdum erant abyssi et ego iam concepta eram necdum fontes aquarum eruperant*

'Even before *the* abyss was,
I *was* already conceived.
'I existed before
the fountains of water
erupted.

8:25 *necdum montes gravi mole constiterant ante colles ego parturiebar*

'Before massive mountains
were piled together,
and before *the* hills,
I was born.

8:26 *adhuc terram non fecerat et flumina et cardines orbis terrae*

'As yet, earth had not
been made,
nor rivers, nor *the* axis
of *the* circles of earth.

8:27 *quando praeparabat caelos aderam quando certa lege et gyro vallabat abyssos*

'I was there when
He prepared *the* heavens,
when He enclosed *the* abyss
by fixed law and by course;

8:28 *quando aethera firmabat sursum et librabat fontes aquarum*

'when He established
the sky above,
and freed *the* fountains of
water;

8:29 *quando circumdabat mari terminum suum et legem ponebat aquis ne transirent fines suos quando adpendebat fundamenta terrae*

'when He prescribed
to *the* sea its limits,
and placed *a* law on waters,
'*They* shall not pass
their limits;'
when He weighed out
the foundation of earth;

8:30 *cum eo eram cuncta conponens et delectabar per singulos dies ludens coram eo omni tempore*

'I was with Him, ordering all,
and I was glad in each day,

---

through him, and without him was not anything made that was made.

playing before Him all *the*
time,

8:31 *ludens in orbe terrarum et deliciae meae esse cum filiis hominum*

'playing in *the* circle of earth,
and my delight was with
the children of men.'

Now, Therefore, Hear Me

8:32 *nunc ergo filii audite me beati qui custodiunt vias meas*

'Now, therefore, children,
hear me!
Those who keep my ways
are blessed!

8:33 *audite disciplinam et estote sapientes et nolite abicere eam*

'Hear discipline, and be wise,
and do not turn away from it!

8:34 *beatus homo qui audit me qui vigilat ad fores meas cotidie et observat ad postes ostii mei*

'*A* man who hears me,
who seeks my gates daily,
and observes *the* doorposts
of my house, *is* blessed.

8:35 *qui me invenerit inveniet vitam et hauriet salutem a Domino*

'Who finds me will find life,
and will drink down health
from *the* Lord,

8:36 *qui autem in me peccaverit laedet animam suam omnes qui me oderunt diligunt mortem*

'but who sins in me
punishes his soul.
All who hate me
delight in death.'

Chapter 9

Wisdom's Solemn Sacrifice

9:1 *sapientia aedificavit sibi domum excidit columnas septem*

Wisdom built herself
a house,
cut down seven columns,

9:2 *immolavit victimas suas miscuit vinum et proposuit mensam suam*

burned her sacrifices,
mixed her wine,
and spread out her table.[86]

9:3 *misit ancillas suas ut vocarent ad arcem et ad moenia civitatis*

She sent her maidens,
that they might call out
from *the* citadels and walls
of *the* city.

9:4 *si quis est parvulus veniat ad me et insipientibus locuta est*

'If someone is young,
come to me.'
To *the* empty-headed
she has spoken.

9:5 *venite comedite panem meum et bibite vinum quod miscui vobis*

'Come, eat my bread,
and drink wine
which I mixed for you.

9:6 *relinquite infantiam et vivite et ambulate per vias prudentiae*

'Give up infancy and live,
and walk in ways of
prudence,

9:7 *qui erudit derisorem ipse sibi facit iniuriam et qui arguit impium generat maculam sibi*

'because he who
teaches *a* scoffer
causes injury to himself,
and *one* who corrects
the lawless
generates dishonor for
himself.

9:8 *noli arguere derisorem ne oderit te argue sapientem*

---

[86]These are the steps taken prior to offering a sacrifice to God. This indicates that Wisdom's search for us is itself a holy obligation, undertaken with the gravest purpose.

et diliget te

'Do not correct *a* scoffer,
lest he hate you.
Correct *the* wise
and he will love you.

9:9 *da sapienti et addetur ei sapientia doce iustum et festinabit accipere*

'Give to *the* wise and wisdom
will be added to him.
Teach *the* fair,
and he will accept it quickly.

9:10 *principium sapientiae timor Domini et scientia sanctorum prudentia*

'*The* fear of *the* Lord
is the beginning of wisdom,
and knowledge of *the* holy
is prudence,

9:11 *per me enim multiplicabuntur dies tui et addentur tibi anni vitae*

for by me your days
will be multiplied,
and years of life
will be added to you.

9:12 *si sapiens fueris tibimet ipsi eris si inlusor solus portabis malum*

'If you are wise,
you will be *wise* for yourself.
If you are *a* mocker,
you only carry harm.

A Loud and Foolish Woman

9:13 *mulier stulta et clamosa plenaque inlecebris et nihil omnino sciens*

There is a loud and foolish
woman, full of allurement,
and, knowing nothing at all.[87]

9:14 *sedit in foribus domus suae super sellam in excelso urbis loco*

She sits by *the* doors
of her house
on *a* seat in *the* high place
of *the* city,[88]

9:15 *ut vocaret transeuntes viam et pergentes itinere suo*

that she may call

---

[87] The figure of the Foolish Woman can be seen as an antitype of Wisdom, rather than as a condemnation of women in general.

[88] The High Places in the Old Testament often were used for ritual prostitution.

those crossing *the* road
and going on their journey.

9:16 *quis est parvulus declinet ad me et vecordi locuta est*

'Let whoever is young
turn aside to me.'
And she has spoken
to *a* wild *youth*,

9:17 *aquae furtivae dulciores sunt et panis absconditus suavior*

'Stolen waters are sweeter,
and hidden bread tastier.'

9:18 *et ignoravit quod gigantes ibi sint et in profundis inferni convivae eius*

And he ignores
that giants may be there,
and her table companions
are in *the* deepest reaches
of *the* inferno.

Chapter 10

The Heart of Wisdom

10:1 *parabolae Salomonis filius sapiens laetificat patrem filius vero stultus maestitia est matris suae*

Parables of Solomon.[89]

A wise son gives joy
to *a* father;
a foolish son, truly,
is *a* grief to his mother.

10:2 *non proderunt thesauri impietatis iustitia vero liberabit a morte*

The treasures of *the* lawless
do not help;
fairness, truly, liberates
from death.

10:3 *non adfliget Dominus fame animam iusti et insidias impiorum subvertet*

The Lord does not afflict
a fair-minded soul
with hunger;
yet *he* subverts *the* schemes
of *the* lawless.

---

[89] Chapter 10 begins a new section of the book.

10:4 *egestatem operata est manus remissa manus autem fortium divitias parat*

Poverty is *the* work
of *a* lazy hand,
but *a* strong hand
prepares riches.

10:5 *qui congregat in messe filius sapiens est qui autem stertit aestate filius confusionis*

One who gathers in harvest
is *a* wise son;
but *one* who snores away
summer is *a* son of trouble.

10:6 *benedictio super caput iusti os autem impiorum operit iniquitatem*

Blessing *flows* over *the* head
of *the* fair man;
but *the* mouth of *the* lawless
works treachery.

10:7 *memoria iusti cum laudibus et nomen impiorum putrescet*

The memory of *the* fair man
is sung with praises,
but *the* name of *the* lawless
will rot.

10:8 *sapiens corde praecepta suscipiet stultus caeditur labiis*

The wise in heart
accepts precepts;
a fool is cut down
by *his* lips.

10:9 *qui ambulat simpliciter ambulat confidenter qui autem depravat vias suas manifestus erit*

One who walks simply,
walks confidently;
but *one* who perverts his way
will be made known.

10:10 *qui annuit oculo dabit dolorem stultus labiis verberabitur*

Who nods with *the* eye
gives pain;
because of *his* lips,
a fool will be beaten.

10:11 *vena vitae os iusti et os impiorum operiet iniquitatem*

The mouth of *the* fair man
is a vein of life,
and *the* mouth of *the* lawless
will work treachery.

10:12 *odium suscitat rixas et universa delicta operit caritas*

Hatred awakens brawls,
yet love covers all faults.

10:13 *in labiis sapientis invenietur sapientia et virga in dorso eius qui indiget corde*

Wisdom is found
in *the* lips of *the* wise,
and *a* rod in his back
who lacks judgment.

10:14 *sapientes abscondunt scientiam os autem stulti confusioni proximum est*

The wise shelter knowledge,
but *the* mouth of *a* fool
is *a* neighbor's confusion.

10:15 *substantia divitis urbs fortitudinis eius pavor pauperum egestas eorum*

The substance of *the* rich
is his strong city;
the fear of *the* poor *is* their lack.

10:16 *opus iusti ad vitam fructus impii ad peccatum*

The work of *the* fair man
leads to life;
the fruit of *the* lawless to sin.

10:17 *via vitae custodienti disciplinam qui autem increpationes relinquit errat*

Keeping discipline
is the way of life ,
but *one* who dismisses rebukes errs.

10:18 *abscondunt odium labia mendacia qui profert contumeliam insipiens est*

Lying lips hide hatred;
who offers up contention
is empty-headed.

10:19 *in multiloquio peccatum non deerit qui autem moderatur labia sua prudentissimus est*

In many words
sin is not lacking,
but *one* who is measured
in his lips is most prudent.

10:20 *argentum electum lingua iusti cor impiorum pro nihilo*

The tongue of *the* fair

is choice silver;
the heart of *the* lawless
is good for nothing.

10:21 *labia iusti erudiunt plurimos qui autem indocti sunt in cordis egestate morientur*

The lips of *the* fair
will teach many,
but *those* who are
unlearned in heart
will die in poverty.

10:22 *benedictio Domini divites facit nec sociabitur ei adflictio*

The blessing of *the* Lord
makes rich,
nor will He share affliction
with him.

10:23 *quasi per risum stultus operatur scelus sapientia autem est viro prudentia*

A fool works crime
as if for *a* laugh,
but wisdom is prudence
to man.

10:24 *quod timet impius veniet super eum desiderium suum iustis dabitur*

What *a* lawless *man* fears
will come upon him;
the fair-minded will be given
their desire.

10:25 *quasi tempestas transiens non erit impius iustus autem quasi fundamentum sempiternum*

Like *a* passing storm,
the lawless will not be,
but, like *an* enduring
foundation,
the fair-minded *endure*.

10:26 *sicut acetum dentibus et fumus oculis sic piger his qui miserunt eum*

Like vinegar to teeth
and smoke to eyes,
thus *a* lazy *man*
to those who sent him.

10:27 *timor Domini adponet dies et anni impiorum breviabuntur*

Fear of *the* Lord adds days,
yet *the* years of *the* lawless
will be shortened.

10:28 *expectatio iustorum laetitia spes autem impiorum peribit*

The expectation
of *the* fair-minded
is happiness,
but *the* hope of *the* lawless
will perish.

10:29 *fortitudo simplicis via Domini et pavor his qui operantur malum*

The way of *the* Lord
is the strength of *the* simple,
and *the* fear of those
who work evil.

10:30 *iustus in aeternum non commovebitur impii autem non habitabunt in terram*

The fair *man*
will not be moved in eternity,
but *the* lawless will not live
in *the* land.

10:31 *os iusti parturiet sapientiam lingua pravorum peribit*

The mouth of *the* fair-minded
gives birth to wisdom;
the tongue of *the* dishonest
will perish.

10:32 *labia iusti considerant placita et os impiorum perversa*

The lips of *the* fair-minded
consider *what is* pleasing,
but *the* mouth of *the* lawless
what is perverse.

Chapter 11

11:1 *statera dolosa abominatio apud Dominum et pondus aequum voluntas eius*

A deceitful scale
is an abomination
with *the* Lord,
and *an* equal measure
is His will.

11:2 *ubi fuerit superbia ibi erit et contumelia ubi autem humilitas ibi et sapientia*

Where pride is,
there also will be contention,
but where humility *is*,
there also *is* wisdom.

11:3 *simplicitas iustorum diriget eos et subplantatio perversorum vastabit illos*

The simplicity
of *the* fair-minded
guides them,
and *the* dishonesty
of *the* perverse
devastates them.

11:4 *non proderunt divitiae in die ultionis iustitia autem liberabit a morte*

Riches don't matter
on *the* day of vengeance,
but fairness will liberate
from death.

11:5 *iustitia simplicis diriget viam eius et in impietate sua corruet impius*

The fairness of *the* simple
guides his way,
and *the* lawless will be ruined
in his lawlessness.

11:6 *iustitia rectorum liberabit eos et in insidiis suis capientur iniqui*

The fairness of *the* honest
will free him.
The treacherous
will be caught
in their *own* treacheries.

11:7 *mortuo homine impio nulla erit ultra spes et expectatio sollicitorum peribit*

At *the* death of *an* unfair man
there will be no further hope;
The hope and expectation
of *the* anxious will perish.

11:8 *iustus de angustia liberatus est et tradetur*

impius pro eo

The fair is freed
from anguish,
and *the* unfair is handed over
in his place.

11:9 *simulator ore decipit amicum suum iusti autem liberabuntur scientia*

A liar deceives his friend
through his words,
but *the* fair-minded are set
free by knowledge.

11:10 *in bonis iustorum exultabit civitas et in perditione impiorum erit laudatio*

A city will exult
in *the* good of *the* fair,
there will be praise
at *the* destruction
of *the* unfair.

11:11 *benedictione iustorum exaltabitur civitas et ore impiorum subvertetur*

A city will be exalted
by *the* blessing of *the* fair,
and subverted by *the* mouth
of *the* unfair.

11:12 *qui despicit amicum suum indigens corde est vir autem prudens tacebit*

One who disdains his friend
lacks heart,
but *a* prudent man
will keep silent.

11:13 *qui ambulat fraudulenter revelat arcana qui autem fidelis est animi celat commissum*

One who walks deceitfully
reveals secrets,
but *one* who is faithful in
soul keeps secret
what is entrusted.

11:14 *ubi non est gubernator populus corruet salus autem ubi multa consilia*

Where *there* is no guide,
the people come to grief,
but safety *is found*
in many counsels.

11:15 *adfligetur malo qui fidem facit pro extraneo qui autem cavet laqueos securus erit*

One who makes pledge
for *a* stranger

will be afflicted by evil,
but *one* who takes
precautions against traps
will be secure.

11:16 *mulier gratiosa inveniet gloriam et robusti habebunt divitias*

A graceful woman
will find glory,
and *the* robust
will have riches.

11:17 *benefacit animae suae vir misericors qui autem crudelis est et propinquos abicit*

A merciful man
blesses his *own* soul,
but *one* who is cruel
debases even neighbors.

11:18 *impius facit opus instabile seminanti autem iustitiam merces fidelis*

The lawless
does *an* unsteady work,
but to one sowing fairness
there will be a faithful
reward

11:19 *clementia praeparat vitam et sectatio malorum mortem*

Mercy prepares life,
and *the* seeking of evil death.

11:20 *abominabile Domino pravum cor et voluntas eius in his qui simpliciter ambulant*

A deceitful heart
is hateful to *the* Lord,
and his will *is* with
one who walks in simplicity.

11:21 *manus in manu non erit innocens malus semen autem iustorum salvabitur*

The evil will not be innocent,
even hand in hand,
but *the* seed of *the* just
will be saved.

11:22 *circulus aureus in naribus suis mulier pulchra et fatua*

Like a gold ring
in *a* hog's nose
is a beautiful
and empty-headed woman.

11:23 *desiderium iustorum omne bonum est praestolatio impiorum furor*

The desire of *the* fair man
is all good;
the expectation of *the* unfair
is fury.

11:24 *alii dividunt propria et ditiores fiunt alii rapiunt non sua et semper in egestate sunt*

Some divide
their own *possessions*
and become richer;
others carry off
what is not *their* own,
yet are always in need.

11:25 *anima quae benedicit inpinguabitur et qui inebriat ipse quoque inebriabitur*

A soul which blesses
will prosper,
and one who drinks
will himself also get drunk.

11:26 *qui abscondit frumenta maledicetur in populis benedictio autem super caput vendentium*

One who hides grain
will be cursed
among *the* people,
but blessing *will be*
on *the* head of *one* selling.

11:27 *bene consurgit diluculo qui quaerit bona qui autem investigator malorum est opprimetur ab eis*

He rises well at daybreak
who seeks good,
but one who searches out evil
is weighed down by it.

11:28 *qui confidet in divitiis suis corruet iusti autem quasi virens folium germinabunt*

One who confides
in his riches falls to ruin,
but *a* fair-minded man,
like *a* green leaf,
will spring up.

11:29 *qui conturbat domum suam possidebit ventos et qui stultus est serviet sapienti*

One who troubles
his own house
will possess *the* wind,
and *one* who *is a* fool
will serve *the* wise.

11:30 *fructus iusti lignum vitae et qui suscipit animas sapiens est*

The fruit of *the* fair *man*
is a tree of life,

and *one* who sustains souls
is wise.

11:31 *si iustus in terra
recipit quanto magis impius
et peccator*

If *the* fair man
receives on earth,
how much more
the unfair and *the* sinner!

Chapter 12

12:1 *qui diligit disciplinam
diligit scientiam qui autem
odit increpationes insipiens
est*

Who loves discipline
loves knowledge,
but who hates rebukes
is empty-headed.

12:2 *qui bonus est hauriet a
Domino gratiam qui autem
confidit cogitationibus suis
impie agit*

Who is good drinks down
grace from *the* Lord,
but who confides
in his *own* thoughts
works lawlessness.

12:3 *non roborabitur homo
ex impietate et radix
iustorum non commovebitur*

Man is not strengthened
by lawlessness,
and *the* root of *the* fair *man*
will not be moved.

12:4 *mulier diligens corona
viro suo et putredo in ossibus
eius quae confusione res
dignas gerit*

A diligent wife
is the crown of her husband,
yet one who carries on
important business in
confusion *is a* rot
in his bones.

12:5 *cogitationes iustorum iudicia et consilia impiorum fraudulentia*

The thoughts of *the* fair
work judgment,
and *the* counsels of *the*
lawless *are* fraudulent.

12:6 *verba impiorum insidiantur sanguini os iustorum liberabit eos*

The words of *the* lawless
lay traps for blood;
the mouth of *the* fair
will free them.

12:7 *verte impios et non erunt domus autem iustorum permanebit*

Turn again to *the* lawless
and *they* are not *there,*
but *the* house of *the* fair
will endure.

12:8 *doctrina sua noscetur vir qui autem vanus et excors est patebit contemptui*

A man is known
by his teaching,
but *one who* is vain and
stupid will be held
in contempt.

12:9 *melior est pauper et sufficiens sibi quam gloriosus et indigens pane*

Better is *a* poor *man*
who is sufficient to himself,
than *one who is* glorious
and lacking bread.

12:10 *novit iustus animas iumentorum suorum viscera autem impiorum crudelia*

The fair *man* knows
the lives of his animals,
but *the* innermost parts
of *the* lawless are cruel.

12:11 *qui operatur terram suam saturabitur panibus qui autem sectatur otium stultissimus est*

Who works his land
will be satisfied by bread,
but who continually seeks
rest is most foolish.

12:12 *desiderium impii munimentum est pessimorum radix autem iustorum proficiet*

A lawless desire
is *the* worst defense,
but *the* root of *the* fair
will prove sturdy.

12:13 *propter peccata labiorum ruina proximat malo effugiet autem iustus de angustia*

Because of *the* sins of his lips
ruin comes near *the* evil,
but *the* fair *man* will escape
from anguish.

12:14 *de fructu oris sui unusquisque replebitur bonis et iuxta opera manuum suarum retribuetur ei*

From *the* fruit of his lips
each one will be filled
with good,
and, according to *the* works
of his hands, *it* will be repaid
to him.[90]

---

[90] Compare to the "Golden Rule" in the New Testament, Matthew 7:12: *So whatever you wish that men would do to you, do so to them; for this is the law and the prophets.*

12:15 *via stulti recta in oculis eius qui autem sapiens est audit consilia*

The way of *a* fool is right
in his eyes,
but one who is wise
listens to counsel.

12:16 *fatuus statim indicat iram suam qui autem dissimulat iniuriam callidus est*

The mindless quickly
shows his anger,
but *one* who conceals
an injury is clever.

12:17 *qui quod novit loquitur index iustitiae est qui autem mentitur testis est fraudulentus*

One who tells what he knows
is *a* fair informer,
but *one* who lies
is *a* deceptive witness.

12:18 *est qui promittit et quasi gladio pungitur conscientiae lingua autem sapientium sanitas est*

There is one who promises
and who is stabbed

in conscience
as if by *a* sword,
but *the* tongue of *the* wise
brings health.

12:19 *labium veritatis firmum erit in perpetuum qui autem testis est repentinus concinnat linguam mendacii*

A truthful lip
will be established forever,
but *a* witness who is hasty
makes *a* lying tongue.

12:20 *dolus in corde cogitantium mala qui autem ineunt pacis consilia sequitur eos gaudium*

Deceit *is* in *a* heart
considering evil,
but joy follows *those*
who seek out counsels
of peace.

12:21 *non contristabit iustum quicquid ei acciderit impii autem replebuntur malo*

The fair will not be saddened
by anything that might
happen to him,
but *the* lawless will be filled
with regret.

12:22 *abominatio Domino labia mendacia qui autem fideliter agunt placent ei*

Lying lips *are*
an abomination to *the* Lord,
but those who live faithfully
please Him.

12:23 *homo versutus celat scientiam et cor insipientium provocabit stultitiam*

A cunning *man*
hides knowledge,
and *an* uninformed heart
provokes foolishness.

12:24 *manus fortium dominabitur quae autem remissa est tributis serviet*

A strong hand will dominate,
but *one* which is lazy
will live to *pay* taxes.

12:25 *maeror in corde viri humiliabit illud et sermone bono laetificabitur*

Sadness in *a* man's heart
will humble him,
yet by *a* good word
he will be made happy.

12:26 *qui neglegit damnum*

propter amicum iustus est iter autem impiorum decipiet eos

One who overlooks *a* loss
on behalf of *a* friend is fair,
but *the* course of *the* lawless
deceives him.

12:27 *non inveniet fraudulentus lucrum et substantia hominis erit auri pretium*

A deceiver will not find
a profit,
though *the* substance of *a*
man will be precious gold.

12:28 *in semita iustitiae vita iter autem devium ducit ad mortem*

In *a* path of fairness *is* life,
but *the* dishonest course
leads to death.

Chapter 13

13:1 *filius sapiens doctrina patris qui autem inlusor est non audit cum arguitur*

A wise son *learns*
his father's doctrine,
but *one* who is *a* scoffer
does not listen when *it*
is being proven.

13:2 *de fructu oris homo saturabitur bonis anima autem praevaricatorum iniqua*

From *the* fruit
of *the* good mouth
a man will be satisfied,
but *a* lying soul
is treacherous.

13:3 *qui custodit os suum custodit animam suam qui autem inconsideratus est ad loquendum sentiet mala*

Who watches his mouth,
keeps his soul;
but who talks without
consideration will feel harm.

13:4 *vult et non vult piger anima autem operantium inpinguabitur*

A lazy *man* wants
and does not want,
but *a* working soul
will grow prosperous.

13:5 *verbum mendax iustus detestabitur impius confundit et confundetur*

The fair *man*
will detest *the* word of *a* liar;
the lawless confuses
and will be confused.

13:6 *iustitia custodit innocentis viam impietas vero peccato subplantat*

Fairness keeps *the* way
of *the* innocent;
lawlessness, truly,
undermines through sin.

13:7 *est quasi dives cum nihil habeat et est quasi pauper cum in multis divitiis sit*

One is like *the* rich
when he has nothing,
and *another* is like *the* poor
when *he* is amidst much
wealth.

13:8 *redemptio animae viri divitiae suae qui autem pauper est increpationem non sustinet*

The redemption of *a* man's
soul is his riches,
but *one* who is poor
does not receive *a* rebuke.

13:9 *lux iustorum laetificat lucerna autem impiorum extinguetur*

The light of *the* fair man
brings joy,
but *the* lamp of *the* unfair
will be extinguished.

13:10 *inter superbos semper iurgia sunt qui autem agunt cuncta consilio reguntur sapientia*

Between *the* proud
there are always quarrels,
but *those* who do all
by counsel
are guided by wisdom.

13:11 *substantia festinata minuetur quae autem paulatim colligitur manu multiplicabitur*

Wealth gained quickly
will waste away,
but that which is gathered

bit by bit, by hand,
will be increased.

13:12 *spes quae differtur adfligit animam lignum vitae desiderium veniens*

Hope which is humiliated
afflicts *the* soul;
an approaching desire
is *a* tree of life.

13:13 *qui detrahit alicui rei ipse se in futurum obligat qui autem timet praeceptum in pace
versabitur*

One who drags down
another's business
binds himself in *the* future,
but one who fears *a* precept
will dwell in peace.

13:14 *lex sapientis fons vitae ut declinet a ruina mortis*

The law of *the* wise
is a fountain of life,
that *he* may turn back
from death by catastrophe.

13:15 *doctrina bona dabit gratiam in itinere contemptorum vorago*

Good doctrine gives grace;
a deep hole *blocks the* way
of *the* scornful.

13:16 *astutus omnia agit cum consilio qui autem fatuus est aperit stultitiam*

The astute does all
with counsel,
but one who is mindless
uncovers foolishness.

13:17 *nuntius impii cadet in malum legatus fidelis sanitas*

An lawless messenger
falls into evil;
a faithful representative
is health.

13:18 *egestas et ignominia ei qui deserit disciplinam qui autem adquiescit arguenti glorificabitur*

Poverty and ill-repute
come to one who
abandons discipline,
but one who quiets
accusations will be praised.

13:19 *desiderium si conpleatur delectat animam detestantur stulti eos qui fugiunt mala*

A desire, if fulfilled,
delights *the* soul;
fools detest those
who flee evil.

13:20 *qui cum sapientibus graditur sapiens erit amicus stultorum efficietur similis*

One who walks with *the* wise
will be wise;
a friend of fools
will become like them.

13:21 *peccatores persequetur malum et iustis retribuentur bona*

Harm pursues sinners,
and good will be repaid
to *the* fair *man*.

13:22 *bonus relinquet heredes filios et nepotes et custoditur iusto substantia peccatoris*

The good leave
behind inheritances,
children, and grandchildren,
but *the* substance of sinners
will be kept by *the* fair.

13:23 *multi cibi in novalibus patrum et alii congregantur absque iudicio*

Much food *can be grown*
in *a* father's unplowed fields,
but *it* will be gathered by
others without judgment.

13:24 *qui parcit virgae suae odit filium suum qui autem diligit illum instanter erudit*

Who withholds his
punishment hates his son,
but who loves him
teaches insistently.

13:25 *iustus comedit et replet animam suam venter autem impiorum insaturabilis*

The fair *man* eats
and fills his soul,
but *the* belly of *the* lawless
cannot be satisfied.

Chapter 14

14:1 *sapiens mulier aedificavit domum suam insipiens instructam quoque destruet manibus*

A wise woman
builds her house,
and *a* fool will destroy
the building with her hands.

14:2 *ambulans recto itinere et timens Deum despicitur ab eo qui infami graditur via*

Walking rightly on *the*
journey and fearing God
is despised by one
who travels *a* shameful way.

14:3 *in ore stulti virga superbiae labia sapientium custodiunt eos*

The staff of pride
is in *a* fool's mouth;
the lips of *the* wise
guard them.

14:4 *ubi non sunt boves praesepe vacuum est ubi autem plurimae segetes ibi manifesta fortitudo bovis*

The feed troughs are empty
where *there* are no oxen;
but where *there* are many
crops, there *the* strength
of *the* oxen *is* manifest.

14:5 *testis fidelis non mentietur profert mendacium testis dolosus*

A faithful witness
will not lie;
a deceitful witness
gives out *a* lie.

14:6 *quaerit derisor sapientiam et non inveniet doctrina prudentium facilis*

A mocker seeks wisdom
and will not find it;
the doctrine of *the* prudent
is easy.

14:7 *vade contra virum stultum et nescito labia prudentiae*

Test *a* foolish man,
and he will not know
about prudent lips.

14:8 *sapientia callidi est intellegere viam suam et inprudentia stultorum errans*

The wisdom of *the* clever

is to know his way,
and *the* imprudence of *a* fool
is erring.

14:9 *stultis inludet peccatum inter iustos morabitur gratia*

He will mock *the* sin
of *a* fool;
grace will remain
with *the* fair.

14:10 *cor quod novit amaritudinem animae suae in gaudio eius non miscebitur extraneus*

A heart which knows
the bitterness of his soul,
a stranger will not confuse
in his joy.

14:11 *domus impiorum delebitur tabernacula iustorum germinabunt*

The house of *the* lawless
will be destroyed;
the dwelling of *the* fair *man*
will spring up.

14:12 *est via quae videtur homini iusta novissima autem eius deducunt ad mortem*

There is *a* way
which seems fair to *a* man,
but its end leads to death.

14:13 *risus dolore miscebitur et extrema gaudii luctus occupat*

Laughter will be mixed
with pain,
and grief takes over
the end of joy.

14:14 *viis suis replebitur stultus et super eum erit vir bonus*

A fool will be filled
by his ways,
and *a* good man
will be over him.

14:15 *innocens credit omni verbo astutus considerat gressus suos*

The innocent believe
every word;
the clever considers his steps.

14:16 *sapiens timet et declinat malum stultus transilit et confidit*

The wise fears
and turns away harm;
a fool leaps over and trusts.

14:17 *inpatiens operabitur stultitiam et vir versutus odiosus est*

The impatient
will work foolishness,
and *an* insincere man
is hated.

14:18 *possidebunt parvuli stultitiam et astuti expectabunt scientiam*

The young
will possess foolishness,
and *the* clever
will expect knowledge.

14:19 *iacebunt mali ante bonos et impii ante portas iustorum*

The evil will be thrown down
before *the* good,
and *the* lawless before *the*
doors of the fair *man*.

14:20 *etiam proximo suo pauper odiosus erit amici vero divitum multi*

The poor will be hated
even by his neighbor;
wealth, truly, *has* many
friends.

14:21 *qui despicit proximum suum peccat qui autem miseretur pauperi beatus erit*

One who despises
his neighbor sins,
but *one* who is
compassionate
to *the* poor will be blessed.

14:22 *errant qui operantur malum misericordia et veritas praeparant bona*

They do wrong who do harm;
mercy and truth
prepare good *things*.

14:23 *in omni opere erit abundantia ubi autem verba sunt plurima frequenter egestas*

In much work,
there will be abundance,
but where words are many,
there is often poverty.

14:24 *corona sapientium divitiae eorum fatuitas stultorum inprudentia*

The crown of *the* wise
is their wealth;
the stupidity of *a* fool
is imprudence.

14:25 *liberat animas testis fidelis et profert mendacia versipellis*

A faithful witness frees souls,
and *a* double-dealer
gives out lies.

14:26 *in timore Domini fiducia fortitudinis et filiis eius erit spes*

The confidence of *the* strong
is in *the* fear of *the* Lord,
and *there* will be hope
for his children.

14:27 *timor Domini fons vitae ut declinet a ruina mortis*

The fear of *the* Lord
is a fountain of life,
that one may turn back
from *the* ruin of death.

14:28 *in multitudine populi dignitas regis et in paucitate plebis ignominia principis*

The dignity of *a* ruler
is in *a* multitude of people,
and in *a* scarcity of people,
a ruler's shame.

14:29 *qui patiens est multa gubernatur prudentia qui autem inpatiens exaltat stultitiam suam*

One who is patient
is guided by much prudence;
one who is impatient
exalts his *own* foolishness.

14:30 *vita carnium sanitas cordis putredo ossuum invidia*

The life of *the* flesh
is *a* healthy heart;
envy *is a* rot in *the* bone.

14:31 *qui calumniatur egentem exprobrat factori eius honorat autem eum qui miseretur pauperis*

One who abuses *the* needy
rebukes *the One*
who made him,
but *He* honors one who
is compassionate to *the* poor.

14:32 *in malitia sua expelletur impius sperat autem iustus in morte sua*

The lawless
will be driven out in his evil,
but *the* fair man will hope
in his death.

14:33 *in corde prudentis requiescit sapientia et indoctos quoque erudiet*

Wisdom abides
in *a* prudent heart,
and will teach *the* unlearned.

14:34 *iustitia elevat gentem miseros facit populos peccatum*

Fairness lifts up *a* nation;
sin makes *a* people
miserable.

14:35 *acceptus est regi minister intellegens iracundiam eius inutilis sustinebit*

An intelligent minister is
accepted by *a* king;
a useless *minister* will
experience his wrath.

Chapter 15

15:1 *responsio mollis frangit iram sermo durus suscitat furorem*

A soft answer calms anger;
a harsh word stirs up fury.

15:2 *lingua sapientium ornat scientiam os fatuorum ebullit stultitiam*

The tongue of *the* wise
displays knowledge;
the mouth of *the* mindless
bubbles up foolishness.

15:3 *in omni loco oculi Domini contemplantur malos et bonos*

The eyes of God
observe *the* good
and *the* evil, everywhere.

15:4 *lingua placabilis lignum vitae quae inmoderata est conteret spiritum*

A tongue which makes peace
is *a* tree of life;
one which is ill-considered
wears out *the* breath.

15:5 *stultus inridet disciplinam patris sui qui autem custodit increpationes astutior fiet*

A fool laughs
at his father's discipline,
but *one* who
considers rebukes
will be made more clever.

15:6 *domus iusti plurima fortitudo et in fructibus impii conturbatur*

The house of *the* fair
is very strong,
yet *it* is disturbed
by lawless gains.

15:7 *labia sapientium disseminabunt scientiam cor stultorum dissimile erit*

The lips of *the* wise
spread knowledge;
the heart of fools
will be different.

15:8 *victimae impiorum abominabiles Domino vota iustorum placabilia*

The offerings of *the* lawless
are disgusting to *the* Lord;
the promises of *the* fair
are appeasing.

15:9 *abominatio est Domino via impii qui sequitur iustitiam diligetur ab eo*

The path of *the* lawless
is disgusting to *the* Lord;
one who pursues fairness
will be favored by Him.

15:10 *doctrina mala deserenti viam qui increpationes odit morietur*

Teaching is offensive
to one deserting *the* way;
one who hates rebukes
will die.

15:11 *infernus et perditio coram Domino quanto magis corda filiorum hominum*

The inferno and destruction
are open before *the* Lord;
how much more *the* hearts
of *the* children of men!

15:12 *non amat pestilens eum qui se corripit nec ad sapientes graditur*

The destructive does not love
one who corrects him,
nor does he walk

toward *the* wise.

15:13 *cor gaudens exhilarat faciem in maerore animi deicitur spiritus*

A rejoicing heart
gladdens *the* face;
the spirit is brought down
by *a* grieving soul.

15:14 *cor sapientis quaerit doctrinam et os stultorum pascetur inperitia*

A wise heart seeks
instruction,
and *a* foolish mouth
feeds on ignorance.

15:15 *omnes dies pauperis mali secura mens quasi iuge convivium*

All days are evil to *the* poor,
but *a* secure mind
is like *a* continuing feast.

15:16 *melius est parum cum timore Domini quam thesauri magni et insatiabiles*

A little with *the* fear
of *the* Lord
is better than great
and unsatisfying treasures.

15:17 *melius est vocare ad holera cum caritate quam ad vitulum saginatum cum odio*

It is better to call on
cabbages with love,
than on *a* fatted calf
with hatred.

15:18 *vir iracundus provocat rixas qui patiens est mitigat suscitatas*

An angry man
provokes brawls;
one who is patient
reduces quarrels.

15:19 *iter pigrorum quasi sepes spinarum via iustorum absque offendiculo*

The way of *the* lazy
is like *a* thorny hedge;
the way of *the* fair
is without obstacle.

15:20 *filius sapiens laetificat patrem et stultus homo despicit matrem suam*

A wise son
makes his father happy,
and *a* foolish man
despises his mother.

15:21 *stultitia gaudium stulto et vir prudens dirigit gressus*

Foolishness is joy to *a* fool,
but *a* prudent man directs
steps.

15:22 *dissipantur cogitationes ubi non est consilium ubi vero plures sunt consiliarii confirmantur*

Ideas dissipate
where *there* is no counsel;
where counselors are many,
they are validated.

15:23 *laetatur homo in sententia oris sui et sermo oportunus est optimus*

Man is made happy
in his opinions,
and *a* timely word is best.

15:24 *semita vitae super eruditum ut declinet de inferno novissimo*

The way of life
is over *the* learned,
that he may avoid
the depth of *the* inferno.

15:25 *domum superborum demolietur Dominus et firmos facit terminos viduae*

The Lord will demolish
the house of *the* proud,
and make *the* widow's
boundaries secure.

15:26 *abominatio Domini cogitationes malae et purus sermo pulcherrimus*

To *the* Lord,
evil thoughts are disgusting,
and purity of speech
most beautiful.

15:27 *conturbat domum suam qui sectatur avaritiam qui autem odit munera vivet*

He disturbs his own home
who follows after greed,
but one who hates bribes
will live.

15:28 *mens iusti meditatur oboedientiam os impiorum redundat malis*

A fair mind
considers obedience;
a lawless mouth
overflows with evil.

15:29 *longe est Dominus ab*

impiis et orationes iustorum exaudiet

The Lord is far
from *the* lawless,
but will hear *the* entreaties
of *the* fair *man*.

15:30 *lux oculorum laetificat animam fama bona inpinguat ossa*

The light of *the* eyes
makes *the* soul happy;
a good reputation
nourishes *the* bones.

15:31 *auris quae audit increpationes vitae in medio sapientium commorabitur*

An ear which listens
to life-giving rebukes
will live in *the* midst
of understanding.

15:32 *qui abicit disciplinam despicit animam suam qui adquiescit increpationibus possessor est cordis*

One who rejects discipline
despises his soul;
one who accepts corrections
has possessed his heart.

15:33 *timor Domini disciplina sapientiae et gloriam praecedit humilitas*

The fear of *the* Lord
is *the* discipline of *the* wise,
and humility precedes glory.

Chapter 16

16:1 *hominis est animum praeparare et Dei gubernare linguam*

It falls to man
to prepare his soul
and to God
to govern *the* tongue.

16:2 *omnes viae hominum patent oculis eius spirituum ponderator est Dominus*

All man's ways
stand open to *God's* eyes,
and *the* Lord is *the* judge
of spirits.

16:3 *revela Domino opera tua et dirigentur cogitationes tuae*

Open your work to *the* Lord,
and your thoughts will be
guided.

16:4 *universa propter semet ipsum operatus est Dominus impium quoque ad diem malum*

The Lord made all
for Himself,
even *the* lawless for *an* evil
day.

16:5 *abominatio Domini omnis arrogans etiam si manus ad manum fuerit non erit innocens*

Every arrogant *person*
is a disgust to *the* Lord;
even if he walks
hand in hand,
he will not be innocent.

16:6 *misericordia et veritate redimitur iniquitas et in timore Domini declinatur a malo*

By mercy and truth
treachery is redeemed
and in *the* fear of *the* Lord
one is turned away from evil.

16:7 *cum placuerint Domino viae hominis inimicos quoque eius convertet ad pacem*

When *the* ways of men
please *the* Lord,
he will convert even enemies
to peace.

16:8 *melius est parum cum iustitia quam multi fructus cum iniquitate*

A little with fairness
is better than many benefits
with treachery.

16:9 *cor hominis disponet viam suam sed Domini est dirigere gressus eius*

A man's heart
will arrange his way,
but to direct his steps
is from *the* Lord.

16:10 *divinatio in labiis regis in iudicio non errabit os eius*

Divination *is* in
the lips of *a* king;
his mouth will not err
in judgment.

16:11 *pondus et statera iudicia Domini sunt et opera eius omnes lapides sacculi*

Weight and scale
are judgments of *the* Lord,
and all *the* weights in *the* bag
are his work.

16:12 *abominabiles regi qui agunt impie quoniam iustitia firmatur solium*

Those who work lawlessness
are disgusting to *a* king,
because fairness establishes
a throne.

16:13 *voluntas regum labia iusta qui recta loquitur diligetur*

Straightforward lips
are a king's will;
he will delight in one
who speaks honestly.

16:14 *indignatio regis nuntii mortis et vir sapiens placabit eam*

A king's anger
is *a* messenger of death,
and *a* wise man
will placate him.

16:15 *in hilaritate vultus regis vita et clementia eius quasi imber serotinus*

A king's appearance
in good humor is life,
and his clemency
like *the* latter rain.

16:16 *posside sapientiam quia auro melior est et adquire prudentiam quia pretiosior est argento*

Possess wisdom,
because *it* is better than gold,
and acquire prudence
because *it* is more precious
than silver.

16:17 *semita iustorum declinat mala custos animae suae servat viam suam*

The way of *the* fair man
turns away evils,
and *the* Keeper of his soul
will guard his way.

16:18 *contritionem praecedit superbia et ante ruinam exaltatur spiritus*

Pride precedes regret,
and *a* spirit is exalted
before ruin.

16:19 *melius est humiliari cum mitibus quam dividere spolia cum superbis*

It is better to be humble
with *the* gentle,
than to divide plunder
with *the* prideful.

16:20 *eruditus in verbo repperiet bona et qui in Domino sperat beatus est*

The learned in word
will discover good *things*,
and one who hopes
in *the* Lord is blessed.

16:21 *qui sapiens corde est appellabitur prudens et qui dulcis eloquio maiora percipiet*

One who is wise in heart
will be called prudent,
and one who is charming
in speech will secure
better *things.*

16:22 *fons vitae eruditio possidentis doctrina stultorum fatuitas*

Learning *is a* fountain of life
to one possessing *it;*
the teaching of fools
is mindless.

16:23 *cor sapientis erudiet os eius et labiis illius addet gratiam*

A wise heart
will teach its mouth,
and will add grace to its lips.

16:24 *favus mellis verba conposita dulcedo animae et sanitas ossuum*

Careful words are
a honeycomb,
sweetness to *the* soul
and health to *the* bones.

16:25 *est via quae videtur*
homini recta et novissimum
eius ducit ad mortem

There is *a* way
which seems right to man,
and its end leads to death.

16:26 *anima laborantis*
laborat sibi quia conpulit
eum os suum

The soul of one laboring
labors for itself,
because its mouth drives it.

16:27 *vir impius fodit malum*
et in labiis eius ignis ardescit

A lawless man digs up evil,
and *a* fire burns in his lips.

16:28 *homo perversus*
suscitat lites et verbosus
separat principes

A perverse man
arranges favorable omens,
and *a* blabber separates
princes.

16:29 *vir iniquus lactat*
amicum suum et ducit eum
per viam non bonam

A treacherous man
leads his friend on,
and takes him down *a* road
that isn't good.

16:30 *qui adtonitis oculis*
cogitat prava mordens labia
sua perficit malum

One who reasons
with awestruck eyes
is dangerous;
one biting his lips
completes *the* evil.

16:31 *corona dignitatis*
senectus in viis iustitiae
repperietur

Old age *is a* crown of dignity,
and *it* will be found
in ways of fairness.

16:32 *melior est patiens viro*
forte et qui dominatur animo
suo expugnatore urbium

The patient is better
than *a* strong man,
and one who controls his soul
than one who conquers cities.

16:33 *sortes mittuntur in sinu sed a Domino temperantur*

Lots are tossed into *a* lap,
but they are combined
by *the* Lord.

Chapter 17

17:1 *melior est buccella sicca cum gaudio quam domus plena victimis cum iurgio*

A dry morsel with joy
is better than *a* house
full of victims with abuse.

17:2 *servus sapiens dominabitur filiis stultis et inter fratres hereditatem dividet*

A wise slave
will dominate *a* foolish son,
and *he* will divide
the inheritance
with brothers.

17:3 *sicut igne probatur argentum et aurum camino ita corda probat Dominus*

Just as silver is proved by fire
and gold by *a* furnace,
so *the* Lord proves *the* heart.

17:4 *malus oboedit linguae iniquae et fallax obtemperat labiis mendacibus*

The evil *person* obeys
a treacherous tongue,

and *a* liar is submissive
to lying lips.

17:5 *qui despicit pauperem exprobrat factori eius et qui in ruina laetatur alterius non erit inpunitus*

One who despises
a poor man
reproaches *the* One
who made him,
and one who is happy
in another's ruin
will not be unpunished.

17:6 *corona senum filii filiorum et gloria filiorum patres sui*

Children's children
are *the* crown of old age,
and *the* glory of children
is their parents.

17: 7 *non decent stultum verba conposita nec principem labium mentiens*

Careful words are not
becoming to *a* fool,
nor lying lips to *a* prince.

17:8 *gemma gratissima expectatio praestolantis quocumque se verterit prudenter intellegit*

A long-awaited expectation
is *a* most beautiful jewel;
wherever he turns himself,
he understands prudently.

17:9 *qui celat delictum quaerit amicitias qui altero sermone repetit separat foederatos*

One who hides wrongs
seeks friendships;
one who repeats
another's conversation
separates companions.

17:10 *plus proficit correptio apud prudentem quam centum plagae apud stultum*

One correction counts
more to *the* prudent
than *a* hundred blows
to *a* fool.

17:11 *semper iurgia quaerit malus angelus autem crudelis mittetur contra eum*

A quarreler always seeks evil,

but *a* cruel angel[91] will be
sent against him.

17:12 *expedit magis ursae occurrere raptis fetibus quam fatuo confidenti sibi in stultitia sua*

It is better to run into
a bear robbed of her cubs,
than *a* mindless *man*
trusting himself
in his foolishness.

17:13 *qui reddit mala pro bonis non recedet malum de domo eius*

Evil will not turn away
from *the* house of one
who returns hurtful for good.

17:14 *qui dimittit aquam caput est iurgiorum et antequam patiatur contumeliam iudicium deserit*

One who lets out water
is *the* source of quarrels,
and judgment deserts him
before he endures conflict.

---

[91] Angel and Messenger are synonyms in Latin, as well as in many other ancient languages.

17:15 *et qui iustificat impium et qui condemnat iustum abominabilis est uterque apud Dominum*

Both one who justifies
the lawless
and one who condemns
the fair
are equally disgusting
to *the* Lord.

17:16 *quid prodest habere divitias stultum cum sapientiam emere non possit*

How does having riches
benefit *a* fool,
when wisdom
cannot be bought?

17:17 *omni tempore diligit qui amicus est et frater in angustiis conprobatur*

One who is *a* friend
loves at every moment,
and *a* brother is proved
in difficult *times.*

17:18 *homo stultus plaudet manibus cum spoponderit pro amico suo*

A foolish man claps *his* hands
when he gives *a* pledge

for his friend.

17:19 *qui meditatur discordiam diligit rixas et qui exaltat ostium quaerit ruinam*

One who obsesses over
discord delights in quarrels,
and one who lifts up *a* door
latch looks for ruin.

17:20 *qui perversi cordis est non inveniet bonum et qui vertit linguam incidet in malum*

One who is perverse in heart
will not find good,
and one who twists *the*
tongue will fall into harm.

17:21 *natus est stultus in ignominiam suam sed nec pater in fatuo laetabitur*

A fool is born in his shame,
and not even *a* father
will be happy
with *a* mindless *child.*

17:22 *animus gaudens aetatem floridam facit spiritus tristis exsiccat ossa*

A joyful soul
makes *the* season bloom;
a mournful spirit
dries out *the* bones.

17:23 *munera de sinu impius accipit ut pervertat semitas iudicii*

A lawless *man* takes *a* bribe
from *his* vest,
that he may pervert
the way of *the* fair.

17:24 *in facie prudentis lucet sapientia oculi stultorum in finibus terrae*

Prudence shines
in *the* face of *the* wise;
the eyes of *a* fool
are in *the* ends of *the* earth.

17:25 *ira patris filius stultus et dolor matris quae genuit eum*

A foolish son
is a father's anger,
and *the* pain of *the* mother
who bore him.

17:26 *non est bonum damnum inferre iusto nec percutere principem qui recta iudicat*

It isn't good to take away

the confiscated goods
of *a* fair-minded *man*,
or to beat *a* leader
who judges rightly.

17:27 *qui moderatur sermones suos doctus et prudens est et pretiosi spiritus vir eruditus*

One who is careful
in his words
is learned and prudent,
and *the* spirit
of *an* educated man
is precious.

17:28 *stultus quoque si tacuerit sapiens putabitur et si conpresserit labia sua intellegens*

Even *a* fool
will be considered wise
if he keeps quiet,
and intelligent if he
closes his lips.

Chapter 18

18:1 *occasiones quaerit qui vult recedere ab amico omni tempore erit exprobrabilis*

He who wants to turn back
from *a* friend
seeks occasions;
every moment he will be
worthy of reproach.

18:2 *non recipit stultus verba prudentiae nisi ea dixeris quae versantur in corde eius*

A fool does not accept
a prudent word,
unless you tell him
what is turning in his heart.

18:3 *impius cum in profundum venerit peccatorum contemnit sed sequitur eum ignominia et obprobrium*

The lawless, when he comes
into *the* depth of sin,
condemns,
but shame and reproach
follow him.

18:4 *aqua profunda verba ex ore viri et torrens redundans* *fons sapientiae*

Words from *a* man's mouth
are deep waters,
and *the* spring of wisdom
is an overflowing torrent.

18:5 *accipere personam impii non est bonum ut declines a veritate iudicii*

It isn't good
to accept *the* lawless,
lest you turn
from truthful judgment.

18:6 *labia stulti inmiscunt se rixis et os eius iurgia provocat*

A fool's lips
mix him up in brawls,
and his mouth
provokes quarrels.

18:7 *os stulti contritio eius et labia illius ruina animae eius*

A fool's mouth is his regret,
and his lips are *the* ruin
of his soul.

18:8 *verba bilinguis quasi simplicia et ipsa perveniunt usque ad interiora ventris*

The words of *a* two-faced
man seem straightforward,
and they lead to *the* inside
of *the* womb.

18:9 *qui mollis et dissolutus est in opere suo frater est sua opera dissipantis*

One who is soft and negligent
in his actions
is *a* brother to one
whose works are wasteful.

18:10 *turris fortissima nomen Domini ad ipsum currit iustus et exaltabitur*

The name of *the* Lord
is *a* strong tower;
the fair man runs to it
and will be exalted.

18:11 *substantia divitis urbs roboris eius et quasi murus validus circumdans eum*

A rich man's substance
is his bulwark,
and *is* like a strong wall,
surrounding him.

18:12 *antequam conteratur exaltatur cor hominis et antequam glorificetur humiliatur*

Before *it* is crushed,
a man's heart is lifted up,
and before *it* is glorified,
it is humbled.

18:13 *qui prius respondit quam audiat stultum se esse demonstrat et confusione dignum*

One who responds
before he listens
shows himself to be *a* fool,
and worthy of confusion.

18:14 *spiritus viri sustentat inbecillitatem suam spiritum vero ad irascendum facilem quis poterit sustinere*

A man's spirit
sustains his weakness;
a spirit quick to anger, truly,
who can sustain?

18:15 *cor prudens possidebit scientiam et auris sapientium quaerit doctrinam*

A prudent heart
will possess knowledge,
and *a* wise ear
seeks teaching.

18:16 *donum hominis dilatat viam eius et ante principes spatium ei facit*

A man's gift
broadens his way,
and makes *a* space for him
before princes.

18:17 *iustus prior est accusator sui venit amicus eius et investigavit eum*

The fair-minded *man*
is his own accuser,
before his friend comes
and investigates him.

18:18 *contradictiones conprimit sors et inter potentes quoque diiudicat*

Lots frustrate contradictions,
and settle conflicts
even among *the* powerful.

18:19 *frater qui adiuvatur a fratre quasi civitas firma et iudicia quasi vectes urbium*

A brother who is helped
by *a* brother
is like a strong city,
and judgment like *the* bars
of *a* city *gate*.

18:20 *de fructu oris viri replebitur venter eius et*

genimina labiorum illius saturabunt eum

By *the* fruit of man's mouth
his belly will be filled,
and what springs forth
from his lips will cover him.

18:21 *mors et vita in manu linguae qui diligunt eam comedent fructus eius*

Death and life *are*
in *the* power of *the* tongue;
those who delight in it,
will eat its fruit.

18:22 *qui invenit mulierem invenit bonum et hauriet iucunditatem a Domino*

Who finds *a* wife finds good,
and will drink down
happiness from *the* Lord.

18:23 *cum obsecrationibus loquetur pauper et dives effabitur rigide*

The poor will speak
with flatteries,
and *the* rich
will answer roughly.

18:24 *vir amicalis ad societatem magis amicus erit quam frater*

A man who is agreeable
in company
will be more *a* friend
than *a* brother.

Chapter 19

19:1 *melior est pauper qui ambulat in simplicitate sua quam torquens labia insipiens*

A poor *man* who walks
in his simplicity
is better than
twisting, foolish lips.

19:2 *ubi non est scientia animae non est bonum et qui festinus est pedibus offendit*

Where *there* is no knowledge
of life, *there* is no good,
and one who is in a hurry
to leave offends.

19:3 *stultitia hominis subplantat gressus eius et contra Deum fervet animo suo*

A man's foolishness
undermines his steps,
yet he will be angry in his
soul against God.

19:4 *divitiae addunt amicos plurimos a paupere autem et hii quos habuit separantur*

Riches add many friends;
but for *a* poor *man,*
even those he had abandon
him.

19:5 *testis falsus non erit inpunitus et qui mendacia loquitur non effugiet*

A false witness
will not be unpunished,
and one who speaks lies
will not escape.

19:6 *multi colunt personam potentis et amici sunt dona tribuenti*

Many worship *the* person
of *the* powerful,
and friends are
to one giving gifts.

19:7 *fratres hominis pauperis oderunt eum insuper et amici procul recesserunt ab eo qui tantum verba sectatur nihil habebit*

The brothers of *a* poor man
hate him as well,
and friends stay
far away from him.
One who only follows
after words will have
nothing,

19:8 *qui autem possessor est mentis diligit animam suam et custos prudentiae inveniet bona*

but one who has possessed
his mind delights his soul,
and *a* keeper of prudence
will find good.

19:9 *testis falsus non erit inpunitus et qui loquitur mendacia peribit*

A false witness
will not be unpunished
and one who speaks lies
will perish.

19:10 *non decent stultum deliciae nec servum dominari principibus*

Luxuries are not fit
for *a* fool,
nor slaves
to dominate masters.

19:11 *doctrina viri per patientiam noscitur et gloria eius est iniqua praetergredi*

A man's learning is known
through patience,
and his glory is in
marching past treachery.

19:12 *sicut fremitus leonis ita et regis ira et sicut ros super herbam ita hilaritas eius*

Like *a* lion's roar,
thus *the* anger of *a* king,
and like dew on grass,
thus his happiness.

19:13 *dolor patris filius stultus et tecta iugiter perstillantia litigiosa mulier*

A foolish son
is his father's pain,
and *a* quarrelsome woman
is a roof caving in.

19:14 *domus et divitiae dantur a patribus a Domino autem proprie uxor prudens*

Home and riches
are given by fathers,
but *a* prudent wife
by *the* Lord himself.

19:15 *pigredo inmittit soporem et anima dissoluta esuriet*

Laziness sends out sleep,
and *a* careless soul
will hunger.

19:16 *qui custodit mandatum custodit animam suam qui autem neglegit vias suas mortificabitur*

One who keeps *a*
commandment keeps his
soul,
but one who neglects his
ways will be ashamed.

19:17 *feneratur Domino qui miseretur pauperis et vicissitudinem suam reddet ei*

One who has mercy
on *a* poor man
lends to *the* Lord,
and *God* will pay back to him
his concern.

19:18 *erudi filium tuum ne desperes ad interfectionem autem eius ne ponas animam tuam*

Teach your son!
Do not despair!
But do not set your soul
to killing him!

19:19 *qui inpatiens est sustinebit damnum et cum rapuerit aliud adponet*

One who is impatient
will sustain loss,
and when *it* is taken away,
he will add another.

19:20 *audi consilium et suscipe disciplinam ut sis sapiens in novissimis tuis*

Listen to counsel
and accept discipline,
that you may be wise
in your purposes.

19:21 *multae cogitationes in corde viri voluntas autem Domini permanebit*

Many ideas *are*
in a man's heart,
but *the* will of *the* Lord
will endure.

19:22 *homo indigens misericors est et melior pauper quam vir mendax*

A needy man is merciful,
and *a* poor man is better
than *a* liar.

19:23 *timor Domini ad vitam et in plenitudine commorabitur absque visitatione pessimi*

The fear of *the* Lord

leads to life,
and it will dwell in plenty,
away from *a* dismal
visitation.

19:24 *abscondit piger manum suam sub ascella nec ad os suum adplicat eam*

A lazy *man* hides his hand
under his arm,
and does not lift it
even to his mouth.

19:25 *pestilente flagellato stultus sapientior erit sin autem corripueris sapientem intelleget disciplinam*

When *a* destructive *man*
is punished,
a fool will be wiser,
but if *a* wise *man* is
corrected,
he learns discipline.

19:26 *qui adfligit patrem et fugat matrem ignominiosus est et infelix*

One who afflicts his father
and chases away his mother
is shameful and unhappy.

19:27 *non cesses fili audire doctrinam nec ignores sermones scientiae*

Do not cease, son,
listening to teaching,
nor ignore knowing words.

19:28 *testis iniquus deridet iudicium et os impiorum devorat iniquitatem*

A deceitful witness
laughs at judgment,
and *a* lawless mouth
devours treachery.

19:29 *parata sunt derisoribus iudicia et mallei percutientes stultorum corporibus*

Judgments are prepared
for scoffers
and pounding hammers
for *the* bodies of fools.

Chapter 20

20:1 *luxuriosa res vinum et tumultuosa ebrietas quicumque his delectatur non erit sapiens*

Wine is *a* luxurious thing
and drunkenness tumultuous;
whoever delights in these
is not wise.

20:2 *sicut rugitus leonis ita terror regis qui provocat eum peccat in animam suam*

Like *the* roar of *a* lion,
so *the* terror of *a* king;
one who provokes him
sins in his soul.[92]

20:3 *honor est homini qui separat se a contentionibus omnes autem stulti miscentur contumeliis*

Honor belongs to *a* man
who separates himself
from quarrels,
but all fools are mixed up
in conflicts.

20:4 *propter frigus piger arare noluit mendicabit ergo aestate et non dabitur ei*

A lazy *man*
does not want to plow
because of *the* cold;
therefore, he will beg in
summer
and nothing will be given
to him.[93]

20:5 *sicut aqua profunda sic consilium in corde viri sed homo sapiens exhauriet illud*

Like deep water,
thus *is* counsel
in *the* heart of *a* man,
but *a* wise man
will draw it out.

20:6 *multi homines misericordes vocantur virum autem fidelem quis inveniet*

Many men are called
merciful,
but who can find *a* faithful
man?

20:7 *iustus qui ambulat in simplicitate sua beatos post*

---

[92] Sin is not abstract here. Sin does damage to one's own life.

[93] Summer is the season prior to the harvest, when the last of the old year's crops are being used.

se filios derelinquet

A fair-minded *man*
who walks in his simplicity
will leave behind him
blessed children.

20:8 *rex qui sedet in solio iudicii dissipat omne malum intuitu suo*

A king who sits
on *a* throne of fairness,
disperses all evil
by his consideration.

20:9 *quis potest dicere mundum est cor meum purus sum a peccato*

Who can say,
'My heart is clean;
I am pure from sin'?

20:10 *pondus et pondus mensura et mensura utrumque abominabile est apud Deum*

Weight and weight,
measure and measure,[94]
both are detestable with God.

20:11 *ex studiis suis intellegitur puer si munda et si recta sint opera eius*

A child is known
by his enthusiasms,
if his works are clean
and honest.

20:12 *aurem audientem et oculum videntem Dominus fecit utrumque*

A hearing ear
and *a* seeing eye,
the Lord made them both.

20:13 *noli diligere somnum ne te egestas opprimat aperi oculos tuos et saturare panibus*

Do not delight in sleep,
so that need
won't oppress you!
Open your eyes
and be filled with bread!

20:14 *malum est malum est dicit omnis emptor et cum recesserit tunc gloriabitur*

'It's bad, it's bad,'
says each buyer,
and when he walks away,
then he will praise *it*.

---

[94] The proverb refers to scales used by merchants to measure goods. With two different weights, they are able to defraud unsuspecting customers.

20:15 *est aurum et multitudo gemmarum vas autem pretiosum labia scientiae*

There is gold
and *a* multitude of gems,
but learned lips
are *a* precious vessel.

20:16 *tolle vestimentum eius qui fideiussor extitit alieni et pro extraneis aufer pignus ab eo*

Take his garment
from him who stands
as *a* guarantor to *a* foreigner,
and gives out *a* pledge
for strangers.

20:17 *suavis est homini panis mendacii et postea implebitur os eius calculo*

The bread of lying
is sweet to *a* man,
but afterwards his mouth
will be filled with gravel.

20:18 *cogitationes consiliis roborantur et gubernaculis tractanda sunt bella*

The ideas of counselors
are strengthened,
and wars are managed
by governments.

20:19 *ei qui revelat mysteria et ambulat fraudulenter et dilatat labia sua ne commiscearis*

Do not mix with one
who tells secrets,
practices deceit,
and puffs himself up.

20:20 *qui maledicit patri suo et matri extinguetur lucerna eius in mediis tenebris*

One who curses
his father and mother,
his lamp will be extinguished
in *the* midst of shadows.

20:21 *hereditas ad quam festinatur in principio in novissimo benedictione carebit*

An inheritance to one
who is hurried
at *the* beginning,
will lack blessing at *the* end.

20:22 *ne dicas reddam malum expecta Dominum et liberabit te*

Do not say

'I will pay back harm.'
Wait for *the* Lord
and he will liberate you.

20:23 *abominatio est apud Deum pondus et pondus statera dolosa non est bona*

With God, weight and weight
is *an* abomination,
and *an* unjust measure
is not good.

20:24 *a Domino diriguntur gressus viri quis autem hominum intellegere potest viam suam*

A man's steps
are directed by *the* Lord,
but what man can understand
his own way?

20:25 *ruina est hominis devorare sanctos et post vota tractare*

It is ruin to man
to devour holy *things*,
and after *a* promise
to have discussions.

20:26 *dissipat impios rex sapiens et curvat super eos fornicem*

A wise king scatters *the* lawless,
and closes *the* vault over them.

20:27 *lucerna Domini spiraculum hominis quae investigat omnia secreta ventris*

The Lord's lamp
is man's opening,
that investigates
all *the* secrets of *the* womb.

20:28 *misericordia et veritas custodiunt regem et roboratur clementia thronus eius*

Compassion and truth
guard *a* king,
and mercy strengthens
his throne.

20:29 *exultatio iuvenum fortitudo eorum et dignitas senum canities*

The exuberance of *the* young
is their strength,
and *the* dignity of *the* old,
gray hair.

20:30 *livor vulneris absterget mala et plagae in*

secretioribus ventris

Bruising around *a* wound
cleans away evil,
as do punishments
in *the* body's secret places.

Chapter 21

21:1 *sicut divisiones aquarum ita cor regis in manu Domini quocumque voluerit inclinabit illud*

Like *the* divisions of water,
thus *the* heart of *a* king
in *the* hand of *the* Lord;
God will incline it
wherever *He* desires.

21:2 *omnis via viri recta sibi videtur adpendit autem corda Dominus*

Every man's way
seems right to him,
but *the* Lord weighs *the* heart.

21:3 *facere misericordiam et iudicium magis placent Domino quam victimae*

To work mercy and judgment
is more pleasing to *the* Lord
than sacrifices.

21:4 *exaltatio oculorum et dilatatio cordis lucerna impiorum peccatum*

Lifting up of *the* eye
and broadening of *the* heart,
the lamp of *the* lawless *is* sin.

21:5 *cogitationes robusti semper in abundantia omnis autem piger semper in egestate*

The thoughts of *the* strong
are always in abundance,
but every lazy *man*
is always in need.

21:6 *qui congregat thesauros lingua mendacii vanus est et inpingetur ad laqueos mortis*

One who gathers treasures
by *a* lying tongue is vain,
and will be thrust against
the snares of death.

21:7 *rapinae impiorum detrahent eos quia noluerunt facere iudicium*

The plunder of *the* lawless
will take them away,
because they did not want
to do what is right.

21:8 *perversa via viri aliena est qui autem mundus est rectum opus eius*

A man's twisted way
is strange,
but one who is clean,
his work *is* straightforward.

21:9 *melius est sedere in angulo domatis quam cum muliere litigiosa et in domo communi*

It is better to sit
in *a* corner of *the* roof,
than with *an* argumentative
woman in *a* common house.

21:10 *anima impii desiderat malum non miserebitur proximo suo*

The soul of *the* lawless
desires evil;
he will not have mercy
on his neighbor.

21:11 *multato pestilente sapientior erit parvulus et si sectetur sapientem sumet scientiam*

A youth will become wiser,
through *the* punishment
of *the* destructive,
and if he pursues *the* wise,
he will obtain understanding.

21:12 *excogitat iustus de domo impii ut detrahat impios in malum*

The fair devises
outside *the* house
of *the* lawless,
how he may carry away
the lawless in harm.

21:13 *qui obturat aurem suam ad clamorem pauperis et ipse clamabit et non exaudietur*

One who closes his ear
to *the* cry of *the* poor,
will himself also cry out
and not be heard.

21:14 *munus absconditum extinguet iras et donum in sinu indignationem maximam*

A hidden bribe
will extinguish wrath,
and *a* gift in *the* vest pocket,
great indignation.

21:15 *gaudium iusto est facere iudicium et pavor operantibus iniquitatem*

To work judgment is joy
to *the* fair,
and fear to workers
of treachery.

21:16 *vir qui erraverit a via doctrinae in coetu gigantum commorabitur*

A man who wanders
from *the* way of teaching,
will live in *a* fearsome
company.

21:17 *qui diligit epulas in egestate erit qui amat vinum et pinguia non ditabitur*

One who loves banquets
will be in need;
one who loves wine
and rich *foods* will not
be enriched.

21:18 *pro iusto datur impius et pro rectis iniquus*

The lawless is given over
for *the* fair *man*,
and *the* treacherous
for *the* honest.

21:19 *melius est habitare in terra deserta quam cum muliere rixosa et iracunda*

It is better to live
in *a* desert land
than with *a* quarrelsome,
angry woman.

21:20 *thesaurus desiderabilis et oleum in*

habitaculo iusti et inprudens homo dissipabit illud

There is desirable treasure
and oil in *the* dwelling
of *the* fair,
and *an* imprudent man
will waste it.

21:21 *qui sequitur iustitiam et misericordiam inveniet vitam et iustitiam et gloriam*

One who follows
fairness and mercy
will find life, fairness
and glory.

21:22 *civitatem fortium ascendit sapiens et destruxit robur fiduciae eius*

The wise ascends
against a strong city,
and destroys *the* strength
of *its* confidence.

21:23 *qui custodit os suum et linguam suam custodit ab angustiis animam suam*

One who guards
his mouth and his tongue,
guards his soul from anguish.

21:24 *superbus et arrogans vocatur indoctus qui in ira operatur superbiam*

An unlearned man
who works disdainfully
in anger,
is called proud and arrogant.

21:25 *desideria occidunt pigrum noluerunt enim quicquam manus eius operari*

Desires kill *a* lazy *man*,
for his hands refused
to do any work at all.

21:26 *tota die concupiscit et desiderat qui autem iustus est tribuet et non cessabit*

All day he lusts and desires,
but one who is fair will give
and will not cease.

21:27 *hostiae impiorum abominabiles quia offeruntur ex scelere*

The offerings of *the* lawless
are detestable,
because they are offered
from wickedness.

21:28 *testis mendax peribit vir oboediens loquitur victoriam*

A lying witness will perish;
an obedient man speaks
success.

21:29 *vir impius procaciter obfirmat vultum suum qui autem rectus est corrigit viam suam*

A lawless man
rashly hardens his outlook,
but one who is honest
corrects his way.

21:30 *non est sapientia non est prudentia non est consilium contra Dominum*

There is no wisdom,
there is no prudence,
there is no counsel
against *the* Lord.

21:31 *equus paratur ad diem belli Dominus autem salutem tribuet*

A horse is prepared
for *the* day of war,
but *the* Lord
will give security.

Chapter 22

22:1 *melius est nomen bonum quam divitiae multae super argentum et aurum gratia bona*

A good name
is better than many riches;
good grace *is* above
silver and gold.

22:2 *dives et pauper obviaverunt sibi utriusque operator est Dominus*

Rich and poor
have met each other,
and *the* Lord made them
both.

22:3 *callidus vidit malum et abscondit se innocens pertransiit et adflictus est damno*

The experienced *man*
has seen evil
and hidden himself;
the inexperienced kept going
and suffered loss.

22:4 *finis modestiae timor Domini divitiae et gloria et vita*

The end result of restraint
is the fear of *the* Lord,
riches, glory and life.

22:5 *arma et gladii in via perversi custos animae suae longe recedit ab eis*

Weapons and swords
are in *the* path of *the* lawless;
one guarding his soul
will back far away
from them.

22:6 *proverbium est adulescens iuxta viam suam etiam cum senuerit non recedet ab ea*

A proverb is *something*
a youth *keeps* close
to his way;
even when he is old,
he will not back away
from it.

22:7 *dives pauperibus imperat et qui accipit mutuum servus est fenerantis*

The rich command *the* poor,
and one who accepts *a* loan
is slave to *the* lender.

22:8 *qui seminat iniquitatem metet mala et virga irae suae consummabitur*

One who plants treachery
reaps evil,
and *the* rod of his anger
will consume him.

22:9 *qui pronus est ad misericordiam benedicetur de panibus enim suis dedit pauperi*

One who is inclined to mercy
will be blessed,
for he gave of his bread
to *the* poor.

22:10 *eice derisorem et exibit cum eo iurgium cessabuntque causae et contumeliae*

Throw *a* scoffer out
and quarrels will leave
with him.
Pretexts and conflicts
will cease.

22:11 *qui diligit cordis munditiam propter gratiam labiorum suorum habebit amicum regem*

One who delights
in cleanness of heart,
because of *the* grace

of his lips,
will have *the* king as friend.

22:12 *oculi Domini custodiunt scientiam et subplantantur verba iniqui*

The eyes of the Lord
guard knowledge
and undermine
treacherous words.

22:13 *dicit piger leo foris in medio platearum occidendus sum*

A lazy *man* says,
'*A* lion is outside
in *the* middle of *the* streets!
I will be killed!'

22:14 *fovea profunda os alienae cui iratus est Dominus incidet in eam*

A stranger's mouth
is *a* gaping hole;
the one *the* Lord is angry
with will fall in it.

22:15 *stultitia conligata est in corde pueri et virga disciplinae fugabit eam*

Foolishness is bound up
in *the* heart of *a* child,
and *the* rod of discipline
will drive it out.

22:16 *qui calumniatur pauperem ut augeat divitias suas dabit ipse ditiori et egebit*

One who abuses *the* poor
that he might increase
his riches,
will himself hand over his
wealth and be in need.

Take Wisdom to Heart[95]

22:17 *inclina aurem tuam et audi verba sapientium adpone autem cor ad doctrinam meam*

Incline your ear
and hear words of wisdom;
and direct *your* heart
to my teaching,

22:18 *quae pulchra erit tibi cum servaveris eam in ventre tuo et redundabit in labiis tuis*

because it will be
beautiful to you
when you serve it
from *the* gut,
and it will overflow
in your lips,

22:19 *ut sit in Domino fiducia tua unde et ostendi eam tibi hodie*

that your faith may be
in *the* Lord,
which is why I have shown it
to you today.[96]

22:20 *ecce descripsi eam tibi tripliciter in cogitationibus et scientia*

Look, I have described it
to you thoroughly,
in thoughts and in
knowledge,

22:21 *ut ostenderem tibi firmitatem et eloquia veritatis respondere ex his illi qui misit te*

that I may show you firmness
and truthful eloquence,
to respond from them
to one who sends you.

Treat the Poor Fairly

22:22 *non facias violentiam pauperi quia pauper est neque conteras egenum in porta*

Do not work violence

---

[95] This begins a new section of the book.)

[96] Wisdom's revelation echoes the Revelation on Sinai. Compare to Exodus 19:10-11 *And the LORD said to Moses, "Go to the people and consecrate them today and tomorrow, and let them wash their garments, 11 and be ready by the third day; for on the third day the LORD will come down upon Mount Sinai in the sight of all the people.*

against *the* poor
because he is poor,
nor grind up *the* needy
at *the* gate.

22:23 *quia Dominus iudicabit causam eius et configet eos qui confixerint animam eius*

because *the* Lord
will judge his cause,
and strike down
those who have struck him.

Beware of Angry People

22:24 *noli esse amicus homini iracundo neque ambules cum viro furioso*

Do not be *a* friend
to *a* wrathful man,
nor walk with *a* furious man,

22:25 *ne forte discas semitas eius et sumas scandalum animae tuae*

lest perhaps you learn
his paths,
and you add scandal
to your soul.

Avoid a Stranger's Debt

22:26 *noli esse cum his qui defigunt manus suas et qui vades se offerunt pro debitis*

Do not be with those
whose hands bewitch,
and who offer themselves
as guarantors for debts.

22:27 *si enim non habes unde restituas quid causae est ut tollat operimentum de cubili tuo*

For if you do not have *money*
to *make* restitution,
why give him cause
to take away *the* cover
of your bed?

Respect Existing Order

22:28 *ne transgrediaris terminos antiquos quos posuerunt patres tui*

Do not remove
the ancient boundaries,
which your fathers
established.

Where the Talented End Up

22:29 *vidisti virum velocem in opere suo coram regibus stabit nec erit ante ignobiles*

Have you considered *a* man
swift in his work?

He will stand before kings,
and will not be before
the ignoble.

Chapter 23

Be Prudent with the Powerful

23:1 *quando sederis ut comedas cum principe diligenter adtende quae posita sunt ante faciem tuam*

When you sit and eat
with *a* prince,
pay attention diligently,
because you have been
positioned before his face,

23:2 *et statue cultrum in gutture tuo si tamen habes in potestate animam tuam*

and put *a* knife to your throat
if you still have your soul
in control.

23:3 *ne desideres de cibis eius in quo est panis mendacii*

Do not long for his bread,
because *it* is *the* bread of lies.

23:4 *noli laborare ut diteris sed prudentiae tuae pone modum*

Don't labor to get rich,
but put on your mode

of prudence.

23:5 *ne erigas oculos tuos ad opes quas habere non potes quia facient sibi pinnas quasi aquilae et avolabunt in caelum*

Do not raise your eyes
toward riches over which
you have no power,
because they will make
wings for themselves,
like an eagle's,
and fly away to *the* sky.

Beware of a Greedy Man

23:6 *ne comedas cum homine invido et ne desideres cibos eius*

Do not eat
with *a* greedy man,
and do not desire his food,

23:7 *quoniam in similitudinem arioli et coniectoris aestimat quod ignorat comede et bibe dicet tibi et mens eius non est tecum*

because, like *a* diviner
and soothsayer,
he guesses at what
he does not know.
'Eat and drink,'
he says to you,
yet his mind is not with you.

23:8 *cibos quos comederas evomes et perdes pulchros sermones tuos*

You will vomit
the meals which you ate,
and you will waste
your pretty speeches.

23:9 *in auribus insipientium ne loquaris quia despicient doctrinam eloquii tui*

Do not speak
in *the* ears of *the* ignorant,
because, despite your
eloquence,
he will despise your teaching.

Do Not Harm the Harmless

23:10 *ne adtingas terminos parvulorum et agrum pupillorum ne introeas*

Do not touch
the boundaries of little ones,
or go into *an* orphan's field,

23:11 *propinquus enim eorum Fortis est et ipse iudicabit contra te causam illorum*

for Strength is his neighbor,
and will Himself judge *the*
orphan's cause against you.

23:12 *ingrediatur ad doctrinam cor tuum et aures tuae ad verba scientiae*

Let your heart go in
toward learning,
and your ears
to knowing words.

Discipline Your Child

23:13 *noli subtrahere a puero disciplinam si enim percusseris eum virga non morietur*

Do not take away discipline
from *a* boy,
for if you beat him
with *a* stick,
he will not die.

23:14 *tu virga percuties eum et animam eius de inferno liberabis*

You will beat him
with *a* stick,
and save his soul
from *the* inferno.

Exhortations to a Son

23:15 *fili mi si sapiens fuerit animus tuus gaudebit tecum cor meum*

My son, if your soul is wise,
my heart will rejoice with
you,

23:16 *et exultabunt renes mei cum locuta fuerint rectum labia tua*

and my kidneys will exult
when your lips
will have spoken rightly.[97]

23:17 *non aemuletur cor tuum peccatores sed in timore Domini esto tota die*

Do not let your heart
imitate sinners,
but abide in *the* fear
of *the* Lord all day,

23:18 *quia habebis spem in novissimo et praestolatio tua non auferetur*

because you will have hope
in *the* end,
and your expectation
will not be taken away.

---

[97] Compare to RSV: *My soul will rejoice when your lips speak what is right.*

23:19 *audi fili mi et esto sapiens et dirige in via animum tuum*

Hear, my son, and be wise,
and direct your soul
in *the* way.

23:20 *noli esse in conviviis potatorum nec in comesationibus eorum qui carnes ad vescendum conferunt*

Do not stay in
the banquets of drunkards,
nor in their feasts,
who bring food to
disputations,

23:21 *quia vacantes potibus et dantes symbola consumentur et vestietur pannis dormitatio*

because those who
idle over drinks
and those giving feasts
will be consumed,
and drowsiness
will be dressed in rags.

23:22 *audi patrem tuum qui genuit te et ne contemnas cum senuerit mater tua*

Listen to your father
who brought you up,
and do not condemn
when your mother has grown old.

23:23 *veritatem eme et noli vendere sapientiam et doctrinam et intellegentiam*

Buy truth and do not sell:
wisdom, learning,
and intelligence.

23:24 *exultat gaudio pater iusti qui sapientem genuit laetabitur in eo*

A father of *the* fair *man*
exults joyfully;
one who brought up *a* wise
son, he will be happy in him.

23:25 *gaudeat pater tuus et mater tua et exultet quae genuit te*

Your father will rejoice
and your mother,
and she who bore you
will exult.

Another Warning Against Whores

23:26 *praebe fili mi cor tuum mihi et oculi tui vias*

meas custodiant

Make your heart
available to me, my son,
and let your eyes
keep my ways.

23:27 *fovea enim profunda est meretrix et puteus angustus aliena*

For *a* whore is *a* deep hole,
and *a* stranger *a* narrow pit.

23:28 *insidiatur in via quasi latro et quos incautos viderit interficit*

She lies in ambush
on *the* way, like *a* robber,
and those careless *fools* she
sees, she kills.

A Warning Against Alcoholism

23:29 *cui vae cuius patri vae cui rixae cui foveae cui sine causa vulnera cui suffusio oculorum*

To whom woe,
to whose father woe,
to whom quarrels,
to whom pits,
to whom wounds without
cause,
to whom bloodshot eyes?

23:30 *nonne his qui morantur in vino et student calicibus epotandis*

Are they not to those
who linger over wine,
and practice draining cups?

23:31 *ne intuearis vinum quando flavescit cum splenduerit in vitro color eius ingreditur blande*

Do not look at wine
when *it* turns gold
and *its* color shimmers
in *the* cup.
It goes smoothly,

23:32 *sed in novissimo mordebit ut coluber et sicut regulus venena diffundet*

but in *the* end
it will bite like *a* cobra,
and like *a* petty prince
will spread its venom.

23:33 *oculi tui videbunt extraneas et cor tuum loquetur perversa*

Your eyes
will see strange *sights*,

and your heart will say
perverse *things*,

23:34 *et eris sicut dormiens in medio mari et quasi sopitus gubernator amisso clavo*

and you will feel
like one sleeping
in *the* middle of *the* sea,
like *a* sleepy helmsman
who lost *the* wheel,

23:35 *et dices verberaverunt me sed non dolui traxerunt me et ego non sensi quando evigilabo et rursum vina repperiam*

and you say,
'They beat me up,
but it didn't hurt.
'They dragged me,
but I didn't feel *it*.
'When will I wake up again?
I want more wine.'

Chapter 24

Warning Against Evil Men

24:1 *ne aemuleris viros malos nec desideres esse cum eis*

Do not imitate evil men,
or desire to be with them,

24:2 *quia rapinas meditatur mens eorum et fraudes labia eorum loquuntur*

because their mind
meditates on plunder,
and their lips speak of frauds.

The Value of Wisdom

24:3 *sapientia aedificabitur domus et prudentia roborabitur*

A house will be built
by wisdom,
and be strengthened
by prudence

24:4 *in doctrina replebuntur cellaria universa substantia pretiosa et pulcherrima*

By education,
a store room is filled
with all precious
and beautiful substance.

24:5 *vir sapiens et fortis est et vir doctus robustus et validus*

A wise man is strong
and *a* learned man
robust and valuable,

24:6 *quia cum dispositione initur bellum et erit salus ubi multa consilia sunt*

because war is begun
by careful planning,
and safety will be
where *there* are many
counselors.

Miscellaneous Proverbs

24:7 *excelsa stulto sapientia in porta non aperiet os suum*

Wisdom *is* too high
for *a* fool;
in *the* gate he will not
open his mouth.

24:8 *qui cogitat malefacere stultus vocabitur*

One who considers
doing harm
will be called *a* fool.

24:9 *cogitatio stulti peccatum est et abominatio hominum detractor*

A fool's idea is sin,
and *a* belittler is disgusting
to men.

24:10 *si desperaveris lassus in die angustiae inminuetur fortitudo tua*

If you despair in exhaustion
on *an* anxious day,
your strength will be
diminished.

24:11 *erue eos qui ducuntur ad mortem et qui trahuntur ad interitum liberare ne cesses*

Rescue those who are
led to death,
and do not cease to free
those who are being dragged
to destruction.

God Will Repay

24:12 *si dixeris vires non suppetunt qui inspector est cordis ipse intellegit et servatorem animae tuae nihil fallit reddetque homini iuxta opera sua*

If you say,
'Strength is not sufficient,'

He who has inspected *the*
heart –
He will understand,
and will be *the* preserver
of your life.
He lacks nothing
and will pay *a* man back
according to his actions.

The Sweetness of Wisdoms

24:13 *comede fili mi mel quia bonum est et favum dulcissimum gutturi tuo*

Eat honey, my son,
because *it* is good,
and *a* honeycomb is
most sweet to your throat.

24:14 *sic et doctrina sapientiae animae tuae quam cum inveneris habebis in novissimis et spes tua non peribit*

So also *is the* teaching of
wisdom to your soul,
which, when you find it,
you will have it to *the* end,
and your hope will not
perish.

The Fair-Minded Man Gets Back Up

24:15 *ne insidieris et quaeras impietatem in domo iusti neque vastes requiem eius*

Do not plot and seek
lawlessness
in *the* house of *the* fair,
nor disturb his peace,

24:16 *septies enim cadet iustus et resurget impii autem corruent in malum*

for *a* fair-minded *man*
will fall seven times
and will get back up,
but *the* lawless
will fall into harm.

Don't Rejoice Over Your Enemy

24:17 *cum ceciderit inimicus tuus ne gaudeas et in ruina eius ne exultet cor tuum*

When your enemy falls,
do not rejoice,
and do not let your heart
exult in his ruin,

24:18 *ne forte videat Dominus et displiceat ei et auferat ab eo iram suam*

unless, perhaps, *the* Lord see
and be displeased with you,
and take *His* wrath

away from him.

The Fate of the Lawless

24:19 *ne contendas cum pessimis nec aemuleris impios*

Do not contend
with *the* worst,
nor imitate *the* lawless,

24:20 *quoniam non habent futurorum spem mali et lucerna impiorum extinguetur*

because *the* harmful
do not have *a* hopeful future,
and *the* light of *the* lawless
will be extinguished.

24:21 *time Dominum fili mi et regem et cum detractoribus non commiscearis*

Fear *the* Lord, my son,
and *the* king,
and do not mingle
with their detractors,

24:22 *quoniam repente consurget perditio eorum et ruinam utriusque quis novit*

because their destruction
will come suddenly,
and who knows
the ruin of both?

More Proverbs

24:23 *haec quoque sapientibus cognoscere personam in iudicio non est bonum*

These also are wise:
to prejudge *a* person
is not good.

24:24 *qui dicit impio iustus es maledicent ei populi et detestabuntur eum tribus*

One who says to *the* lawless,
'You are fair,'
people will lie to him,
and tribes will detest him.

24:25 *qui arguunt laudabuntur et super ipsos veniet benedictio*

Those who contest *him*
will be praised,
and blessing will come
upon them.

24:26 *labia deosculabitur qui recta verba respondet*

The lips of one who responds

honestly will be kissed.

24:27 *praepara foris opus tuum et diligenter exerce agrum tuum ut postea aedifices domum tuam*

Prepare your work outdoors,
and diligently cultivate
your field,
that afterwards you may build
your house.

24:28 *ne sis testis frustra contra proximum tuum nec lactes quemquam labiis tuis*

Do not be *a* witness
without cause
against your neighbor,
nor lead someone on
with your lips.

24:29 *ne dicas quomodo fecit mihi sic faciam ei reddam unicuique secundum opus suum*

Do not say, 'Whatever he did
to me, I will do to him;
I will repay each one
according to his work.'

The Fruit of Laziness

24:30 *per agrum hominis pigri transivi et per vineam viri stulti*

I passed through the field
of *a* lazy man,
and through *the* vineyard
of *a* stupid man,

24:31 *et ecce totum repleverant urticae operuerant superficiem eius spinae et maceria lapidum destructa erat*

and, look, they were all
overgrown with stinging
nettles.
Thorns had overgrown
the building
and *the* retaining wall
had been destroyed.

24:32 *quod cum vidissem posui in corde meo et exemplo didici disciplinam*

Because when I saw,
I set *it* in my heart.
I learned discipline by
example.

24:33 *parum inquam dormies modicum dormitabis pauxillum manus conseres ut quiescas*

I say, 'You will sleep *a* little,

you will slumber
a short time,
your hand will sow
just a little,
so you can rest,

24:34 *et veniet quasi cursor egestas tua et mendicitas quasi vir armatus*

and need will come upon you
like *a* sprinter,
and begging like *an* armed man.

Chapter 25

More of Solomon's Proverbs, via Hezekiah

25:1 *haec quoque parabolae Salomonis quas transtulerunt viri Ezechiae regis Iuda*

These also are
parables of Solomon,
which *the* men of Hezekiah,
king of Judah, copied out.[98]

25:2 *gloria Dei celare verbum et gloria regum investigare sermonem*

The glory of God *is*
to hide *a* matter,
and *the* glory of *a* king
to investigate *its* cause.

25:3 *caelum sursum et terra deorsum et cor regum inscrutabile*

Heaven above
and earth below

[98] Hezekiah, king of Judah from 715 to 687 B.C.E., led a religious and national revival during an epoch of extreme national stress. See, http://en.wikipedia.org/wiki/Hezekiah. Hezekiah's story in scripture may be found beginning at 2 Kings 18 and 2 Chronicles 29.

and *a* king's heart
are unsearchable.

Purifying Silver and Kings

25:4 *aufer robiginem de argento et egredietur vas purissimum*

Take away silver's rust
and it will be *the* purest vessel.

25:5 *aufer impietatem de vultu regis et firmabitur iustitia thronus eius*

Take away lawlessness
from *a* king's appearance
and his throne will be made firm by fairness.

Don't Put on Airs

25:6 *ne gloriosus appareas coram rege et in loco magnorum ne steteris*

Do not appear boasting
before *a* king,
and do not stand
in place of *the* great,

25:7 *melius est enim ut dicatur tibi ascende huc quam ut humilieris coram principe*

for *it* is better that he say to you, 'Come up here,'
than that you be humiliated
before *a* prince.

Keeping Confidences

25:8 *quae viderunt oculi tui ne proferas in iurgio cito ne postea emendare non possis cum dehonestaveris amicum tuum*

Things which your eyes have seen,
do not blurt out quickly during *a* quarrel,
lest afterwards you not be able to make amends
when you have slandered your friend.

25:9 *causam tuam tracta cum amico tuo et secretum extraneo non reveles*

Handle your concern
with your friend,
and do not reveal *his* secret
to *a* stranger,

25:10 *ne forte insultet tibi cum audierit et exprobrare non cesset*

lest, perhaps, he take offense
at you when he hear it,

and not cease to resent *you.*

Various Comparisons

25:11 *mala aurea in lectis argenteis qui loquitur verbum in tempore suo*

Like golden apples
in *a* silver bed
is one who speaks
a timely word.

25:12 *inauris aurea et margaritum fulgens qui arguit sapientem et aurem oboedientem*

Like a golden earring
and *a* brilliant pearl,
so *is* one who tests *the* wise
and *has an* obedient ear.

25:13 *sicut frigus nivis in die messis ita legatus fidelis ei qui misit eum animam illius requiescere facit*

Like cold snow
in *the* day of harvest,
thus *is a* faithful
representative
to one who sent him,
for he puts his soul at ease.

25:14 *nubes et ventus et pluviae non sequentes vir gloriosus et promissa non conplens*

Like clouds and wind
without rain following,
thus is a boasting man
not fulfilling *a* promise.

25:15 *patientia lenietur princeps et lingua mollis confringet duritiam*

A prince will be appeased
by patience,
and *a* soft tongue
breaks up harshness.

25:16 *mel invenisti comede quod sufficit tibi ne forte saturatus evomas illud*

You found honey?
Eat what is sufficient to you,
lest perhaps you eat too much
of it and vomit.

25:17 *subtrahe pedem tuum de domo proximi tui nequando satiatus oderit te*

Take your feet away
from your neighbor's house,
lest when he has had enough,
he hate you.

25:18 *iaculum et gladius et*

sagitta acuta homo qui loquitur contra proximum suum testimonium falsum

Like a spear and sword
and sharp arrow,
so is a man who gives
false testimony against
his neighbor.

25:19 *dens putridus et pes lapsus qui sperat super infideli in die angustiae*

Like a rotten tooth
and *a* lame foot
is one who hopes
in *the* faithless
on *a* day of anguish.

25:20 *et amittit pallium in die frigoris acetum in nitro et qui cantat carmina cordi pessimo*

Like one who loses *a* coat
on *a* cold day,
like vinegar in soda,
is one who sings to
a dismal heart.

How to Treat Your Enemy

25:21 *si esurierit inimicus tuus ciba illum et si sitierit da ei aquam bibere*

If your enemy is hungry,
feed him,
and if *he* is thirsty,
give him water to drink,

25:22 *prunam enim congregabis super caput eius et Dominus reddet tibi*

for you will gather
glowing coals over his head,
and *the* Lord will repay you.[99]

25:23 *ventus aquilo dissipat pluvias et facies tristis linguam detrahentem*

A stormy wind
dissipates showers,
and *a* sad appearance
a disparaging tongue.

25:24 *melius est sedere in angulo domatis quam cum muliere litigiosa et in domo communi*

Better to sit on *a* corner
of *a* roof
than in *a* common house

---

[99] This verse is quoted in Romans 12:20-21: *No, "if your enemy is hungry, feed him; if he is thirsty, give him drink; for by so doing you will heap burning coals upon his head." Do not be overcome by evil, but overcome evil with good.*

with *a* quarrelsome woman.

25:25 *aqua frigida animae sitienti et nuntius bonus de terra longinqua*

Like cold water
to *a* thirsty soul,
so is good news
from *a* distant land.

25:26 *fons turbatus pede et vena corrupta iustus cadens coram impio*

Like water dirtied by feet
and *a* spring corrupted,
so is the fair *man*
falling before *the* lawless.

25:27 *sicut qui mel multum comedit non est ei bonum sic qui scrutator est maiestatis opprimitur gloria*

Just as *it* is not good for
someone who eats too much
honey,
so someone who scrutinizes
greatness is worn down
by fame.

25:28 *sicut urbs patens et absque murorum ambitu ita vir qui non potest in loquendo cohibere spiritum suum*

Like *an* open city,
away from *a* wall's
protection,
thus *is a* man who cannot
silence his passion while
talking.

Chapter 26

26:1 *quomodo nix aestate et pluvia in messe sic indecens est stulto gloria*

Like snow in summer
and rain at harvest,
so fame is not fitting
to *a* fool.

26:2 *sicut avis ad alia transvolans et passer quolibet vadens sic maledictum frustra prolatum in quempiam superveniet*

Like a bird flying
to other *places*
and *a* sparrow going
wherever it pleases,
an empty curse
will come upon someone.

26:3 *flagellum equo et camus asino et virga dorso inprudentium*

A whip for *the* horse,
and *a* muzzle for *an* ass,
and *a* rod for *the* back
of *the* imprudent.

Paradoxical Proverbs

26:4 *ne respondeas stulto iuxta stultitiam suam ne efficiaris ei similis*

Do not respond to *a* fool
according to his foolishness,
lest you be made like him.

26:5 *responde stulto iuxta stultitiam suam ne sibi sapiens esse videatur*

Respond to *a* fool,
according to his foolishness,
lest he seem to be wise
to himself.

Various Comparisons

26:6 *claudus pedibus et iniquitatem bibens qui mittit verba per nuntium stultum*

Like lameness of foot
and swallowing treachery
is one who sends instructions
by *a* foolish messenger.

26:7 *quomodo pulchras frustra habet claudus tibias sic indecens est in ore stultorum parabola*

As *a* lame man has beautiful
legs to no purpose,
thus *a* parable in *the* mouth
of *a* fool is not fitting.

26:8 *sicut qui mittit lapidem*

in acervum Mercurii ita qui tribuit insipienti honorem

As one who throws *a* rock
into *a* pile of mercury,
so *is* one who gives honor
to *a* fool.

26:9 *quomodo si spina nascatur in manu temulenti sic parabola in ore stultorum*

As if *a* thorn grew
in *a* drunk's hand,
so *is a* parable
in *a* fool's mouth.

26:10 *iudicium determinat causas et qui inponit stulto silentium iras mitigat*

Causes determine judgment,
and one who puts *a* fool
to silence reduces anger.

26:11 *sicut canis qui revertitur ad vomitum suum sic inprudens qui iterat stultitiam suam*

Like *a* dog who goes back
to his vomit,
thus *is the* imprudent
who returns to his
foolishness.

26:12 *vidisti hominem sapientem sibi videri magis illo spem habebit stultus*

Have you seen *a* man
who considers himself wise?
A fool will have more hope
than him.

26:13 *dicit piger leaena in via leo in itineribus*

A lazy *man* says,
'*A* lioness is in *the* street!
A lion is on *the* roads!'

26:14 *sicut ostium vertitur in cardine suo ita piger in lectulo suo*

As *a* gate turns on its hinges,
thus *a* lazy *man turns* in his
bed.

26:15 *abscondit piger manus sub ascellas suas et laborat si ad os suum eas converterit*

A lazy *man* hides his hand
under his arm,
and labors *to see*
if he can bring it back
to his mouth.

26:16 *sapientior sibi piger videtur septem viris*

loquentibus sententias

A lazy *man* seems wiser
to himself
than seven men
explaining reasons.

26:17 *sicut qui adprehendit auribus canem sic qui transit et inpatiens commiscetur rixae alterius*

Like one who yanks
on *a* dog's ear,
so *is* one who goes
and, impatient,
gets mixed up
in another's brawl.

I Was Only Joking!

26:18 *sicut noxius est qui mittit lanceas et sagittas et mortem*

As one who throws
lances, arrows, and death
is guilty,

26:19 *sic vir qui fraudulenter nocet amico suo et cum fuerit deprehensus dicit ludens feci*

so *is a* man who deceitfully
harms his friend,
and when he is reproached,
says, 'I was joking.'

Various Proverbs

26:20 *cum defecerint ligna extinguetur ignis et susurrone subtracto iurgia conquiescunt*

When wood is taken away
fire is extinguished,
and *when a* complainer
is removed conflicts are
calmed.

26:21 *sicut carbones ad prunam et ligna ad ignem sic homo iracundus suscitat rixas*

Like coal to live coals
and wood to fire,
thus *is an* angry man
to brawls.

26:22 *verba susurronis quasi simplicia et ipsa perveniunt ad intima ventris*

The words of *a* complainer
seem simple,
and they go down
to *the* innermost parts
of *the* gut.

26:23 *quomodo si argento sordido ornare velis vas*

*fictile sic labia tumentia cum
pessimo corde sociata*

Like *an* earthenware dish
covered with tarnished silver,
thus *are* conceited lips
joined to *a* dismal heart.

How to Know an Enemy

26:24 *labiis suis intellegitur
inimicus cum in corde
tractaverit dolos*

An enemy is known
by his lips,
when he prepares deceit
in his heart.

26:25 *quando submiserit
vocem suam ne credideris ei
quoniam septem nequitiae
sunt in corde illius*

When his voice speaks softly,
do not believe him,
because seven evils
are in his heart.

Various Proverbs

26:26 *qui operit odium
fraudulenter revelabitur
malitia eius in concilio*

The malice of one
who falsely hides hatred
will be made clear in council.

26:27 *qui fodit foveam
incidet in eam et qui volvit
lapidem revertetur ad eum*

One who digs *a* hole
will fall in it,
and one who rolls away
a rock,
has it come back to him.

26:28 *lingua fallax non amat
veritatem et os lubricum
operatur ruinas*

A lying tongue
does not love truth,
and *a* slick mouth
brings about ruin.

Chapter 27

Various Proverbs

27:1 *ne glorieris in crastinum ignorans quid superventura pariat dies*

Do not boast
about tomorrow,
ignorant of what
the coming day will bring.

27:2 *laudet te alienus et non os tuum extraneus et non labia tua*

Let another praise you
and not your mouth,
a stranger, and not your lips.

27:3 *grave est saxum et onerosa harena sed ira stulti utroque gravior*

A rock is heavy
and sand weighty,
but *a* fool's wrath is
heavier than both.

27:4 *ira non habet misericordiam nec erumpens furor et impetum concitati ferre quis poterit*

Wrath does not have mercy,
nor *does* fury boiling forth,
and who can bear *the* force
of one provoked?

27:5 *melior est manifesta correptio quam amor absconditus*

Open correction is better
than hidden love.

27:6 *meliora sunt vulnera diligentis quam fraudulenta odientis oscula*

The blows of *the* loving
are better than
the lying kisses of *the* hating.

27:7 *anima saturata calcabit favum anima esuriens et amarum pro dulce sumet*

A soul that is full
will turn down *a* honeycomb,
yet *a* hungry soul will
consider even *the* bitter
sweet.

27:8 *sicut avis transmigrans de nido suo sic vir qui relinquit locum suum*

Like *a* bird leaving its nest,
so is *a* man who
leaves behind his home.

27:9 *unguento et variis odoribus delectatur cor et bonis amici consiliis anima dulcoratur*

A heart is delighted
by perfume and various odors,
and *a* spirit is sweetened
by *the* counsels of good friends.

27:10 *amicum tuum et amicum patris tui ne dimiseris et domum fratris tui ne ingrediaris in die adflictionis tuae melior est vicinus iuxta quam frater procul*

Do not dismiss your friend
or *a* friend of your father's,
and do not go
to your brother's house
on *the* day of your affliction;
a neighbor nearby is better
than *a* brother far away.

27:11 *stude sapientiae fili mi et laetifica cor meum ut possim exprobranti respondere sermonem*

Apply yourself to wisdom, my son,
and make my heart happy,
that you be able to respond
in word to one who questions *you*.

27:12 *astutus videns malum absconditus est parvuli transeuntes sustinuere dispendia*

The experienced *man*,
seeing harm, hid himself,
but *the* inexperienced,
going forward, suffered loss.

27:13 *tolle vestimentum eius qui spopondit pro extraneo et pro alienis auferto pignus*

Take his garment, who gives
a guarantee for *a* foreigner,
and let him give over *a* bond
for strangers.

27:14 *qui benedicit proximo suo voce grandi de nocte consurgens maledicenti similis erit*

One who blesses his neighbor
in *a* loud voice,
rising up at night,
will be like one cursing.

A Quarrelsome Woman

27:15 *tecta perstillantia in die frigoris et litigiosa mulier* *conparantur*

A broken roof on *a* cold day
and *a* quarrelsome woman
are comparable.

27:16 *qui retinet eam quasi qui ventum teneat et oleum dexterae suae vocabit*

One who keeps her is like
one who tries to hold
the wind,
and he will call *the* oil
of his right hand.[100]

27:17 *ferrum ferro acuitur et homo exacuit faciem amici sui*

Iron is sharpened by iron,
and man sharpens *the* face
of his friend.

27:18 *qui servat ficum comedet fructus eius et qui custos est domini sui glorificabitur*

One who tends *a* fig tree
will eat its fruit,
and one who guards his
master faithfully will be
praised.

27:19 *quomodo in aquis resplendent vultus prospicientium sic corda hominum manifesta sunt prudentibus*

As faces looking in water
are reflected,
so human hearts are revealed
to *the* prudent.

27:20 *infernus et perditio non replentur similiter et oculi hominum insatiabiles*

The inferno and destruction
are never filled;
likewise also man's eyes
are never satisfied.

27:21 *quomodo probatur in conflatorio argentum et in fornace aurum sic probatur homo ore laudantis*

As silver is refined in fire
and gold in *a* furnace,
thus man is proved
by *the* mouth of one who
praises.

27:22 *si contuderis stultum in pila quasi tisanas feriente*

---

[100] Compare to RSV translation from Hebrew: *to restrain her is to restrain the wind or to grasp oil in his right hand.*

desuper pilo non auferetur ab eo stultitia eius

If you grind *a* fool in *a* pestle,
like barley struck
from above,
you will not grind
his foolishness out of him.

Consider Diligently

27:23 *diligenter agnosce vultum pecoris tui tuosque greges considera*

Diligently know
the appearance of your cattle,
and think about your flocks,

27:24 *non enim habebis iugiter potestatem sed corona tribuetur in generatione generationum*

for you will not have
strength forever.
But *a* crown will be given
in each generation.

It's There for You

27:25 *aperta sunt prata et apparuerunt herbae virentes et collecta sunt faena de montibus*

Meadows are open
and green grass is evident,
and the wildlife of *the*
mountains is collected.

27:26 *agni ad vestimentum tuum et hedi agri pretium*

A lamb *is* for your coat,
and young goats of *the* fields
are rewards.

27:27 *sufficiat tibi lac caprarum in cibos tuos in necessaria domus tuae et ad victum ancillis tuis*

May the milk of your goats
be sufficient for you:
for your food,
for *the* necessities
of your house,
and for *the* support
of your slave girls.

Chapter 28

Various Proverbs

28:1 *fugit impius nemine persequente iustus autem quasi leo confidens absque terrore erit*

The lawless flees
though no one pursues,
but *the* fair *man,* like *a* lion,
will be confident, without
terror.

28:2 *propter peccata terrae multi principes eius et propter hominis sapientiam et horum scientiam quae dicuntur vita ducis longior erit*

Because of earth's sin,
there are many princes,
and because of wisdom
and those who teach their
knowledge, *a* leader's life
will be longer.

28:3 *vir pauper calumnians pauperes similis imbri vehementi in quo paratur fames*

A poor man
who abuses *the* poor
is like *a* violent storm
in which famine is prepared.

28:4 *qui derelinquunt legem laudant impium qui custodiunt succenduntur contra eum*

Those who abandon *the* law
praise *the* lawless;
those who keep *it*
are set ablaze against him.

28:5 *viri mali non cogitant iudicium qui autem requirunt Dominum animadvertunt omnia*

Bad men do not
consider fairness,
but those who seek *the* Lord
pay attention to everything.

28:6 *melior est pauper ambulans in simplicitate sua quam dives pravis itineribus*

A poor *man*
walking in simplicity
is better than *a* rich *man*
perverting *his* paths.

28:7 *qui custodit legem filius sapiens est qui pascit comesatores confundit patrem suum*

One who keeps *the* law
is *a* wise son;
one who feeds carousers
humiliates his father.

28:8 *qui coacervat divitias usuris et fenore liberali in pauperes congregat eas*

One who piles up riches
by usury and interest,
gathers them for one
who will be generous
to *the* poor.

28:9 *qui declinat aurem suam ne audiat legem oratio eius erit execrabilis*

One who turns his ear away
lest he hear *the* law,
his prayer will be detestable.

28:10 *qui decipit iustos in via mala in interitu suo corruet et simplices possidebunt bona*

One who deceives
the fair man
in *an* evil course
will topple to his destruction,
and *the* simple will possess
his goods.

28:11 *sapiens sibi videtur vir dives pauper autem prudens scrutabitur eum*

A rich man seems
wise to himself,
but *a* prudent poor *man*
will figure him out.

28:12 *in exultatione iustorum multa gloria regnantibus impiis ruinae hominum*

In *the* joy of *the* fair *man*
is much praise;
in *the* reign of *the* lawless
is man's ruin.

28:13 *qui abscondit scelera sua non dirigetur qui confessus fuerit et reliquerit ea misericordiam consequetur*

One who hides his
wickedness will not be led;
one who has confessed
and abandoned it,
is followed by mercy.

28:14 *beatus homo qui semper est pavidus qui vero mentis est durae corruet in malum*

A man who is always wary

is blessed;
truly, one whose mind
is hardened falls into harm.

28:15 *leo rugiens et ursus esuriens princeps impius super populum pauperem*

A lawless prince
over *a* poor people
is like *a* roaring lion
and *a* hungry bear.

28:16 *dux indigens prudentia multos opprimet per calumniam qui autem odit avaritiam longi fient dies eius*

A leader lacking prudence
will oppress many
by abusive accusation,
but one who hates greed,
his days will be made long.

28:17 *hominem qui calumniatur animae sanguinem si usque ad lacum fugerit nemo sustentet*

One who falsely accuses
the blood *of a* man[101] in *his* soul,
even if he flees to *a* lake,
no one will sustain *him.*

28:18 *qui ambulat simpliciter salvus erit qui perversis ingreditur viis concidet semel*

One who walks simply
will be saved;
one who walks
by twisted paths
will be cut down suddenly.

28:19 *qui operatur terram suam saturabitur panibus qui sectatur otium replebitur egestate*

One who works his field
will be satisfied with bread;
one who pursues leisure
will be filled with need.

28:20 *vir fidelis multum laudabitur qui autem festinat ditari non erit innocens*

Many will praise
a faithful man,
but one who hurries to get
rich will not be innocent.

28:21 *qui cognoscit in iudicio faciem non facit bene*

---

[101] An accusation against "the blood of a man" indicates a capital crime, one that could be punished by death.

iste et pro buccella panis deserit veritatem

One who knows *a* face
in judgment[102] does not
do well;
he, for *a* morsel of bread,
deserts truth.

28:22 *vir qui festinat ditari et aliis invidet ignorat quod egestas superveniat ei*

A man who hurries to get rich
and envies others,
does not know that need
will overcome him.

28:23 *qui corripit hominem gratiam postea inveniet apud eum magis quam ille qui per linguae blandimenta decipit*

One who corrects *a* man
will find grace
with him afterward,
more than one who,
by *a* flattering tongue,
deceives.

28:24 *qui subtrahit aliquid a patre suo et matre et dicit hoc non est peccatum particeps homicidae est*

One who takes something
away from his father
and mother,
then says, 'This is not *a* sin,'
is *the* partner of *a* murderer.

28:25 *qui se iactat et dilatat iurgia concitat qui sperat in Domino saginabitur*

One who is conceited and
swollen up stirs up conflict;
one who hopes in *the* Lord
will be fed.

28:26 *qui confidit in corde suo stultus est qui autem graditur sapienter iste salvabitur*

One who trusts
in his own heart is *a* fool,
but one who walks wisely –
he will be saved.

28:27 *qui dat pauperi non indigebit qui despicit deprecantem sustinebit penuriam*

One who gives to *the* poor
will not beg;
one who despises *a* beggar

[102] This indicates one who gives a favorable judgment to someone he knows, rather than deciding on the merits of the situation.

will suffer poverty.

28:28 *cum surrexerint impii abscondentur homines cum illi perierint multiplicabuntur iusti*

When *the* lawless rise,
men hide themselves;
when they perish,
the fair-minded are prosperous.

Chapter 29

Various Proverbs

29:1 *viro qui corripientem dura cervice contemnit repentinus superveniet interitus et eum sanitas non sequitur*

Destruction will come
suddenly to *a* man who,
with *a* stiff neck,
condemns one
who corrects him;
health will not follow him.

29:2 *in multiplicatione iustorum laetabitur vulgus cum impii sumpserint principatum gemet populus*

Ordinary people will rejoice
at *the* prosperity of *the* fair;
but when *the* lawless
take up kingship,
the populace moans.

29:3 *vir qui amat sapientiam laetificat patrem suum qui autem nutrit scorta perdet substantiam*

A man who loves wisdom
makes his father happy,
but one who feeds prostitutes
will lose *his* substance.

29:4 *rex iustus erigit terram*
vir avarus destruet eam

A fair-minded king
builds *the* land;
a greedy man destroys it.

29:5 *homo qui blandis*
fictisque sermonibus loquitur
amico suo rete expandit
gressibus eius

A man who speaks
to his friend
with smooth and lying words,
throws *a* net at his feet.

29:6 *peccantem virum*
iniquum involvet laqueus et
iustus laudabit atque
gaudebit

A trap will catch
a sinful, treacherous man,
and *the* fair *man* will praise,
and even rejoice.

29:7 *novit iustus causam*
pauperum impius ignorat
scientiam

The fair *man* knows
the cause of *the* poor;
the lawless ignores
knowledge.

29:8 *homines pestilentes*
dissipant civitatem sapientes
avertunt furorem

Destructive men
weaken a city;
the wise turn away fury.

29:9 *vir sapiens si cum*
stulto contenderit sive
irascatur sive rideat non
inveniet requiem

Whether he is angry
or whether he laughs,
a wise man
will not find peace
when he contends
against *a* fool.

29:10 *viri sanguinum*
oderunt simplicem iusti
quaerunt animam eius

Bloody men hate
the straightforward;
the fair seek his soul.

29:11 *totum spiritum suum*
profert stultus sapiens differt
et reservat in posterum

A fool offers up all his spirit;
a wise man holds back
and reserves *it* for later.

29:12 *princeps qui libenter audit verba mendacii omnes ministros habebit impios*

A prince who gladly hears
lying words,
will have only lawless
ministers.

29:13 *pauper et creditor obviam fuerunt sibi utriusque inluminator est Dominus*

The poor and *the* creditor
were on *the* way to each
other,
and *the* Lord illuminated
them both.

29:14 *rex qui iudicat in veritate pauperes thronus eius in aeternum firmabitur*

A king who judges
the poor truthfully,
his throne will be established
in eternity.

29:15 *virga atque correptio tribuet sapientiam puer autem qui dimittitur voluntati suae confundet matrem suam*

A rod and even correction
will teach wisdom,
but *a* boy who is left
to his own will
will humiliate his mother.

29:16 *in multiplicatione impiorum multiplicabuntur scelera et iusti ruinas eorum videbunt*

In *the* prosperity
of *the* lawless,
crimes will be multiplied,
yet *the* fair-minded
will see their ruin.

29:17 *erudi filium tuum et refrigerabit te et dabit delicias animae tuae*

Teach your son
and he will preserve you,
and give delights to your
soul.

29:18 *cum prophetia defecerit dissipabitur populus qui custodit legem beatus est*

When prophecy vanishes
a people is scattered;
one who keeps *the* law
is blessed.

29:19 *servus verbis non potest erudiri quia quod dicis intellegit et respondere* *contemnit*

A slave cannot be taught
by words,
because he understands
what you say
and refuses to respond.

29:20 *vidisti hominem velocem ad loquendum stulti magis speranda est quam illius correptio*

Have you seen *a* man
quick to speak?
Foolishness is more to be
hoped for from him than
correction.

29:21 *qui delicate a pueritia nutrit servum suum postea illum sentiet contumacem*

One who tenderly nourishes
his slave in childhood,
afterwards will feel
his disobedience.

29:22 *vir iracundus provocat rixas et qui ad indignandum facilis est erit ad peccata proclivior*

An angry man
provokes brawls,
and one who is easily
indignant
will be inclined to sin.

29:23 *superbum sequitur humilitas et humilem spiritu suscipiet gloria*

Humility follows arrogance,
yet glory will sustain
the humble in spirit.

29:24 *qui cum fure partitur odit animam suam adiurantem audit et non indicat*

One who shares with *a* thief
hates his *own* soul;
he hears *an* oath
but does not answer.

29:25 *qui timet hominem cito corruet qui sperat in Domino sublevabitur*

One who fears man
will quickly fall;
one who hopes in *the* Lord
will be lifted up.

29:26 *multi requirunt faciem principis et a Domino iudicium egreditur singulorum*

Many seek *the* face

of *a* prince,
yet *the* judgment on each one
comes forth from *the* Lord.

29:27 *abominantur iusti virum impium et abominantur impii eos qui in recta sunt via*

The fair *man*
detests *the* lawless,
and *the* lawless detest
those who are in
an honest way.

Chapter 30

Words of the Gatherer

30:1 *verba Congregantis filii Vomentis visio quam locutus est vir cum quo est Deus et qui Deo secum morante confortatus ait*

The words of the Gatherer,
son of *the* Vomiter.[103]
The vision which *a* man
spoke, *a man* with whom *the*
Lord is, and who is
comforted, because *the* Lord
is with him.

He says,

30:2 *stultissimus sum virorum et sapientia hominum non est mecum*

'I am *the* stupidest of men,
and human wisdom is not

---

[103] No record exists telling us who this was, beyond the inscription in the Latin text. The Revised Standard Version attributes this chapter to "Agur son of Jakeh of Massa." A debate has swirled since ancient times as to whether the original Hebrew words underlying "Gatherer" and "Vomiter" should be transcribed as names or translated according to their actual meanings. Jerome, obviously, decided to translate the names. See Peake's Commentary on the Bible, Matthew Black, ed, Thomas Nelson, Nashville, 1962, pg. 457.

with me!

30:3 *non didici sapientiam et non novi sanctorum scientiam*

I did not learn wisdom
or understand knowledge
of *the* holy.

Who Made All This?

30:4 *quis ascendit in caelum atque descendit quis continuit spiritum manibus suis quis conligavit aquas quasi in vestimento quis suscitavit omnes terminos terrae quod nomen eius et quod nomen filii eius si nosti*

Who ascended in *the* sky
and who descended?
Who secured *the* wind
in his hands?
Who bound *the* waters
like *a* garment?
Who stirred up all *the* ends
of *the* earth?
What *is* his name,
and what *is* his son's name,
if you know?[104]

God's Word

30:5 *omnis sermo Dei ignitus clypeus est sperantibus in se*

Every word of God
is *a* flaming shield
to those hoping in Him.

30:6 *ne addas quicquam verbis illius et arguaris inveniarisque mendax*

Do not add anything
to his words,
lest you be contradicted
and found *a* liar.

Two Things I Ask

30:7 *duo rogavi te ne deneges mihi antequam moriar*

Two things I pray you.
Do not deny me before I die.

30:8 *vanitatem et verba mendacia longe fac a me mendicitatem et divitias ne dederis mihi tribue tantum victui meo necessaria*

Make me far from vanity
and lying words.

[104] Compare to God's answer to Job: Job 38:4-5 *Where were you when I laid the foundation of the earth? Tell me, if you have understanding. Who determined its measurements -- surely you know! Or who stretched the line upon it?*

Do not give me poverty
or riches.
Grant only as much food
as necessary,

30:9 *ne forte saturatus inliciar ad negandum et dicam quis est Dominus et egestate conpulsus furer et peierem nomen Dei mei*

lest, perhaps, *when I am* full,
I be tempted to deny
and I say, 'Who is the Lord?'
and, compelled by need,
I steal and perjure
the name of my God.

A Proverb

30:10 *ne accuses servum ad dominum suum ne forte maledicat tibi et corruas*

Do not accuse *a* slave
to his master,
lest, perhaps, he curse you
and you fall.

A Dismal Generation

30:11 *generatio quae patri suo maledicit et quae non benedicit matri suae*

This is a generation
that curses its father
and does not bless its mother,

30:12 *generatio quae sibi munda videtur et tamen non est lota a sordibus suis*

a generation
that seems clean to itself,
yet nevertheless is not
washed from its filth,

30:13 *generatio cuius excelsi sunt oculi et palpebrae eius in alta subrectae*

a generation
whose eyes and eyelids
are lifted up
to *the* highest heights,

30:14 *generatio quae pro dentibus gladios habet et commandit molaribus suis ut comedat inopes de terra et pauperes ex hominibus*

a generation which possesses
swords for teeth,
and with its molars
grinds to devour
the powerless from *the* earth,
and *the* poor from among
men!

Four Things that Are Never Satisfied

30:15 *sanguisugae duae sunt*

filiae dicentes adfer adfer
tria sunt insaturabilia et
quartum quod numquam dicit
sufficit

Bloodsuckers have
two daughters who say,
'Give me, give me,'
three who are insatiable,
and a fourth who never says,
'Enough':

30:16 *infernus et os vulvae*
et terra quae non satiatur
aqua ignis vero numquam
dicit sufficit

the inferno;
the mouth of *the* vulva;
earth, which is not satisfied
with water;
and fire which, truly,
never says, 'Enough.'

30:17 *oculum qui subsannat*
patrem et qui despicit partum
matris suae effodiant corvi de
torrentibus et comedant illum
filii aquilae

Let *the* crows of *the* rapids
dig out *an* eye
which insults its father
and which despises
the womb of its mother!
Let young eagles eat it!

Four Mysterious Ways

30:18 *tria sunt difficilia mihi*
et quartum penitus ignoro

Three things are
difficult to me,
and I am completely ignorant
of *a* fourth:

30:19 *viam aquilae in caelo*
viam colubri super petram
viam navis in medio mari et
viam viri in adulescentula

the way of *an* eagle
in *the* sky;
the way of *a* cobra
over *a* rock;
the way of *a* ship
in *the* middle of *the* sea;
and *the* way of *a* man
with *a* young woman.

30:20 *talis est via mulieris*
adulterae quae comedit et
tergens os suum dicit non
sum operata malum

Such is *the* way
of *an* adulterous woman,
who eats and, wiping her
mouth, says,
'I have done nothing wrong.'

Four Things that Move Earth

30:21 *per tria movetur terra et quartum non potest sustinere*

Earth *is* moved
by three *things*,
and *a* fourth it cannot sustain:

30:22 *per servum cum regnaverit per stultum cum saturatus fuerit cibo*

by *a* slave when he reigns;
by *a* fool when he is full
of food;

30:23 *per odiosam mulierem cum in matrimonio fuerit adsumpta et per ancillam cum heres fuerit dominae suae*

by *a* hateful woman
when she is taken in
marriage;
and by *a* slave woman
when she inherits from
her mistress.

Four Small but Wise Things

30:24 *quattuor sunt minima terrae et ipsa sunt sapientiora sapientibus*

Four *things* are
small on earth,
yet they are wiser
than *the* wise:

30:25 *formicae populus infirmus quae praeparant in messe cibum sibi*

ants, *a* weak people,
who gather food for
themselves in harvest;

30:26 *lepusculus plebs invalida quae conlocat in petra cubile suum*

the rabbit,
a powerless commoner
which makes its home
in *a* rock;

30:27 *regem lucusta non habet et egreditur universa per turmas*

the locust, *who* has no king,
yet all march in ranks;

30:28 *stilio manibus nititur et moratur in aedibus regis*

the lizard, who struggles
in *one's* hands
yet lives in *a* king's palace.

Three Things and a Fourth

30:29 *tria sunt quae bene gradiuntur et quartum quod incedit feliciter*

There are three *things*
which walk proudly,
and *a* fourth,
which advances happily:

30:30 *leo fortissimus bestiarum ad nullius pavebit occursum*

the lion, strongest of beasts,
who will fear no encounter;

30:31 *gallus succinctus lumbos et aries nec est rex qui resistat ei*

a rooster, preparing his loins
for action;
a ram;
and *a* king, *for there* is no
one who resists him.

30:32 *et qui stultus apparuit postquam elatus est in sublime si enim intellexisset ori inposuisset manum*

There is one who was seen
to be a fool,
only after he rose
to *a* high position.
For if he knew,
he should have covered
his mouth with his hand.

A Comparison

30:33 *qui autem fortiter premit ubera ad eliciendum lac exprimit butyrum et qui vehementer emungitur elicit sanguinem et qui provocat iras producit discordias*

But one who strongly
squeezes *the* tit to bring milk
squeezes out butter,
and one who violently
wipes *the* nose draws blood,
and one who provokes
passions produces conflicts.

Chapter 31

31:1 *verba Lamuhel regis visio qua erudivit eum mater sua*

The words of King Lemuel,[105]
the vision which his mother
taught him

31:2 *quid dilecte mi quid dilecte uteri mei quid dilecte votorum meorum*

What, my beloved?
What, beloved of my uterus?
What, beloved of my
promises?

31:3 *ne dederis mulieribus substantiam tuam et vias tuas ad delendos reges*

Do not give your substance
to women,
or your energies
to destroying kings.

Who Should Drink Alcohol

31:4 *noli regibus o Lamuhel noli regibus dare vinum quia nullum secretum est ubi regnat ebrietas*

Refuse to give wine
to kings, O Lemuel,
because, where drunkenness
reigns, *there* are no secrets.
Refuse *to give wine* to kings,

31:5 *ne forte bibat et obliviscatur iudiciorum et mutet causam filiorum pauperis*

lest, perhaps, he drink
and forget judgment
and pervert *the* cause
of *the* children of *the* poor.

31:6 *date siceram maerentibus et vinum his qui amaro sunt animo*

Give strong drink
to *the* grieving,
and wine to those
who are bitter in soul.

31:7 *bibant ut obliviscantur egestatis suae et doloris non recordentur amplius*

They may drink
and forget their need,
and not remember their pain
any more.

---

[105] Other than the reference here, King Lemuel is unkown. New Oxford Annotated Bible, Third Edition, New Revised Standard Version, Oxford, Oxford, 2001, pg. 942.

Open Your Mouth

31:8 *aperi os tuum muto et causis omnium filiorum qui pertranseunt*

Open your mouth
for *the* voiceless,
and *for the* causes of all
the children who pass by.

31:9 *aperi os tuum decerne quod iustum est et iudica inopem et pauperem*

Open your mouth,
determine what is fair,
and judge *the* powerless
and *the* poor.

An Acrostic Poem in Praise of a Good Wife[106]

31:10 *aleph mulierem fortem quis inveniet procul et de ultimis finibus pretium eius*

Who can find *a* strong wife?
Far away and from
the farthest limits
is her price!

31:11 *beth confidit in ea cor viri sui et spoliis non indigebit*

Her husband's heart
trusts in her,
and he will not require spoils.

31:12 *gimel reddet ei bonum et non malum omnibus diebus vitae suae*

She will return good to him,
and not evil,
all *the* days of his life.

31:13 *deleth quaesivit lanam et linum et operata est consilio manuum suarum*

She sought wool and linen,
and worked by *the* counsel
of her hands.

31:14 *he facta est quasi navis institoris de longe portat panem suum*

She is like *a* merchant's ship;
she brings her bread
from far away.

31:15 *vav et de nocte surrexit deditque praedam domesticis suis et cibaria ancillis suis*

While it was yet night

---

[106] An acrostic poem is "one in which each successive verse begins with the successive letter in the Hebrew alphabet." Ibid, pg. 942.

she rose
and gave meat to her
servants,
and food to her slave women.

31:16 *zai consideravit agrum et emit eum de fructu manuum suarum plantavit vineam*

She considered *a* field,
and bought it;
from *the* fruit of her hands,
she planted *a* vineyard.

31:17 *heth accinxit fortitudine lumbos suos et roboravit brachium suum*

She girded her loins
with power,
and strengthened her arm.

31:18 *teth gustavit quia bona est negotiatio eius non extinguetur in nocte lucerna illius*

She made sure
that her business was good;
her lamp will not go out
at night.

31:19 *ioth manum suam misit ad fortia et digiti eius adprehenderunt fusum*

She put out her hand
to *the* powerful,
and her fingers laid hold
of *the* spindle.

31:20 *caph manum suam aperuit inopi et palmas suas extendit ad pauperem*

She opened her hand
to *the* powerless,
and extended her palms
to *the* poor.

31:21 *lameth non timebit domui suae a frigoribus nivis omnes enim domestici eius vestiti duplicibus*

She will not fear
for her house *the* cold
of snow,
for all her servants
are dressed doubly.

31:22 *mem stragulam vestem fecit sibi byssus et purpura indumentum eius*

She made herself
a cloth covering;
her garment is fine linen
and purple cloth.

31:23 *nun nobilis in portis vir eius quando sederit cum* *senatoribus terrae*

Her husband is respected
when he sits in *the* gate
with *the* elders of *the* land.

31:24 *samech sindonem fecit et vendidit et cingulum tradidit Chananeo*

She made fine linen
and sold *it*,
and traded *a* sash
to *the* Canaanite.

31:25 *ain fortitudo et decor indumentum eius et ridebit in die novissimo*

Strength and beauty
are her covering,
and she will laugh
on *the* last day.

31:26 *phe os suum aperuit sapientiae et lex clementiae in lingua eius*

Her mouth opened
to wisdom,
and *the* law of mercy
was on her tongue.

31:27 *sade considerat semitas domus suae et panem otiosa non comedet*

She considers *the* paths
of *those in* her household,
and will not eat *the* bread
of idleness.

31:28 *coph surrexerunt filii eius et beatissimam praedicaverunt vir eius et laudavit eam*

Her children rose up
and proclaimed her
most blessed,
and her husband
praised her also.

31:29 *res multae filiae congregaverunt divitias tu supergressa es universas*

'Many daughters
have gathered riches;
you have surpassed *them* all!'

31:29 *sin fallax gratia et vana est pulchritudo mulier timens Dominum ipsa laudabitur*

Grace is deceptive
and beauty is vain;
but a woman
who fears *the* Lord,
she will be praised!

31:30 *thau date ei de fructu*

manuum suarum et laudent
eam in portis opera eius

Give her from *the* fruit
of her hands,
and let her works praise her
in *the* gate.

The Book of Ecclesiastes

Introduction to Ecclesiastes

Ecclesiastes begins with the phrase,

> *Words of the proclaimer,*
> *son of David,*
> *king in Jerusalem*

Subsequent verses make clear that the King was Solomon, who ruled Israel from Jerusalem between 971 BCE and 931 BCE.[107] Originally written in Hebrew, the book was translated into Greek in the 3rd Century, B.C.E. It entered the canon of the Western church through Jerome's translation of it into Latin, some four centuries after Christ. I have translated into English from Jerome's Latin version, making this work a translation of a translation.

Both the Jewish and Christian traditions long accepted that Solomon himself authored the work. Though his authorship has come into question among some modern scholars, the book nevertheless represents itself as Solomon's thoughts.

Therefore, to understand Ecclesiastes, we first need to know something about Solomon. We will leave aside for now the question of his authorship. Whether the words were his own or were placed in his mouth by a later writer, they are best understood against the backdrop of Solomon's tumultuous background and life.

Solomon's Birth

Solomon's life was in danger literally from the moment he was conceived. His father, David, was King of Israel. His mother, Bathsheba, had been another man's wife. How they came to be Solomon's parents is one of the more sordid stories in scripture.

Bathsheba's husband, Uriah, was one of David's "*mighty*

---

[107] http://en.wikipedia.org/wiki/Solomon

men," leaders of his army.[108] Uriah, scripture notes, was a foreigner, a Hittite. At the time of David and Bathsheba's first meeting, Uriah was with Israel's army, taking part in a siege of the city of Rabbah. Scripture notes that the army had already "*ravaged the Ammonites*."[109]

Kingship was not for the faint of heart. Springtime meant war, almost without fail. Yet David was not at the front, leading his troops. He was in Jerusalem, enjoying his comfort.

One late afternoon, as David walked on the flat roof of his house, he saw Bathsheba bathing. She was "*very beautiful*," as scripture notes. David was King. He did whatever he chose to do.[110]

He ordered his "*messengers*" to bring the woman to him. He had his way with her. Then he sent her home. It was just another one night stand for David, at least at first. A few weeks later, though, Bathsheba sent a message to him: "I'm pregnant."

David had a dilemma on his hands. Bathsheba was a married woman now pregnant, whose husband clearly could not have been the father of her unborn child. As such, she faced execution for adultery on his return.[111] Uriah would return, know that the child was not his, and do what honor required.

David had the option of doing nothing. He could let the event unfold. The Law required Bathsheba's death. Who would believe her if she claimed David was the father? David's reputation for holiness would protect him.

He wasn't quite cynical enough to let that happen. Instead, he sent for Uriah. He consulted with him, then sent him home, hoping that Uriah

---

[108] 1 Chronicles 11:41

[109] 2 Samuel 11:1

[110] 2 Samuel 11:2

[111] Leviticus 20:10: *"If a man commits adultery with the wife of his neighbor, both the adulterer and the adulteress shall be put to death."*

would do to Bathsheba what David himself had done. David would be off the hook. Uriah would have had relations with his wife. Everyone would assume he was the unborn child's father.

Uriah slept outside, though. His soldiers were sleeping in the field. The Ark of the Covenant, God's own holy place, lay under the stars, not under a roof. Uriah's conscience wouldn't let him go in to his beautiful wife under the circumstances.

In the morning, David's men told him Uriah hadn't had sex with his wife. David called him in and asked him why. Uriah answered,

The ark and Israel and Judah dwell in booths; and my lord Joab and the servants of my lord are camping in the open field; shall I then go to my house, to eat and to drink, and to lie with my wife? As you live, and as your soul lives, I will not do this thing.[112]

David kept Uriah with him in Jerusalem two more days, still hoping Uriah would solve his problem. He wouldn't. Uriah refused out of loyalty to David to make love to his own wife.

On the third day, seeing no other way out, David wrote a letter to Joab, who commanded the army in his absence. *Set Uriah in the forefront of the hardest fighting, and then draw back from him, that he may be struck down, and die.*[113]

Uriah himself carried the letter, ignorant of its contents. Shortly thereafter, he was killed in action.

David made a show of taking the grieving widow into his own house. The country applauded. Here was a King who took care of the families of the fallen.

David's court prophet, Nathan, did not reach his exalted position at David's side by being a rabble-rouser. He was fierce denouncing the King's enemies, but seldom troubled

---

[112] 2 Samuel 11:4

[113] 2 Samuel 11:15

the King. If wagging tongues noticed the odd circumstances of Bathsheba's pregnancy, David thought he could count on Nathan to not make trouble in God's name.

According to the story, God had other plans. Scripture tells us, "*The Lord sent Nathan to David.*[114]"
The Bible doesn't tell us how God sent this message to Nathan, only that He did. So Nathan went to the King and, like a good preacher, told him a story. A rich man had great herds and flocks, Nathan said. His poor neighbor had only one lamb, which he loved and tended.

The rich man had a guest one night. Instead of feeding him with a lamb from his own flocks, he ordered his men to take the poor man's lamb. They killed it, cooked it, and set it in front of the rich man's guest for dinner.

David was furious. "*As the LORD lives, the man who has done this deserves to die*," he shouted.[115]

Nathan said to him, "*You are the man.*"[116]

Nathan, the court prophet, spoke on:

Thus says the LORD, the God of Israel, `I anointed you king over Israel, and I delivered you out of the hand of Saul; and I gave you your master's house, and your master's wives into your bosom, and gave you the house of Israel and of Judah; and if this were too little, I would add to you as much more. Why have you despised the word of the LORD, to do what is evil in his sight? You have smitten Uriah the Hittite with the sword, and have taken his wife to be your wife, and have slain him with the sword of the Ammonites.

No one else had the nerve to call the King's bluff. David was King, after all. Those who angered him often paid with their lives.

---

[114] 2 Samuel 12:1

[115] 2 Samuel 12:5

[116] 2 Samuel 12:7

Yet Nathan wasn't done.

Now therefore the sword shall never depart from your house, because you have despised me, and have taken the wife of Uriah the Hittite to be your wife.' Thus says the LORD, `Behold, I will raise up evil against you out of your own house; and I will take your wives before your eyes, and give them to your neighbor, and he shall lie with your wives in the sight of this sun. For you did it secretly; but I will do this thing before all Israel, and before the sun.

David did not kill Nathan, as most tyrants would have. Instead, David repented and begged God's forgiveness. Nathan told the King, "*The LORD also has put away your sin; you shall not die.*"

Then Nathan offered a grim prediction. "*Nevertheless, because by this deed you have utterly scorned the LORD, the child that is born to you shall die.*"[117]

The child, a baby boy, died a week after his birth.

David and Bathsheba's second child was Solomon.

How Solomon Became David's Heir

Solomon came into the world as David's family began to destroy itself. As was the custom of the time, David had many wives and a multitude of children. One of his daughters, Tamar, was a beauty. Tamar's half-brother, Amnon, also David's child, lusted after her as wholeheartedly as David lusted after Bathsheba.

Amnon pretended to be sick. The King came to him and asked what he could do. Caring fathers do such things, of course. Amnon's request was, *Pray let my sister Tamar come and make a couple of cakes in my sight, that I may eat from her hand.*[118]

When she came, he ordered her to order his slaves from

[117] 2 Samuel 12:13-14

[118] 2 Samuel 13:6

the room. When she did, he raped her, despite her pleas. When the deed was done, he despised her even more than he had longed for her. Scripture does not tell us why his sentiment changed so dramatically.

He sent her away in disgust, commanding his slaves to, "*Put this woman out of my presence, and bolt the door after her.*"[119]

Tamar fled to the home of her full brother, Absalom, where she lived the rest of her life as *a desolate woman.*[120]

This was the treatment women in her situation received from their society, whether the women consented to the sex leading to pregnancy or not. No reliable birth control, other than abstinence, seems to have existed.

Scripture tells us, "*When King David heard of all these things, he was very angry.*"[121] Despite his anger, he did nothing. Absalom, Tamar's full brother, was not so forgiving.

After biding his time for two years, Absalom invited the King to a celebration. The King declined, not wanting to burden his son.

"*If not,*" Absalom asked the King, "*pray let my brother Amnon go with us.*"[122]

David relented. Amnon and his brothers, Solomon presumably among them, went to Absalom's celebration.

2 Samuel 13:28 tells the rest:

Then Absalom commanded his servants, "Mark when Amnon's heart is merry with wine, and when I say to you, `Strike Amnon,' then kill him. Fear not; have I not commanded you? Be courageous and be valiant."

At Absalom's command, they

[119] 2 Samuel 13:17

[120] 2 Samuel 13:20

[121] 2 Samuel 13:21

[122] 2 Samuel 13:26

did what they were told. Amnon paid with his life for raping his sister.

Absalom, the King's firstborn son and heir, fled into exile, fearing for his life. David's anger and grief gave way in time. He had suffered not only the loss of Amnon, he realized, but of Absalom as well. Persuaded by Joab, David forgave Absalom and brought him home again.

David's faults as King grew more obvious with the passing years, though. He had won not only renown but, ultimately, the kingdom by his skill as a warrior. He possessed no similar skill when it came to governing his people.

The people of the land came up to David in Jerusalem, his capital, seeking justice, just as people today go to the courts for justice. It seems that David did not provide such justice often enough.

Absalom, seeing the lack, began to act as an impartial judge for those who came to see his father. By doing so, 2 Samuel 15:6 tells us, "*Absalom stole the hearts of the men of Israel.*"

After four years, Absalom led an uprising against his father. The people rejected David in Absalom's favor, and David fled across the Jordan River into the desert. Absalom was King in his place.

Fooled by bad advice, Absalom set out with an army to hunt his father in the Judean desert. This was a crucial mistake. However inept David may have been as a domestic ruler, he and his army remained fearsome opponents. Despite Absalom's numerical advantage, David's men crushed the young rebel's army on the battlefield.

Absalom, caught in a low-hanging tree while fleeing the battle, was killed by Joab, despite David's order to spare him.

Only then, after the deaths of both Amnon and Absalom, did Solomon become David's heir.

Solomon's Path to Kingship

Solomon's childhood was marred by violence. One older brother Amnon, raped his own half-sister, Tamar. Two years later, Absalom, another older half-brother to Solomon, murdered Amnon in revenge.

Absalom himself died battling his father for the throne. Before his death in battle, Absalom had driven King David and his followers (presumably including Bathsheba and Solomon), from Jerusalem into the Judean desert.

David had been in the desert before, as a young man, fleeing King Saul.[123] No doubt it galled him having to make the trip again in middle age, after getting a taste for the softer life of Jerusalem.

David and his family seldom hesitated to kill to forward their political ambitions. Solomon, wise kid that he was, could not have been ignorant of what his father's death would mean either to himself or to his mother.

David prevailed in battle and returned to Jerusalem. Solomon and Bathsheba lived to see another day.

In the ensuing years, David gathered the materials for a Temple to Yahweh in Jerusalem. He did not attempt to build it himself, having been warned by his court prophet not to. He left it for his successor-to-be, Solomon.

Solomon still had a rival to the throne, though: another older brother named Adonijah.[124] One day, when David seemed to be dying of extreme old age, Adonijah proclaimed himself King. Solomon and Bathsheba heard the news while attending David.

Bathsheba spoke to the aged king nervously,

My lord, you swore to your maidservant by the LORD your God, saying, `Solomon your son shall reign after me, and he shall sit upon my

---

[123] I Samuel 22:1ff.

[124] I Kings 1 ff.

throne.'

And now, behold, Adonijah is king, although you, my lord the king, do not know it.[125]

David affirmed that he had, indeed, made Solomon his heir. Such was David's authority, still, that Adonijah immediately obeyed and sought Solomon's forgiveness. So it was that Solomon officially inherited his father's kingship.

David ordered Solomon to carry out a violent revenge following the elderly King's death. It thus fell to Solomon to avenge his father against Joab, David's cousin and the commander of his army. Joab killed both Abner, a rival military commander, and Absalom, against the King's orders in both cases.

Solomon also avenged David against other old enemies, including a kinsman of King Saul who had cursed David as he fled from Absalom. Solomon took his own preemptive revenge against Adonijah. His young throne was baptized in blood, most of which Solomon was responsible for shedding.

When God asked him what gift he desired with his new kingship, Solomon did the unexpected. Instead of asking for long life, riches, or the deaths of more enemies, he asked for wisdom:

At Gibeon the LORD appeared to Solomon in a dream by night; and God said, "Ask what I shall give you." And Solomon said, "Thou hast shown great and steadfast love to thy servant David my father, because he walked before thee in faithfulness, in righteousness, and in uprightness of heart toward thee; and thou hast kept for him this great and steadfast love, and hast given him a son to sit on his throne this day. And now, O LORD my God, thou hast made thy servant king in place of David my father, although I am but a little child; I do not know how to go out or come in. And thy servant is in the midst of thy people whom thou hast chosen, a great people, that

[125] I Kings 1:17-18.

cannot be numbered or counted for multitude. Give thy servant therefore an understanding mind to govern thy people, that I may discern between good and evil; for who is able to govern this thy great people?"[126]

Solomon, during his kingship, erected the Temple his father dreamed of. He solidified the kingdom, marrying a daughter of Pharaoh. In addition, according to 1 Kings 11:3, *He had seven hundred wives, princesses, and three hundred concubines*.

Yet Solomon was the last Judean King over a united Israel. His success, so impressive in its day, did not continue in his absence. Given his insight, he no doubt anticipated the hazards that lay ahead, once his shrewd hand was removed from the wheel.

Solomon's wisdom was proverbial, as scripture attests:

And God gave Solomon wisdom and understanding beyond measure, and largeness of mind like the sand on the seashore, so that Solomon's wisdom surpassed the wisdom of all the people of the east, and all the wisdom of Egypt. For he was wiser than all other men, wiser than Ethan the Ezrahite, and Heman, Calcol, and Darda, the sons of Mahol; and his fame was in all the nations round about. He also uttered three thousand proverbs; and his songs were a thousand and five. He spoke of trees, from the cedar that is in Lebanon to the hyssop that grows out of the wall; he spoke also of beasts, and of birds, and of reptiles, and of fish. And men came from all peoples to hear the wisdom of Solomon, and from all the kings of the earth, who had heard of his wisdom.[127]

Solomon's View of Women

Solomon, like many other biblical writers, does not seem to have had a exalted opinion of women. This calls into question for many the value of any insights presented in his

[126] I Kings 3:5-9

[127] I Kings 4:29-34.

name. His voice may be indeed yet one more among the patriarchs who long kept women shackled in inferior social positions.

There is no getting around what he says, though. In Ecclesiastes 7:27-29, he warns his hearers against predatory women:

and I found more bitter than death a woman who is a hunter's snare, her heart a drag-net. Her hands are chains. One who pleases God avoids her, but a sinner is captured by her.

Difficult as the words seem, he speaks a truth that the wealthy and powerful have learned again and again through the generations. There are those in the world, male and female alike, who are "*more bitter than death.*"

We can also understand the text symbolically. The unnamed woman represents any of the endless varieties of vice that can put chains on our souls. Experiences of this sort certainly aren't limited to males.

Solomon speaks of women again in Ecclesiastes 7:28-29:

"Look, I found this," said the Proclaimer, "one after another, that I may find reason, which until now my soul seeks and I did not find. I have found one man in a thousand. I did not find one woman at all."

The text contains a curious ambiguity. We know from it that Solomon does not consider himself to have found a final reason or purpose. That is stated clearly. We know he has "*found one man in a thousand,*" yet "*did not find one woman at all.*"

Yet he does not quite tell us what he was looking for in those men and women. Did he look for someone who understood wisdom? Did he look for friendship, companionship, faith? We don't know. We know only that, whatever it was he was seeking, he did not find it among women.

In Ecclesiastes 9:9, the message is less harsh, yet still directed toward males:

Enjoy life with a wife whom you love all the days of your unstable life, which are given you under the sun, all the time of your vanity, for this is your portion in life, and in your labor at which you labor under the sun.

On reflection, the passage speaks generically to humans, of whatever gender. One does equally well to "*enjoy life with*" husband, partner, or dear friends, as well. The passage restates a central theme of the book: that being able to enjoy the fruit of one's labors, including another's love, is a blessing from God, not to be disdained. He does not share in greater detail the ways in which one should "*Enjoy life with a wife whom you love . . .*"

Solomon's understanding of women needs to understood against the backdrop of his culture, of course. Women's rights under Jewish law were limited, though according to many these rights exceeded those of women in the Greco-Roman culture of the New Testament era. Solomon seems no more or less misogynistic than his companions in the canon.

There are many ways of responding to Solomon's position. We can dismiss him and the patriarchy he represents entirely, because of his unenlightened views. We can ignore the offending passages, consider them aberrations, and try to understand the work apart from them. In Ecclesiastes, certainly, but even more so with Proverbs, that will excise significant parts of the work.

We can acknowledge the texts as being scripture, which indeed they are, then wrestle with ways in which wisdom still shines through them to us. In what senses are they true in our experience? Is there a value in them that speaks to us, though we find the language uncomfortable?

However we choose to interpret them, the passages say what they say. We can dismiss them, ignore them, or deal with them. We are not free to rewrite them.

Solomon's Authorship

The Rabbinic and Christian traditions considered the book of Ecclesiastes to be one of Solomon's "*songs*," referred to in the text above. Tradition also dates the writing of the book to the latter years of Solomon's reign, when the inevitable end of his life and stewardship loomed before him.

This view came into question during and after the Enlightenment of the 18th Century of the Common Era. Critical biblical scholarship in the 18th- and 19th-Centuries in Europe and North America offered revisions to the traditional understanding.

Many contemporary critical scholars believe Ecclesiastes was written pseudonymously, several centuries after Solomon's death.[128] They draw this conclusion, in part, from the presence in the text of Hebrew words borrowed from Persian and Aramaic. According to scholars, neither language was common in Canaan during Solomon's reign.[129] Both became common during the years of Persian imperial rule. Charles Ryrie, a prominent, contemporary, evangelical Bible scholar, calls the linguistic evidence "inconclusive."[130]

Whoever wrote Ecclesiastes in Hebrew "spoke Hebrew with an Aramaic accent."[131] This does not eliminate Solomon as a possible author, since Hebrews and Arameans, speakers of Aramaic, had a long history. In Deuteronomy 26:5, Moses commands

---

[128] Pseudonymous authorship is the name given by modern scholars to the ancient practice of writing a book in the name of another. The author puts his own words on the lips of a famous hero, hoping for a wider audience than what he could reach in his own name.

[129] The New Oxford Annotated Bible Third Edition, New Revised Standard Version with the Apocrypha, Michael Coogan, ed, Oxford University Press, Oxford, 2001, pgs. 944-945.

[130] The Ryrie Study Bible, New International Version, Charles Caldwell Ryrie, ed, Moody Press, Chicago, 1986, pg. 891.

[131] Interpreter's Dictionary of the Bible, E-J, Abingdon Press, Nashville, 1962, pg. 8.

Israelites to identify themselves to others as follows:

And you shall make response before the LORD your God, `A wandering Aramean was my father; and he went down into Egypt and sojourned there, few in number; and there he became a nation, great, mighty, and populous.

Whoever its author may have been, the book had been considered scripture among the Jews long enough to have been included in the Septuagint, the first known translation of the Hebrew Bible into ancient Greek.[132] The presence in the text of Persian and Aramaic, but not Greek, loan words suggests a date of composition prior to the emergence of Greek as a significant Near Eastern language, before Alexander the Great's conquests in the 4th Century, B.C.E.[133] Ecclesiastes may well be older than that. Given the linguistic evidence, though, it is not likely to be younger.

A case certainly can be made that Ecclesiastes came from Solomon directly. Ecclesiastes presents a radical view of God and of the purpose of human life. Like Job, its kinsman in the canon, Ecclesiastes presents a God who is not necessarily fair from a human perspective. Both books recognize that the truisms of religious piety sometimes ring horribly false.

Life is no picnic, according to both books. From the point of view of Ecclesiastes, the best someone can hope for is the opportunity to enjoy the works of his or her hands. Only God's works last forever. Everything we make, everything we are, everything we hope for, comes to an end in oblivion.

These views have led many throughout the centuries to reject outright Ecclesiastes' value, much less its place in the canon of scripture. Given

---

[132] http://en.wikipedia.org/wiki/Septuagint.

[133] http://en.wikipedia.org/wiki/Alexander_the_great.

how unpalatable the work seems on the surface, I find it difficult to conceive of Ecclesiastes having remained in the canon had it not been connected so intimately to Solomon.

In any event, whoever wrote the "*song*" of Ecclesiastes did so intending that Solomon should sing it. Understanding his life and context places the book in a context from which its strange-seeming theology is seen more clearly.

Seven Pillars of Solomon's Theology

We in North America are experiencing a long-term, gradual decline in religious participation.[134] In such an environment, church leaders concerned about a shrinking market face a natural temptation to soften the biblical message about God. The rise of Islamic terrorism in the name of *Allah* has only heightened this tendency.

One such softening effort has been an increased focus on the unconditional love of God.[135] In this picture, God loves all of us without preconditions, regardless of our actions. Many preach God as if He were an indulgent parent. God, we are told, does not judge or rebuke and would never punish. The God of unconditional love conforms to us and our needs, rather than calling us to conform to Him.

I feel safe in saying such a view of God has next to nothing in common with the view of God expressed in Ecclesiastes. The God of Ecclesiastes is not soft, warm, or inclusive. He is not a God humans approach casually or invoke lightly.

Solomon's view of God reflects the austerity of Israel's nomadic origins. God reveals Himself in the harshness of the

---

[134] See http://www.barna.org/FlexPage.aspx?Page=BarnaUpdate&BarnaUpdateID=280.

[135] See http://en.wikipedia.org/wiki/Unconditional_love

desert, where the immutable laws of nature almost always prevail against the foolishness of all living beings. Even sages die of thirst in Sinai. The God who made Himself known to Israel in the remote past did so against a fierce backdrop: withering heat by day; an endless ocean of stars in an ink-black sky by night.

In the vast epic of desert life, individual human life counts remarkably little. True, wisdom's principles help both individuals and larger communities survive the hardship. Those who share their water and bread with other wanderers, for instance, sustain life. Their generosity may, or may not, be returned. Living according to wisdom does not grant an exemption from suffering. Nevertheless, Solomon decided to live by wisdom and contemplate Truth, despite the ambiguity. Solomon's understanding of divinity has seven pillars, which are outlined below:

1. God, by wisdom, creates all that is real.

God is both the source of and the underlying reason for what exists. Yet what seems permanent enough from our perspective – natural forms, the order of day and night, the flow of seasons – is often merely longer-lived than we are. What exactly is it we consider real?

The wise, as Solomon makes clear, can't tell us what wisdom is, exactly. They can, however, understand the difference between what really exists and what our tendency to self-deception leads us to wish existed.

Whatever "it" is that God has created, we cannot mistake it for the sights we see with our eyes.

2. God's works endure forever.

Here is the test. If God made it, it endures forever. Even when it seems to be fading, it will be restored. What do we know of that fits that description?

It is easier to say what doesn't

fit the description. Anything that has a beginning and end, that changes, that is time-bound, does not endure forever. Therefore, any such thing is not something God has made.

What doesn't change? Presumably, the fundamental laws of physics endure as long as the universe does: the laws of Conservation of Energy and of Entropy both seem permanent. Still, does the basic wisdom that causes the dance of electrons cause the dance at the high school on Saturday night as well?

No object we can think of lasts forever. Yet as long as there is any object at all, logic tells us there will be a subject around to know it. Only the process seems to endure, not the forms within it. The wise learn to distinguish between what endures and what doesn't.

3. God is immensely great and immensely holy.

It seems harder for city dwellers to catch the sense of God's holiness that flashed through the desert experience, surrounded as we are by the work of human hands. We tend to shrink our world and our imagination to the size of the people and problems around us. We look for gods who are like us, suspicious of anything that makes us feel unimportant or small. Solomon's God is not like that.

The immensity of Solomon's God needs to be understood once again against the backdrop of the desert: the vastness of the night sky; the grandeur of earth; the sweep of time; the smallness of human life. Such sights continually remind those whose eyes see them of the majesty of One who encompasses all things. Experiencing God's holiness and greatness keeps human life in perspective.

4. God, by wisdom, judges all actions.

The same wisdom that guides the motion of stars and planets also judges our actions.

Humanity, collectively, reaps what it sows on earth. But the process isn't necessarily personal. It isn't aimed at us directly. As Solomon tells us in Ecclesiastes 9:11, "*time and chance work in all.*"

We are not directly responsible for all the things we suffer, any more than for all the blessings that come our way. But life as a whole cannot escape the consequences of its actions. This order of cause and effect, built into the fabric of nature, is nothing more and nothing less than the wisdom of God.

5. God's purposes go beyond our understanding.

We ask questions. We want answers. Sometimes the answers don't satisfy us. Sometimes, as Solomon tells us, there are no answers at all, at least that we can understand. As befits a being so much greater than us, God's ways go beyond our comprehension.

An example may help. My dog may learn from living with me what my expectations of him are. He perhaps realizes the need to stay off the couch, to relieve himself outside, and not to jump on strangers. As he gets used to these things, we find we can live comfortably together. I'm pretty sure I couldn't teach him calculus, though.

In the same way, we may learn how to live more peacefully with God and others. We may advance in knowledge and understanding of the world around us. But I am sure we would not comprehend the deepest thoughts of a Being who encompasses the entire universe, even if told.

6. God is fearsome.

Contemporary believers are uncomfortable with fearing God. Yet the God Solomon knew was fearsome, as any reader of the Old Testament knows. To begin with, He is infinitely greater and holier than we are. Our caution is, in part, that of an ant among bulldozers. One does not saunter casually into His presence.

Solomon warns us against speaking careless words to God (5:1). He advises us to keep our promises to God (5:3), telling us we would be better off not making them, than not keeping them. He cautions us against assuming either that God doesn't hear our promises or that our words don't matter.

Solomon instructs us not to express ignorant doubts about God's providence (5:5). He tells us of the finality of God's judgment (7:14). This is no God to trifle with.

7. God is not accountable to man.

Solomon reminds us that God does not answer to human beings, acknowledging that the world seems unfair at times from our perspective. "*The learned die just like the unlearned*," he laments in 2:16, and one fate awaits all, whether wise or foolish.

Yet in 7:15, he tells us that God has created in such a way that humanity cannot "*find a justifiable complaint against him.*" However unfair life may seem, God feels no obligation to apologize or explain.

Solomon's God, in His surpassing greatness, does not bend to meet our needs. He is not a passive enabler. While His constancy may be on display throughout the universe, no one is safe taking His favor for granted, and no one is exempt from life's hardships.

The believer may well ask what comfort can be found in a God like this. He offers us neither guarantees in this life, nor promises for the life to come. This God is either an interior comfort, or no comfort at all.

What Is the Value of Ecclesiastes?

In light of this, why should Ecclesiastes be in the Bible, other than for its now-doubted connection to Solomon? Simply put, Ecclesiastes remedies *hubris*, a Greek word meaning "excessive self-importance." *Hubris* is an ongoing affliction in human life.

Solomon himself, for all his wisdom and great accomplishment, understood the vanity of his own life. Though the consequences of our actions may outlive us, we as individuals do not continue on in some changeless Paradise to enjoy them. Solomon's wisdom points this out clearly, calling the reader to consider what actions and attitudes in life may be worthwhile in light of it.

Solomon's wisdom also points us to the here-and-now. Too often, believers overlook what is present and tangible in favor of what they imagine is to come. In contrast, Solomon reminds us of the only thing that is certain in our future: our demise. He asserts that living a decent life and enjoying the fruit of our labor is a gift from God.

Solomon's wisdom dignifies what many disdain as common and ordinary. For many, wisdom's blessing of the ordinary is liberating in itself. Yet these factors alone hardly qualify the work for the canon.

What separates Ecclesiastes from a work of mere practical nihilism is the difficult truth it teaches about God and about ourselves. Life as we commonly live it does not offer the rewards for which we long. We do not find enduring satisfaction in the work of our hands. We do not establish an unchanging identity through either our successes or our failures.

Too often, our impulse is to cover up these difficult truths, to put make-up on the pig of our actual situation and pretend it is other than it is. Solomon refuses to do that. In taking away our customary deceptions and poking a hole in the bubble of our *hubris*, he points to a deeper truth. Amidst the vanity of human preoccupations, God's truth stands transcendent. In the vortex of ceaseless change, where no relative identity endures, One who does not change abides.

As Solomon makes clear, God is beyond our ability either to comprehend fully or to manipulate to our ends. The wise know enough of God, though, to seek to conform to His wisdom. They are clever enough to stand in awe of Him. What they fail to understand intellectually, they seek to contemplate in their souls. This sense, of the unchanging, diamond Truth of divinity, is the transcendent message of Ecclesiastes.

Suffering humanity is as inclined now as in Solomon's day to ignore difficult truths and chase pipe dreams that lead only to further disappointment. Through it all, though, the vision of God abides, a pillar of fire guiding those who will look up through the desert night of existence. Those who receive Solomon's wisdom, and wake up to their genuine situation, discover the comfort of an abiding Truth.

We cannot build such a truth ourselves. It is neither inherent in us nor available in the world as we know it. It exists purely and simply by the nature and grace of God, whose ways are too often otherwise totally mysterious to us. For all we cannot do in relationship to this Truth, there remains one action we can take: we can surrender ourselves to it. Doing so, we can anchor ourselves in it. We can maintain our perspective through it. We can guide our lives by it.

This is not enough for some, of course. Many times it is not enough for us either. Yet it remains as a floor, a foundation, beneath the flimsy structures of belief we build on top of it.

Ecclesiastes is not a "feel-good" book. It will never be the preferred scripture for those whose lives are going well. Yet for those who suffer, those who have bumped up against the disappointments and heartaches of life, it offers transcendent insights. In it, we hear the voice of a wise fellow sufferer, pointing to One whose mystery and wonder endure forever.

That, for many, is value enough.

Chapter 1

Introduction

1:1 *verba*[136] *Ecclesiastes filii David*[137] *regis Hierusalem*[138]

Words of *the* proclaimer,[139]
son *of* David,
King *in* Jerusalem

---

[136] *Verba*, in Latin, is understand in this sense as a solemn, truthful proclamation, expressed by the highest authority. Its truthfulness is transcendent, leading beyond itself to Truth itself. *Verba* also appears in the Prologue to the Gospel of John, John 1:1-18, associated with the Second Person of the Trinity, Jesus Christ. *Verba* is both that which is proclaimed, and that which later will be the Proclaimer.

[137] The biblical tradition teaches that Solomon, King David's son and heir, wrote this book. Solomon's story may be found in 1 Kings and II Chronicles. See: http://en.wikipedia.org/wiki/Ecclesiastes.

[138] Latin was not the original language of "Ecclesiastes." The book, written in Hebrew several centuries before Christ, was translated into Latin by St. Jerome, around the 4th Century of the Common Era. See http://en.wikipedia.org/wiki/Jerome.

[139] "Ecclesiastes is the name given to the book of Holy Scripture which follows Proverbs; the Hebrew *Qoheleth* probably has the same meaning. The word *preacher,* however, is not meant to suggest a congregation or a public speech, but only the solemn announcement of sublime truths. . ." See Catholic Encyclopedia Online, "Ecclesiastes," http://www.newadvent.org/cathen/05244b.htm

The Nature of Existence

1:2 *vanitas vanitatum dixit Ecclesiastes vanitas vanitatum omnia vanitas*

"Vanity *of* vanities,[140]
the Proclaimer said,
"Vanity *of* vanities.
All *is* vanity."

1.3 *quid habet amplius homo de universo labore suo quod laborat sub sole*

What more does man have
from all his labor
at which he labors
under *the* Sun?

1:4 *generatio praeterit et generatio advenit terra vero in aeternum stat*

A generation goes
and *a* generation comes;
earth, truly, stands in eternity.

1:5 *oritur sol et occidit et ad locum suum revertitur ibique renascens*

The sun rises and sets,
and returns to his place,
from there rising again.

1:6 *gyrat per meridiem et flectitur ad aquilonem lustrans universa circuitu pergit spiritus et in circulos suos regreditur*

He turns with *the* south
and is turned to *the* north,
passing all.
Spirit goes by circuit,
and, in its circles,
returns.

1:7 *omnia flumina intrant mare et mare non redundat ad locum unde exeunt flumina revertuntur ut iterum fluant*

All rivers enter *the* sea,
and *the* sea does not
overflow.
To *the* place
where they leave,
rivers are returned,
that they may flow again.

1:8 *cunctae res difficiles non*

---

[140] The phrasing *vanitas vanitatum* echoes an ancient Hebraic poetic form. The "Holy of Holies" in both the Tent of Meeting in the Wilderness and in Solomon's Temple in Jerusalem was considered supremely sacred, the place where the Ark of the Covenant was stored. See Exodus 25:10ff, 1 Kings 6:19. "Vanity of vanities," then, would signify something supremely vain, utterly pointless.

potest eas homo explicare sermone non saturatur oculus visu nec auris impletur auditu

All *things are* difficult!
Man cannot explain them
by words;
the eye is not satisfied
with seeing,
nor *the* ear filled by hearing.

1:9 *quid est quod fuit ipsum quod futurum est quid est quod factum est ipsum quod fiendum est*

What exists?
What was is the same
as what will be.
What exists?
What was done is the same
as what will be done.

1:10 *nihil sub sole novum nec valet quisquam dicere ecce hoc recens est iam enim praecessit in saeculis quae fuerunt ante nos*

Nothing under *the* sun
is new;
nor is *he* truthful who says,
"Look, this is recent;"
for *it* already preceded us
in *the* ages which were
before us.

1:11 *non est priorum memoria sed nec eorum quidem quae postea futura sunt erit recordatio apud eos qui futuri sunt in novissimo*

Neither does a memory
of prior *events* exist,
nor will one be recorded
of any of them who will be
afterward, in *the* future,
not even to *the* end.

Ecclesiastes' Quest

1:12 *ego Ecclesiastes fui rex Israhel in Hierusalem*

I, *the* Proclaimer,
was King of Israel
in Jerusalem,[141]

1:13 *et proposui in animo meo quaerere et investigare sapienter de omnibus quae fiunt sub sole hanc occupationem pessimam*

---

[141]Only two kings reigned over all Israel from Jerusalem: David and his son, Solomon. Following Solomon's death, the united Israelite monarchy fell apart, resulting in two separate kingdoms: Judah, based in Jerusalem, and Israel, which ultimately built its capital at Samaria. Accounts of Israel's division following Solomon's death may be found in 1 Kings 14 and 2 Chronicles 10.

dedit Deus filiis hominum ut occuparentur in ea

and proposed in my soul[142]
to question and
investigate wisely
from all that is done
under *the* sun.

God gave this dismal
occupation
to *the* sons *of* men,
that *they* be overtaken by it.

1:14 *vidi quae fiunt cuncta sub sole et ecce universa vanitas et adflictio spiritus*

I saw all that was done
under *the* sun,
and, look, all *is* vanity
and affliction of spirit.

1:15 *perversi difficile corriguntur et stultorum infinitus est numerus*

The lawless are corrected
with difficulty,
and *the* number of fools
is infinite.

1:16 *locutus sum in corde meo dicens ecce magnus effectus sum et praecessi sapientia omnes qui fuerunt ante me in Hierusalem et mens mea contemplata est multa sapienter et didicit*

I spoke in my heart, saying,
"Look, I have become
very powerful
and exceeded in wisdom
all who came before me
in Jerusalem,
and my mind has
contemplated
many things by wisdom
and I have learned.

1:17 *dedique cor meum ut scirem prudentiam atque doctrinam erroresque et stultitiam et agnovi quod in his quoque esset labor et adflictio spiritus*

And I gave my heart
to know prudence
and learning,

---

[142]The word "soul" translates the Latin *anima*, which can also be rendered as "life force." Anima refers to one's inner experience of life, as opposed to the outward perspective others have of us. Soul is not separate from the body, in Hebrew thought, but is the product of the union between the natural "stuff" which constitutes our bodies and the life-giving Spirit of God.

According to Genesis 2:7: *And the LORD God formed man of the dust of the ground, and breathed into his nostrils the breath of life; and man became a living soul.*

and even errors
and foolishness,
and I knew that in this also
was labor and affliction
of spirit,

1:18 *eo quod in multa sapientia multa sit indignatio et qui addit scientiam addat et laborem*

for this reason:
because in much wisdom
is also much outrage,
and *one* who acquires
knowledge acquires also
labor.

Chapter 2

Testing Pleasure

2:1 *dixi ego in corde meo vadam et affluam deliciis et fruar bonis et vidi quod hoc quoque esset vanitas*

I said in my heart,
"Let me go
and abound in pleasure
and delight
in attractive *things*,
and I saw that this also
was vanity.

2:2 *risum reputavi errorem et gaudio dixi quid frustra deciperis*

I considered laughter *an* error
and sensual delight, I said,
deceives to no purpose.

Testing Abstinence

2:3 *cogitavi in corde meo abstrahere a vino carnem meam ut animum meum transferrem ad sapientiam devitaremque stultitiam donec viderem quid esset utile filiis hominum quod facto opus est sub sole numero dierum vitae suae*

I decided in my heart

to keep wine away
from my body,[143]
that my soul might go
to wisdom,
and I might avoid
foolishness,
until I could consider what
was useful to *a* man's son,
what work was necessary
under *the* sun,
the number of *the* days
of his life.

Testing Accomplishment
2:4 *magnificavi opera mea*
aedificavi mihi domos
plantavi vineas

I magnified my works.
I built myself homes.
I planted vineyards.[144]

2:5 *feci hortos et pomeria et*
consevi ea cuncti generis
arboribus

I made gardens and orchards,
and planted them
with all species of trees.

2:6 *extruxi mihi piscinas*
aquarum ut inrigarem silvam
lignorum germinantium

I built for myself
pools of water,
that I might irrigate
a forest of seedling trees.

2:7 *possedi servos et*
ancillas multamque familiam
habui armenta quoque et
magnos ovium greges ultra
omnes qui fuerunt ante me in
Hierusalem

I owned male slaves
and female slaves,
and *a* large family.
I had herds
and great flocks of sheep,
more than all who
were before me in Jerusalem.

2:8 *coacervavi mihi*
argentum et aurum et
substantias regum ac
provinciarum feci mihi
cantores et cantrices et

---

[143] Solomon chooses sobriety in order to develop wisdom. Sobriety is not an end in itself, since "wine" is one of the gifts God has given humanity (See Psalm 104:15). Nevertheless, there are times when we choose to forgo pleasure in pursuit of a higher purpose.

[144] Interestingly, Solomon does not list what scripture considers to be his greatest work: the building of the Temple in Jerusalem. Perhaps he leaves it out because he performed that work at the behest of his father, as an act of faith. It was not, in that sense, his work. Some consider the absence of a reference to the Temple as an indication that Solomon was not the author.

delicias filiorum hominum
scyphos et urceos in
ministerio ad vina fundenda

I heaped up for myself
silver, gold, royal substances,
and provinces.

I acquired for myself
male and female singers
and *the* delights
of *the* children of men:
goblets and pitchers
made for serving wine.

2:9 *et supergressus sum*
opibus omnes qui fuerunt
ante me in Hierusalem
sapientia quoque
perseveravit mecum

And I exceeded in riches
all who were before me
in Jerusalem,
and yet wisdom
remained with me.

The Results of the Tests

2:10 *et omnia quae*
desideraverunt oculi mei non
negavi eis nec prohibui cor
quin omni voluptate frueretur
et oblectaret se in his quae
paraveram et hanc ratus sum
partem meam si uterer labore
meo

And all that my eyes desired
I did not deny them,
nor did I keep *my* heart
from enjoying every desire
and amusing itself
in that which I had provided.

And I have considered
my portion of these *things*,
whether I might enjoy
my work.

2:11 *cumque me*
convertissem ad universa
opera quae fecerant manus
meae et ad labores in quibus
frustra sudaveram vidi in
omnibus vanitatem et
adflictionem animi et nihil
permanere sub sole

And I turned to all *the* work
which my hands had done,
and to *the* labors in which
I sweat to no purpose.
I saw in all *things* vanity
and affliction of soul,
and nothing endured
under *the* sun.

Testing Wisdom

2:12 *transivi ad*
contemplandam sapientiam
erroresque et stultitiam quid
est inquam homo ut sequi
possit regem factorem suum

I turned to contemplate
wisdom, errors,
and foolishness,
saying, "What is *it*
a man can pursue
after a King's own work?"

2:13 *et vidi quia tantum praecederet sapientia stultitiam quantum differt lux tenebris*

And I saw that wisdom
only exceeds foolishness
to *the* degree light
dispels darkness.[145]

2:14 *sapientis oculi in capite eius stultus in tenebris ambulat et didici quod unus utriusque esset interitus*

There is an eye in the head
of *the* wise;
a fool walks in darkness.
Yet I knew that
one is destroyed
like *the* other.

2:15 *et dixi in corde meo si unus et stulti et meus occasus erit quid mihi prodest quod maiorem sapientiae dedi operam locutusque cum mente mea animadverti quod hoc quoque esset vanitas*

And I said in my heart,
If one death will befall
both *a* fool and me,
what does *it matter*
that I gave *myself* more
to *a* work of great wisdom?
In my thought
I understood that this,
also, is vanity.

2:16 *non enim erit memoria sapientis similiter ut stulti in perpetuum et futura tempora oblivione cuncta pariter obruent moritur doctus similiter et indoctus*

For there will be
no more memory
of *the* wise in eternity
than of *the* fool,
and in future time
together equally
they will be covered up
in oblivion.[146]
The learned die
just like *the* unlearned.

---

[145] Light does indeed dispel darkness. In most instances, though, it cannot do so without leaving behind shadows. Thus, our wisdom is almost always limited.

[146] Oblivion here is similar to the Buddhist concept of Emptiness.

Life Is Wearisome
2:17 *et idcirco taeduit me vitae meae videntem mala esse universa sub sole et cuncta vanitatem atque adflictionem spiritus*

And for this,
my life wearied me,
seeing all *things are* evil
under *the* sun,
and altogether vanity
and affliction of spirit.

2:18 *rursum detestatus sum omnem industriam meam quae sub sole studiosissime laboravi habiturus heredem post me*

In return I detested
all my hard work
at which I labored so greatly
under *the* sun,
having *an* heir after me

2:19 *quem ignoro utrum sapiens an stultus futurus sit et dominabitur in laboribus meis quibus desudavi et sollicitus fui et est quicquam tam vanum*

whom I do not know.[147]
Whether in *the* future
he be wise or foolish,
yet he will have dominion
in my labors,
over which I sweat
and was anxious,
and *this* is utterly vain.

2:20 *unde cessavi renuntiavitque cor meum ultra laborare sub sole*

From this *realization,*
I gave up,
and my heart renounced
further labor under *the* sun.

2:21 *nam cum alius laboret in sapientia et doctrina et sollicitudine homini otioso quaesita dimittit et hoc ergo vanitas et magnum malum*

For when one works
in wisdom, learning,
and anxiety,
he leaves *his* acquisitions
to *an* idle man,
and this, therefore, *is*
vanity and great evil.

---

[147] Solomon's heir, Rehoboam, triggered a rebellion in the early days of his reign that resulted in the division of Solomon's kingdom into two separate states. See 1 Kings 12 and 2 Chronicles 12.

2:22 *quid enim proderit homini de universo labore suo et adflictione spiritus qua sub sole cruciatus est*

For what benefit will there be
for man from all his labor
and affliction of spirit
by which he is tortured
under *the* sun?

2:23 *cuncti dies eius doloribus et aerumnis pleni sunt nec per noctem mente requiescit et haec non vanitas est*

All his days *are full* of pains,
and hardships are abundant.
Not even at night
does *the* mind rest,
and is this not vanity?

Enjoy the Good

2:24 *nonne melius est comedere et bibere et ostendere animae suae bona de laboribus suis et hoc de manu Dei est*

Is it not better
to eat and drink
and demonstrate *the* good
of his labors to his soul?
And this is from
the hand of God.

2:25 *quis ita vorabit et deliciis affluet ut ego*

Who thus will eat
and quietly pursue pleasures
as I *do*?

2:26 *homini bono in conspectu suo dedit Deus sapientiam et scientiam et laetitiam peccatori autem dedit adflictionem et curam superfluam ut addat et congreget et tradat ei qui placuit Deo sed et hoc vanitas et cassa sollicitudo mentis*

To *a* man good in His sight,
God gave wisdom,
understanding, and
happiness.
But to *the* sinner he gave
affliction and needless care,
that he may add and gather
and hand *it* over
to one who pleases God.
Yet even this is vain
and *a* worthless anxiety
of mind.

Chapter 3

Times and Intervals

3:1 *omnia tempus habent et suis spatiis transeunt universa sub caelo*

All *things* have *a* time
and all pass through
their intervals under *the* sky:

3:2 *tempus nascendi et tempus moriendi tempus plantandi et tempus evellendi quod plantatum est*

time to be born
and time to die;
time to plant
and time to pluck up
what is planted;

3:3 *tempus occidendi et tempus sanandi tempus destruendi et tempus aedificandi*

time for killing
and time for healing;
time for destroying
and time for building;

3:4 *tempus flendi et tempus ridendi tempus plangendi et tempus saltandi*

time for weeping
and time for laughing;
time for bitter grieving
and time to leap for joy;

3:5 *tempus spargendi lapides et tempus colligendi tempus amplexandi et tempus longe fieri a conplexibus*

time for scattering rocks
and time for gathering;
time for embracing
and time to hold back
from embracing;

3:6 *tempus adquirendi et tempus perdendi tempus custodiendi et tempus abiciendi*

time for acquiring
and time for losing;
time for caring
and time for casting aside;

3:7 *tempus scindendi et tempus consuendi tempus tacendi et tempus loquendi*

time for cutting apart
and time for sewing together;
time for keeping silent
and time for speaking;

3:8 *tempus dilectionis et*

tempus odii tempus belli et tempus pacis

time to delight
and time to hate;
time to make war
and time for peace.

3:9 *quid habet amplius homo de labore suo*

What more does man have
from his labor?

God's Ways Are Beyond Knowing

3:10 *vidi adflictionem quam dedit Deus filiis hominum ut distendantur in ea*

I saw *the* affliction
which God gave
to *the* children of men,
that they be stretched out
in it.[148]

3:11 *cuncta fecit bona in tempore suo et mundum tradidit disputationi eorum ut non inveniat homo opus quod operatus est Deus ab initio usque ad finem*

[148] One is "stretched out" here in the sense of being strapped down to an instrument of torture.

He made everything good
in its time,
yet handed *the* world over
to their disputation,
that man may not discover
the work God has done from
beginning to end.

3:12 *et cognovi quod non esset melius nisi laetari et facere bene in vita sua*

And I understood that
nothing is better or happier
than to do well in one's life.

3:13 *omnis enim homo qui comedit et bibit et videt bonum de labore suo hoc donum Dei est*

To every man
who eats and drinks
and sees good from his labor,
this is a gift from God.

3:14 *didici quod omnia opera quae fecit Deus perseverent in perpetuum non possumus eis quicquam addere nec auferre quae fecit Deus ut timeatur*

I learned that all *the* works
which God made
endure forever.

We cannot even add
or take away from these
which God made,
that *God* may be feared.

3:15 *quod factum est ipsum permanet quae futura sunt iam fuerunt et Deus instaurat quod abiit*

What was made endures;
what will be in the future
already was;
and God restores
that which passes away.

The Riddle of Lawlessness
3:16 *vidi sub sole in loco iudicii impietatem et in loco iustitiae iniquitatem*

I saw under *the* sun
in *the* place of judgment,
lawlessness,
and in *the* place of fairness,
treachery.

3:17 *et dixi in corde meo iustum et impium iudicabit Deus et tempus omni rei tunc erit*

And I said in my heart,
"God will judge *the* fair
and *the* lawless,
and *a* time will be then
for all these *things*."

Death Rules over All
3:18 *dixi in corde meo de filiis hominum ut probaret eos Deus et ostenderet similes esse bestiis*

I said in my heart
of the children of men,
that God will prove them
and show that they are
like beasts,

3:19 *idcirco unus interitus est hominis et iumentorum et aequa utriusque condicio sicut moritur homo sic et illa moriuntur similiter spirant omnia et nihil habet homo iumento amplius cuncta subiacent vanitati*

because one destruction
exists for men and beasts,
and their condition is equal.
As man dies, so they die.
All likewise breathe
and man has nothing more
than beast.
Together they lie exposed
as vanity,

3:20 *et omnia pergunt ad unum locum de terra facta sunt et in terram pariter* *revertentur*

and all go to one place.
They are made of dirt,
and equally will return
to dirt.

3:21 *quis novit si spiritus filiorum Adam ascendat sursum et si spiritus iumentorum descendat deorsum*

Who knows if *the* spirit
of *the* children of Adam
ascends above,
or if *the* spirit of beasts
descends below?

Again, Enjoy Life

3:22 *et deprehendi nihil esse melius quam laetari hominem in opere suo et hanc esse partem illius quis enim eum adducet ut post se futura cognoscat*

And I recognized that
nothing is better for *a* man
than to be happy in his work,
and his portion is this.
For who can show him that
after him *the* future may
know?

Chapter 4

The Dead and the Living

4:1 *verti me ad alia et vidi calumnias quae sub sole geruntur et lacrimas innocentum et consolatorem neminem nec posse resistere eorum violentiae cunctorum auxilio destitutos*

I turned myself another way,
and saw *the* lies which are
carried on under *the* sun,
and *the* tears of *the* innocent,
and *they have* no comforter,
nor can they resist their
violence,
entirely destitute of help.

4:2 *et laudavi magis mortuos quam viventes*

And I praised more *the* dead
than the living,

4:3 *et feliciorem utroque iudicavi qui necdum natus est nec vidit mala quae sub sole fiunt*

and I judged happier
than both
one who is as yet unborn,
and has not seen *the* evils
which are done

under *the* sun.

Envy and Hatred

4:4 *rursum contemplatus omnes labores hominum et industrias animadverti patere invidiae proximi et in hoc ergo vanitas et cura superflua est*

Again contemplating
all *the* labors of men,
I noticed *their* hard work
laid bare to *the* hatred
of neighbor,
and in this, therefore,
is vanity and needless care.

A Fool's Excuse

4:5 *stultus conplicat manus suas et comedit carnes suas dicens*

A fool folds his hands
and eats his meal, saying,

4:6 *melior est pugillus cum requie quam plena utraque manus cum labore et adflictione animi*

"Better is *a* handful
with respite
than two full hands
with labor and affliction
of spirit."[149]

Working for Nothing

4:7 *considerans repperi et aliam vanitatem sub sole*

Considering, I have found
yet another vanity
under the sun:

4:8 *unus est et secundum non habet non filium non fratrem et tamen laborare non cessat nec satiantur oculi eius divitiis nec recogitat dicens cui laboro et fraudo animam meam bonis in hoc quoque vanitas est et adflictio pessima*

One is *alone*,
and has no second,
neither child, nor brother.
Even so he does not stop
laboring,
nor are his eyes satisfied
with riches,
nor does he reflect, saying,
'For whom am I working
and defrauding my soul

---

[149] In the Latin text, these verses are placed in the mouth of a fool. In English translations like the RSV, they stand alone, rather than as quotations. In the Latin, the verses are to be understood as truisms, excuses used by those who think themselves wise, rather than as proverbs themselves.

of good?'
In this as well is vanity
and dismal affliction.

The Value of Companionship

4:9 *melius ergo est duos simul esse quam unum habent enim emolumentum societatis suae*

Therefore, two together
are better than one,
for they have *the* comfort
of their companionship.

4:10 *si unus ceciderit ab altero fulcietur vae soli quia cum ruerit non habet sublevantem*

If one should fall,
she will find support
from the other.

Woe to one alone!

She has none to lift her
up when *she* falls.

4:11 *et si dormierint duo fovebuntur mutuo unus quomodo calefiet*

And if two sleep together,
they warm each other.
How can one *alone* be
warmed?

4:12 *et si quispiam praevaluerit contra unum duo resistent ei funiculus triplex difficile rumpitur*

And should someone prevail
against one,
two will resist him.
A three-fold cord is broken
with difficulty.

Wisdom Better than Power

4:13 *melior est puer pauper et sapiens rege sene et stulto qui nescit providere in posterum*

Better is *a* poor
but wise youth
than *an* old and foolish King,
who does not know
how to provide for *the* future,

4:14 *quod et de carcere catenisque interdum quis egrediatur ad regnum et alius natus in regno inopia consumatur*

because, sometimes
even from prison and chains,
someone comes to kingship,
while another,

born to kingship,
is consumed by poverty.

Ambition
4:15 *vidi cunctos viventes qui ambulant sub sole cum adulescente secundo qui consurgit pro eo*

I saw all *the* living
who walk under *the* sun
with *a* younger follower,
who rises up before them.

4:16 *infinitus numerus est populi omnium qui fuerunt ante eum et qui postea futuri sunt non laetabuntur in eo sed et hoc vanitas et adflictio spiritus*

The number of people
who do not delight in him
is without limit;
all who were before him
and who will be after him.
Yet this, also, *is* vanity
and affliction of spirit.

4:17 *custodi pedem tuum ingrediens domum Dei multo enim melior est oboedientia quam stultorum victimae qui nesciunt quid faciant mali*

Guard your step going
into *the* house of God,
for obedience is much better
than *the* offerings of fools,
who do not realize
that they are doing evil.

Chapter 5

Words before God

5:1 *ne temere quid loquaris neque cor tuum sit velox ad proferendum sermonem coram Deo Deus enim in caelo et tu super terram idcirco sint pauci sermones tui*

Do not speak rashly,
nor let your heart be quick
to offer words before God,
for God *is* in heaven
and you *are* on earth.

Therefore, let your words be few.

Dreams and Foolishness

5:2 *multas curas sequuntur somnia et in multis sermonibus invenitur stultitia*

Dreams follow many cares,
and in many words
foolishness is revealed.

Promises and Payment

5:3 *si quid vovisti Deo ne moreris reddere displicet enim ei infidelis et stulta promissio sed quodcumque voveris redde*

If you have promised
something to God,
do not be slow to deliver,
for unfaithful and foolish
promises displease him.
Whatever you promise, pay.

5:4 *multoque melius est non vovere quam post votum promissa non conplere*

It is much better, rather,
not to promise,
than not to pay
after making *a* promise.

5:5 *ne dederis os tuum ut peccare faciat carnem tuam neque dicas coram angelo non est providentia ne forte iratus Deus super sermone tuo dissipet cuncta opera manuum tuarum*

Don't let your mouth
make your body sin,
nor say before *a* messenger
"*There* is no providence,"
lest by chance God
be provoked by your talk
and scatter all *the* works
of your hands.

5:6 *ubi multa sunt somnia plurimae vanitates et sermones innumeri tu vero*

Deum time

Where dreams are many,
there are many vanities
and innumerable words.

You, instead, fear God.

Oppression

5:7 *si videris calumnias egenorum et violenta iudicia et subverti iustitiam in provincia non mireris super hoc negotio quia excelso alius excelsior est et super hos quoque eminentiores sunt alii*

If you see oppressions
against *the* poor,
violent judgment,
and subverted justice
in *a* province,
don't be amazed
at this business,
because over *the* high
authority
is one who is higher still,
and over those,
others who are
still more eminent.

5:8 *et insuper universae terrae rex imperat servienti*

And over *the* whole land
a King commands *his*
servants.

Greed Is not Satisfied

5:9 *avarus non implebitur pecunia et qui amat divitias fructus non capiet ex eis et hoc ergo vanitas*

A greedy *person* will not
be filled by money,
and one who loves riches
will not capture fruit
from them,
and this, therefore, *is* vanity.

5:10 *ubi multae sunt opes multi et qui comedant eas et quid prodest possessori nisi quod cernit divitias oculis suis*

Where *there* are many riches,
there are also many
who eat them,
and what value does
the possessor have,
other than to sift riches
with his eyes?

5:11 *dulcis est somnus operanti sive parum sive multum comedat saturitas autem divitis non sinit dormire eum*

A laborer's sleep is sweet
whether he eats little
or much,
but *the* 'satisfaction'
of *a* rich *man*
will not allow him to sleep.

Holding on to Riches
5:12 *est et alia infirmitas pessima quam vidi sub sole divitiae conservatae in malum domini sui*

There is another
grim infirmity
which I saw under *the* sun:
riches conserved
to *the* harm of their owner;

5:13 *pereunt enim in adflictione pessima generavit filium qui in summa egestate erit*

for *the riches* perish
in dismal affliction.
The rich man has *a* child
who will be in utter poverty.

5:14 *sicut egressus est nudus de utero matris suae sic revertetur et nihil auferet secum de labore suo*

Just as he came out naked
from his mother's womb,
so he will return,
and will carry nothing
with him from his labor.

5:15 *miserabilis prorsus infirmitas quomodo venit sic revertetur quid ergo prodest ei quod laboravit in ventum*

A most miserable sickness!
As he came out,
so he will return.
What, then,
does it benefit him
that he labored in *the* wind?

5:16 *cunctis diebus vitae suae comedit in tenebris et in curis multis et in aerumna atque tristitia*

All *the* days of his life
he eats in shadows
and in many cares, in toil,
and even in sadness.

Once More, Enjoy Life
5:17 *hoc itaque mihi visum est bonum ut comedat quis et bibat et fruatur laetitia ex labore suo quod laboravit ipse sub sole numerum dierum vitae suae quos dedit ei Deus et haec est pars illius*

And so this, to my sight,

is good:
that someone eat and drink
and delight in happiness
from his labor,
which he himself performed
under *the* sun,
all the days of *the* life
which God gave him,
and this is his portion.

5:18 *et omni homini cui dedit Deus divitias atque substantiam potestatemque ei tribuit ut comedat ex eis et fruatur parte sua et laetetur de labore suo hoc est donum Dei*

And every man
to whom God gave
riches and substance,
and gave also power to him,
that he may eat from them
and enjoy his portion,
and delight in his labor;
this is *a* gift from God.

5:19 *non enim satis recordabitur dierum vitae suae eo quod Deus occupet deliciis cor eius*

For *he* will not remember
enough *the* days of his life,
because God occupied his
heart with pleasures.[150]

[150] Compare to RSV: "*For he will not much remember the days of his life because God keeps him occupied with joy in his heart.*"

Chapter 6

Power that Serves No Purpose

6:1 *est et aliud malum quod vidi sub sole et quidem frequens apud homines*

There is yet another evil
which I have seen
under *the* sun,
and which is frequent
among men:

6:2 *vir cui dedit Deus divitias et substantiam et honorem et nihil deest animae eius ex omnibus quae desiderat nec tribuit ei potestatem Deus ut comedat ex eo sed homo extraneus vorabit illud hoc vanitas et magna miseria est*

a man to whom God gave
riches, substance, and honor,
and his soul lacking nothing
of all that he desired.
Yet God did not grant him
power that he might eat
from it,
but *a* stranger
will consume it.
This is vanity
and great misery.

An Aborted Child

6:3 *si genuerit quispiam centum et vixerit multos annos et plures dies aetatis habuerit et anima illius non utatur bonis substantiae suae sepulturaque careat de hoc ego pronuntio quod melior illo sit abortivus*

If someone should reach
the age of a hundred,
see many years and
have many days of life,
yet his soul *does* not enjoy
the pleasure of his substance,
and he lacks also
a *loving* burial,
from this I say
that an aborted *child*
is better than him,

6:4 *frustra enim venit et pergit ad tenebras et oblivione delebitur nomen eius*

for it came to no purpose,
and it goes to shadows,
and in oblivion its name
will be forgotten.

6:5 *non vidit solem neque cognovit distantiam boni et mali*

It has not seen *the* sun,
nor known *the* distance
between good and evil.

6:6 *etiam si duobus milibus annis vixerit et non fuerit perfruitus bonis nonne ad unum locum properant omnia*

Even if he sees
two thousand years,
but does not manage
to enjoy good *things*,
do all not hurry to one place?

6:7 *omnis labor hominis in ore eius sed anima illius non impletur*

All man's labor *goes*
to fill his mouth,
but his soul is not filled.

What More Do the Wise Have

6:8 *quid habet amplius sapiens ab stulto et quid pauper nisi ut pergat illuc ubi est vita*

What more does *a* wise
person have than *a* fool,
or what *does a* poor *person,*
except that *he* goes there,
where life is?

Beware of Dreams

6:9 *melius est videre quod cupias quam desiderare quod nescias sed et hoc vanitas est et praesumptio spiritus*

It is better to see
what you want,
than to long for what
you do not know,
yet even this is vanity
and presumption of spirit.

The Future

6:10 *qui futurus est iam vocatum est nomen eius et scitur quod homo sit et non possit contra fortiorem se in iudicio contendere*

One who will be
in *the* future?
His name already is spoken,
and what man can be
is known,
and *he* cannot contend
in judgment against *those*
who are mightier than him.

6:11 *verba sunt plurima multa in disputando habentia vanitatem*

There are many
meaningless words
in arguments.

Chapter 7

What the Future Holds

7:1 *quid necesse est homini maiora se quaerere cum ignoret quid conducat sibi in vita sua numero dierum peregrinationis suae et tempore quo velut umbra praeterit aut quis ei poterit indicare quid post eum futurum sub sole sit*

Why is it necessary
that *a* man question
things greater than himself,
when he ignores
what benefits him
in *the* days of his pilgrimage,
and time passes
like *a* shadow?
Or who can tell him
what will happen
under *the* sun after him,
in *the* future?

A Good Name

7:2 *melius est nomen bonum quam unguenta pretiosa et dies mortis die nativitatis*

A good name is better
than precious ointment,
and *the* day of death
than *the* day of birth.

Mourning

7:3 *melius est ire ad domum luctus quam ad domum convivii in illa enim finis cunctorum admonetur hominum et vivens cogitat quid futurum sit*

It is better to go to
the house of mourning
than to *the* house of feasting,
for in it *is the* end of all men.
Mourning admonishes a man,
and, *while* living,
he considers what *the* future
might be.

Anger

7:4 *melior est ira risu quia per tristitiam vultus corrigitur animus delinquentis*

Anger is better than laughter,
because by sadness
of outlook
the straying soul is corrected.

Where Is Your Heart?

7:5 *cor sapientium ubi tristitia est et cor stultorum ubi laetitia*

The heart of *the* wise
abides where sadness is,
but *the* heart of *a* fool

where happiness.

The Value of a Rebuke
7:6 *melius est a sapiente corripi quam stultorum adulatione decipi*

Being rebuked
by *a* wise *person*
is better than being deceived
by *the* praise of fools,

7:7 *quia sicut sonitus spinarum ardentium sub olla sic risus stulti sed et hoc vanitas*

because as *the* sound of
thorns burning under *a* pot,
thus *the* laughter of *a* fool,
and this *is* vanity.

False Accusation
7:8 *calumnia conturbat sapientem et perdet robur cordis illius*

Oppression disturbs *the* wise,
and he loses *the* resolve
of his heart.

Patience and Arrogance
7:9 *melior est finis orationis quam principium melior est patiens arrogante*

The end of *a* speech
is better than *the* beginning.
The patient is better
than *the* arrogant.

Temper
7:10 *ne velox sis ad irascendum quia ira in sinu stulti requiescit*

Don't be quick to anger,
because anger rests
in *the* innards of *a* fool.

Good Old Days?
7:11 *ne dicas quid putas causae est quod priora tempora meliora fuere quam nunc sunt stulta est enim huiuscemodi interrogatio*

Don't say, "Why
were earlier times better
than today,"
for *it* is foolishness
to question in this manner.

Wisdom and Riches
7:12 *utilior est sapientia cum divitiis et magis prodest videntibus solem*

Wisdom is more useful
than riches,
and *it* greatly helps
those seeing *the* sun,

7:13 *sicut enim protegit sapientia sic protegit pecunia hoc autem plus habet eruditio et sapientia quod vitam tribuunt possessori suo*

for just as wisdom protects,
money also protects.
Yet learning and wisdom
have this more:
that they give life
to one possessing them.

Consider God's Work
7:14 *considera opera Dei quod nemo possit corrigere quem ille despexerit*

Consider God's work,
because no one can reclaim
someone God has disdained.

Eyes Open
7:15 *in die bona fruere bonis et malam diem praecave sicut enim hanc sic et illam fecit Deus ut non inveniat homo contra eum iustas querimonias*

In *a* good day,
delight in good *things*,
and guard against *a* bad day;
for just as God made one,
thus also *the* other,
that man might not find
a justifiable complaint
against him.[151]

Unrecognized Worth
7:16 *haec quoque vidi in diebus vanitatis meae iustus perit in iustitia sua et impius multo vivit tempore in malitia sua*

This also I saw
in *the* days of my vanity:
an honest person dies
in his honesty
and *a* liar lives *a* long time
in his lie.

7:17 *noli esse iustus multum neque plus sapias quam necesse est ne obstupescas*

Don't be too fair,
or wiser than is necessary,
and don't be stupid.

7:18 *ne impie agas multum et noli esse stultus ne moriaris in tempore non tuo*

Don't carry on in *a* lie,
and don't be *a* fool,
so that you do not die

---

[151] Similar to God's statement in Job 38:1-5.

at *a* time not *meant for* you.

Support the Straightforward

7:19 *bonum est te sustentare iustum sed et ab illo ne subtrahas manum tuam quia qui Deum timet nihil neglegit*

It's good to sustain
the honest,
but don't take your support
away from him,
because one who fears God
ignores nothing.

Wisdom Comforts

7:20 *sapientia confortabit sapientem super decem principes civitatis*

Wisdom comforts *the* wise
more than ten princes *a* city,

7:21 *non est enim homo iustus in terra qui faciat bonum et non peccet*

but *there* is not
an honest man on earth
who does good
and does not sin.

Ignore Foolish Words

7:22 *sed et cunctis sermonibus qui dicuntur ne accommodes cor tuum ne forte audias servum tuum maledicentem tibi*

But do not adjust your heart
to fit all *the* words
which *others* say.
You might hear
your servant cursing you,

7:23 *scit enim tua conscientia quia et tu crebro maledixisti aliis*

but your conscience knows
that you cursed others too.

Wisdom Is Far Away

7:24 *cuncta temptavi in sapientia dixi sapiens efficiar et ipsa longius recessit a me*

I tested all by wisdom.
I said, "I will be wise!"
Yet *wisdom* withdrew
further from me,

7:25 *multo magis quam erat et alta profunditas quis inveniet eam*

much more than it was,
and *at a* great depth.
Who can find it?

More Bitter than Death

7:26 *lustravi universa animo meo ut scirem et considerarem et quaererem sapientiam et rationem et ut cognoscerem impietatem stulti et errorem inprudentium*

I passed through all
in my soul,
that I might know
and consider
and seek wisdom and reason,
and that I might know
the failure of *a* fool
and *the* error
of *the* imprudent,

7:27 *et inveni amariorem morte mulierem quae laqueus venatorum est et sagena cor eius vincula sunt manus illius qui placet Deo effugiet eam qui autem peccator est capietur ab illa*

and I found
more bitter than death
a woman who is
a hunter's snare,
her heart a drag-net.
Her hands are chains.
One who pleases God
avoids her,
but *a* sinner
is captured by her.

One in a Thousand

7:28 *ecce hoc inveni dicit Ecclesiastes unum et alterum ut invenirem rationem*

"Look, I found this,"
said the Proclaimer,
"one after another,
that I may find reason,

7:29 *quam adhuc quaerit anima mea et non inveni virum de mille unum repperi mulierem ex omnibus non inveni*

"which until now
my soul seeks
and I did not find.
I have found one man
in a thousand.
I did not find one woman
at all."

God Made Humanity Upright

7:30 *solummodo hoc inveni quod fecerit Deus hominem rectum et ipse se infinitis miscuerit quaestionibus quis talis ut sapiens est et quis cognovit solutionem verbi*

"I only found this:
that God made man upright,
but he stirred up for himself

endless questions."

Who is like *the* wise,
and who understands
a solution to *a* problem?

Chapter 8

Wisdom Shines Forth
8:1 *sapientia hominis lucet in vultu eius et potentissimus faciem illius commutavit*

The wisdom of *a* man
shines in his face,
and the mightiest
changes his expression.

Dealing with the Powerful
8:2 *ego os regis observo et praecepta iuramenti Dei*

I observe *the* mouth of Kings
and *the* precepts of *the* laws
of God.

8:3 *ne festines recedere a facie eius neque permaneas in opere malo quia omne quod voluerit faciet*

Don't hurry to withdraw
from his presence,
and don't stay in evil works,
because everything he
desires,
he does,

8:4 *et sermo illius potestate plenus est nec dicere ei quisquam potest quare ita facis*

and his word is full of power.
No one can say to him,
"Why are you doing this?"

Keep Precepts
8:5 *qui custodit praeceptum*
non experietur quicquam
mali tempus et responsionem
cor sapientis intellegit

One who keeps *a* precept
does not experience
any punishment.
The heart of *the* wise
understands *the* time
and response.

8:6 *omni negotio tempus est*
et oportunitas et multa
hominis adflictio

To every activity
there is time and opportunity,
and many afflictions to men.

Don't Bother Trying to Warn
8:7 *quia ignorat praeterita*
et ventura nullo scire potest
nuntio

Because he ignores
the past and *the* future,
he won't understand anything
by *a* messenger.

Human Limits
8:8 *non est in hominis*
dicione prohibere spiritum
nec habet potestatem in die
mortis nec sinitur quiescere
ingruente bello neque
salvabit impietas impium

There is no authority in man
to stop *the* breath,
nor does he have power
in *the* day of death,
nor is he permitted
to remain uninvolved
when war threatens,
nor will *a* lie save *a* liar.

Guidance for Public Life
8:9 *omnia haec consideravi*
et dedi cor meum in cunctis
operibus quae fiunt sub sole
interdum dominatur homo
homini in malum suum

All these I considered,
and gave my heart
in all works
which are done
under *the* sun.
Sometimes *a* man
dominates *another* man
to his *own* harm.

8:10 *vidi impios sepultos qui*
etiam cum adviverent in loco
sancto erant et laudabantur

in civitate quasi iustorum
operum sed et hoc vanitas est

I saw liars buried
who, when *they* were alive,
were in *the* holy place,
and were praised in *the* city
like *a* work of justice.
Yet this too is vanity.

8:11 *etenim quia non*
profertur cito contra malos
sententia absque ullo timore
filii hominum perpetrant
mala

Because judgment
is not pronounced quickly
against wrongdoers,
the children of men
perpetrate harm
without any fear.

8:12 *attamen ex eo quod*
peccator centies facit malum
et per patientiam sustentatur
ego cognovi quod erit bonum
timentibus Deum qui
verentur faciem eius

Nevertheless, though *a* sinner
do harm *a* hundred times
and is borne with patiently,
I knew that good will be
for those fearing God,
who respect his presence.

8:13 *non sit bonum impio*
nec prolongentur dies eius
sed quasi umbra transeant
qui non timent faciem Dei

May it not be well for *a* liar,
nor let his days be prolonged.

But like *a* shadow
may they pass away
who do not fear
the presence of God.

Being Misunderstood
8:14 *est et alia vanitas quae*
fit super terram sunt iusti
quibus multa proveniunt
quasi opera egerint impiorum
et sunt impii qui ita securi
sunt quasi iustorum facta
habeant sed et hoc
vanissimum iudico

And *there* is another vanity
which is done on earth:
many are decent,
whose works have results
as if done by liars;
and *there* are liars who are
as secure as if their works
had been done fairly.
I consider this utterly
pointless.

Do Enjoy Life
8:15 *laudavi igitur laetitiam*

quod non esset homini bonum
sub sole nisi quod comederet
et biberet atque gauderet et
hoc solum secum auferret de
labore suo in diebus vitae
quos dedit ei Deus sub sole

I praised happiness,
as a result,
because what *else*
could be good
for man under *the* sun,
except that he eat, drink,
and even rejoice,
and this only he might carry
with him from his labor
in *the* days of his life,
which God gave him
under *the* sun.

8:16 *et adposui cor meum ut*
scirem sapientiam et
intellegerem distentionem
quae versatur in terra est
homo qui diebus ac noctibus
somnum oculis non capit

And I set my heart
that it know wisdom
and understand *a* spasm
which writhes on earth:
a man whose eyes
capture no sleep day
and night.

Not Even the Wise Know

8:17 *et intellexi quod*
omnium operum Dei nullam
possit homo invenire
rationem eorum quae fiunt
sub sole et quanto plus
laboraverit ad quaerendum
tanto minus inveniat etiam si
dixerit sapiens se nosse non
poterit repperire

And I understood that *a* man
can find no reason
for every work of God,
for those which are done
under *the* sun,
and *the* more he labors
in seeking,
the less he finds.[152]
Even if *the* wise
should claim he knows,
he won't be able to find out.

---

[152] Again, Solomon stresses the inscrutability of the divine will. Similar expressions of man's inability to know the divine will are found in The Upanishads and Tao Te Ching, written during the same general era in India and China, respectively.

Chapter 9

Limits of Moral Knowledge

9:1 *omnia haec tractavi in corde meo ut curiose intellegerem sunt iusti atque sapientes et opera eorum in manu Dei et tamen nescit homo utrum amore an odio dignus sit*

All this I examined
in my heart,
that, by curiosity,
I might understand.
The fair-minded[153] are wise,
and their works *are*
in *the* hand of God.
Nevertheless, man does not
know whether another
deserves love or hatred.

Our Fate

9:2 *sed omnia in futuro servantur incerta eo quod universa aeque eveniant iusto et impio bono et malo mundo et inmundo immolanti victimas et sacrificia contemnenti sicut bonus sic et peccator ut periurus ita et ille qui verum deierat*

Yet all *things* in *the* future
are surrounded by
uncertainly,
because all *things*
turn out *the* same:
to *the* truthful and *the* liar,
the good and *the* bad,
the clean and *the* unclean,
the one burning offerings,
and *the* one
condemning sacrifices,
as with *the* good,
so with *the* sinner,
as with *the* perjurer,
thus with one
who swears truthfully.

9:3 *hoc est pessimum inter omnia quae sub sole fiunt quia eadem cunctis eveniunt unde et corda filiorum hominum implentur malitia et contemptu in vita sua et post haec ad inferos deducentur*

This is worst
among all things
which are done
under *the* sun,
because these come
to all of them together,
from which even *the* hearts

---

[153] I have translated the Latin *iustus* as "fair" or "fair-minded," rather than "just." In our contemporary idiom, "just" can seem lofty and vague. "Fair-minded," on the other hand, seems more practical and down-to-earth. Solomon does not traffic in abstractions. His advice, here as elsewhere, is oriented to practical living.

of *the* children of men
are filled with malice
and contempt in their life;
and after them they are
sucked down to *the* dead.

9:4 *nemo est qui semper vivat et qui huius rei habeat fiduciam melior est canis vivens leone mortuo*

There is no one
who lives forever,
and who has confidence
in this thing.
A living dog is better
than *a* dead lion,

9:5 *viventes enim sciunt se esse morituros mortui vero nihil noverunt amplius nec habent ultra mercedem quia oblivioni tradita est memoria eorum*

for the living know
that they must die.
The dead, in truth,
know nothing more,
nor do they have
a further reward,
because their memory
is handed over to oblivion.

9:6 *amor quoque et odium et invidia simul perierunt nec habent partem in hoc saeculo et in opere quod sub sole geritur*

Their love and even
their hatred and envy
perish together,
nor do they have part
in this time,
and in *the* work
which is done
under *the* sun.

Be Sure to Enjoy Life

9:7 *vade ergo et comede in laetitia panem tuum et bibe cum gaudio vinum tuum quia Deo placent opera tua*

Hurry, therefore!
Eat your bread in happiness,
and drink your wine
with rejoicing,
because your works
are pleasing to God.

9:8 *omni tempore sint vestimenta tua candida et oleum de capite tuo non deficiat*

At all times let your
clothing be beautiful,
and do not lack ointment
for your head.

9:9 *perfruere vita cum uxore quam diligis cunctis diebus vitae instabilitatis tuae qui dati sunt tibi sub sole omni tempore vanitatis tuae haec est enim pars in vita et in labore tuo quod laboras sub sole*

Enjoy life
with *a* wife whom you love
all *the* days
of your unstable life,
which are given you
under *the* sun,
all *the* time of your vanity,
for this is your portion in life,
and in your labor
at which you labor
under *the* sun.

9:10 *quodcumque potest manus tua facere instanter operare quia nec opus nec ratio nec scientia nec sapientia erunt apud inferos quo tu properas*

So, whatever your hand
is able to do,
do *it* quickly,
because neither work,
nor reason,
nor understanding,
nor wisdom
are with *the* dead,
where you are going.

Accidents Happen

9:11 *verti me alio vidique sub sole nec velocium esse cursum nec fortium bellum nec sapientium panem nec doctorum divitias nec artificum gratiam sed tempus casumque in omnibus*

I turned myself
to another *topic*,
and saw also under *the* sun,
that *a* race is not to *the* swift
nor *a* battle to *the* strong,
nor bread to *the* wise,
nor riches to *the* learned,
nor popularity to *the* skilled,
but time and chance *work*
in all.

9:12 *nescit homo finem suum sed sicut pisces capiuntur hamo et sicut aves conprehenduntur laqueo sic capiuntur homines tempore malo cum eis extemplo supervenerit*

Man does not know his end,
but as fish are captured
by *a* hook,
and as birds are trapped
by *a* snare,
thus men are captured

by evil time, immediately,
when it comes upon them.

Wisdom Isn't Always Appreciated

9:13 *hanc quoque vidi sub sole sapientiam et probavi maximam*

And I also saw this wisdom
under the sun,
and I proved it greatly:

9:14 *civitas parva et pauci in ea viri venit contra eam rex magnus et vallavit eam extruxitque munitiones per gyrum et perfecta est obsidio*

There was a small city
and in it few men.
A great King came against it,
and surrounded it,
and piled up weapons
by turn,
and *the* siege was total.

9:15 *inventusque in ea vir pauper et sapiens liberavit urbem per sapientiam suam et nullus deinceps recordatus est hominis illius pauperis*

But *a* wise and poor man
was found in it,
who freed *the* city
by his wits.
And nothing thereafter
was recorded
of this poor man.

9:16 *et dicebam ego meliorem esse sapientiam fortitudine quomodo ergo sapientia pauperis contempta est et verba eius non sunt audita*

and I said, "Wisdom
is better than strength.
How is it, then,
a poor *man's* wisdom
is despised,
and his words are not heard?"

Where Wisdom Is Heard

9:17 *verba sapientium audiuntur in silentio plus quam clamor principis inter stultos*

Words of *the* wise
are heard in silence
more than *in the* shouting
of *a* leader among fools.

9:18 *melior est sapientia quam arma bellica et qui in uno peccaverit multa bona perdet*

Wisdom is better

than weapons of war,
and a person who sins
in one *thing*
loses many good *things*.

Chapter 10

Various Proverbs

10:1 *muscae morientes perdunt suavitatem unguenti pretiosior est sapientia et gloria parva ad tempus stultitia*

Dying flies ruin
the aroma of *the* ointment.
Wisdom and glory
are more precious
than *a* brief moment
of foolishness.

10:2 *cor sapientis in dextera eius et cor stulti in sinistra illius*

The heart of *the* wise
is in his right *hand*,
but *the* heart of *a* fool
in his left,[154]

10:3 *sed et in via stultus ambulans cum ipse insipiens sit omnes stultos aestimat*

and *a* fool
walking in *the* way,
considers all *others* fools

---

[154] In this instance, the right hand represents what is open, honest, and straightforward. The left represents was is dishonest and hidden.

because he *himself* is a fool.

10:4 *si spiritus potestatem habentis ascenderit super te locum tuum ne dimiseris quia curatio cessare faciet peccata maxima*

If *a* spirit having power
should ascend over you,
do not give up your place,
because planning makes
great sins cease.

10:5 *est malum quod vidi sub sole quasi per errorem egrediens a facie principis*

An evil which I saw
under *the* sun is
going out by mistake
from *the* presence
of *a* prince.

10:6 *positum stultum in dignitate sublimi et divites sedere deorsum*

A fool *is* placed
in sublime dignity,
and *the* rich set below him.

10:7 *vidi servos in equis et principes ambulantes quasi servos super terram*

I saw slaves on horseback
and princes walking
on the ground like slaves.

10:8 *qui fodit foveam incidet in eam et qui dissipat sepem mordebit eum coluber*

One who digs *a* pit
will fall in it,
and *a* snake will bite
one who tears down *a* fence.

10:9 *qui transfert lapides adfligetur in eis et qui scindit ligna vulnerabitur ab eis*

One who moves rocks
will be hurt by them,
and one who splits trees
will be wounded by them.

10:10 *si retunsum fuerit ferrum et hoc non ut prius sed hebetatum erit multo labore exacuatur et post industriam sequitur sapientia*

If iron is blunted
and is not as it was before,
but is *made* blunt,
it will *only* be sharpened
by much labor,
and wisdom will follow
after *the* work *is done*.

10:11 *si mordeat serpens in silentio nihil eo minus habet qui occulte detrahit*

If *a* snake bites in silence,
he does nothing less
who disparages in secret.

10:12 *verba oris sapientis gratia et labia insipientis praecipitabunt eum*

Words from *the* mouths
of *the* wise are pleasing,
and *the* lips of fools
throw them down headlong.

10:13 *initium verborum eius stultitia et novissimum oris illius error pessimus*

The beginning of his words
is foolishness,
and *the* end of his speech
a grave error.

10:14 *stultus verba multiplicat ignorat homo quid ante se fuerit et quod post futurum est quis illi poterit indicare*

A fool multiplies words.
Man ignores what was
before him,
and who can tell him
what will be in the future?

10:15 *labor stultorum adfliget eos qui nesciunt in urbem pergere*

The labor of *a* fool harms
them
who do not know how
to go to *the* city.

The Need for Experienced, Sober Leaders

10:16 *vae tibi terra cuius rex est puer et cuius principes mane comedunt*

Woe to you,
land whose King is a boy,
and whose leaders feast
in *the* morning.

10:17 *beata terra cuius rex nobilis est et cuius principes vescuntur in tempore suo ad reficiendum et non ad luxuriam*

Happy *the* land
whose King is noble,
and whose leaders eat
in their time,
for replenishment,
and not for luxury.

Various Proverbs II

10:18 *in pigritiis humiliabitur contignatio et in infirmitate manuum perstillabit domus*

By laziness, *the* upper floors
will fall,
and by *a* slack hand
a house leaks.

10:19 *in risu faciunt panem ac vinum ut epulentur viventes et pecuniae oboedient omnia*

In laughter, they make
bread and wine
that *the* living
may dine sumptuously;
and all *people* obey money.

10:20 *in cogitatione tua regi ne detrahas et in secreto cubiculi tui ne maledixeris diviti quia avis caeli portabit vocem tuam et qui habet pinnas adnuntiabit sententiam*

Do not disparage *the* King
even in your thought,
and do not speak ill
of *the* rich,
even in your bed in secret,
because *a* bird of *the* air
will carry your voice,
and *the* one who has feathers
will tell *your* opinion.

Chapter 11

Generosity

11:1 *mitte panem tuum super transeuntes aquas quia post multa tempora invenies illum*

Send your bread
over flowing waters,
because after *a* long time
you will find it.

11:2 *da partem septem necnon et octo quia ignoras quid futurum sit mali super terram*

Give a portion to seven,
or even to eight,
because you do not know
what evil future may be
on *the* earth.

11:3 *si repletae fuerint nubes imbrem super terram effundent si ceciderit lignum ad austrum aut ad aquilonem in quocumque loco ceciderit ibi erit*

If clouds are full,
they will pour out
rain over *the* earth.
If *a* tree falls to *the* south
or to *the* north,
in whatever place it fell,
there it will be.

Quit Daydreaming

11:4 *qui observat ventum non seminat et qui considerat nubes numquam metet*

One who watches *the* wind
does not sow,
and one who considers
the clouds, never reaps.

The Mystery of God's Work

11:5 *quomodo ignoras quae sit via spiritus et qua ratione conpingantur ossa in ventre praegnatis sic nescis opera Dei qui fabricator est omnium*

Just as you do not know
which is *the* way of *the* wind,
or by what understanding
bones are formed
in *a* pregnant womb,
even so you do not know
the works of God,
who made all.

Again, Get to Work

11:6 *mane semina sementem tuam et vespere ne cesset manus tua quia nescis quid magis oriatur hoc an illud et si utrumque simul melius erit*

In *the* morning,
sow your seed,
and in *the* evening
do not cease your work,
because you do not know
which *is* better.
This may spring up, or that,
or even both together
at *the* same time will be best.

Light and Vanity
11:7 *dulce lumen et delectabile est oculis videre solem*

Light is sweet,
and *it* is delightful
for eyes to see *the* sun.

11:8 *si annis multis vixerit homo et in omnibus his laetatus fuerit meminisse debet tenebrosi temporis et dierum multorum qui cum venerint vanitatis arguentur praeterita*

If a man sees many years
and has happiness
in all of them,
he must remember
the gloomy time,
and many days which,
when they come,
arguing about *the* past
will be pointless.

Advice to the Young
11:9 *laetare ergo iuvenis in adulescentia tua et in bono sit cor tuum in diebus iuventutis tuae et ambula in viis cordis tui et in intuitu oculorum tuorum et scito quod pro omnibus his adducet te Deus in iudicium*

Be happy, therefore,
young *person*, in your youth,
and let your heart dwell
in *the* good in *the* days
of your youth,
and walk in *the* strength
of your heart
and in *the* intuition
of your eyes.
Yet know that for all these
God will bring you
to judgment.

11:10 *aufer iram a corde tuo et amove malitiam a carne tua adulescentia enim et voluptas vana sunt*

Put away anger
from your heart
and remove malice
from your flesh,
for youth and lust are vain.

Chapter 12

The Coming Days

12:1 *memento creatoris tui in diebus iuventutis tuae antequam veniat tempus adflictionis et adpropinquent anni de quibus dicas non mihi placent*

Remember your creator
in *the* days of your youth,
before times of affliction
come,
and years draw near
of which you say,
"*They* are not pleasant
to me;"

12:2 *antequam tenebrescat sol et lumen et luna et stellae et revertantur nubes post pluviam*

before *the* sun is darkened
and *the* light and *the* moon
and *the* stars;
and clouds return after *the*
rain;

12:3 *quando commovebuntur custodes domus et nutabuntur viri fortissimi et otiosae erunt molentes inminuto numero et tenebrescent videntes per foramina*

when *the* keepers
of *the* house are moved;
and *the* strongest men
give way;
and *the* grinders will be idle,
being diminished in number;
and *the* ones peering
through *the* opening
are obscured;

12:4 *et claudent ostia in platea in humilitate vocis molentis et consurgent ad vocem volucris et obsurdescent omnes filiae carminis*

and they shut *the* doorways
to *the* street
at *the* weakness of
the grinder's voice;
and they are startled at
the voice of *a* bird;
and all *the* daughters of song
become deaf;

12:5 *excelsa quoque timebunt et formidabunt in via florebit amigdalum inpinguabitur lucusta et dissipabitur capparis quoniam ibit homo in domum aeternitatis suae et circumibunt in platea* *plangentes*

and they will fear greatly
and be afraid in *the* way;
the almond will flourish
and *the* locust be fattened;
and *the* caper plant
will be scattered;
because man will go
to his eternal home,
and mourners will go about
in *the* street.

12:6 *antequam rumpatur funis argenteus et recurrat vitta aurea et conteratur hydria super fontem et confringatur rota super cisternam*

Before *the* silver bowl
is broken,
and *the* golden band returns,
and *the* water pot crumbles
over *the* spring,
and *the* rotor is broken
over *the* well,

12:7 *et revertatur pulvis in terram suam unde erat et spiritus redeat ad Deum qui dedit illum*

and dust returns to its earth,
where *it* was,
and *the* spirit returns
to God who gave it.

12:8 *vanitas vanitatum dixit Ecclesiastes omnia vanitas*

"Vanity of vanities,"
the Proclaimer said,
"all *is* vanity."

Summary

12:9 *cumque esset sapientissimus Ecclesiastes docuit populum et enarravit quae fecerit et investigans conposuit parabolas multas*

Along with being most wise,
the Proclaimer taught
the people
and recorded
what he had done,
and, investigating,
composed many parables,[155]

12:10 *quaesivit verba utilia et conscripsit sermones rectissimos ac veritate plenos*

and sought useful words
and wrote most accurate
words
and full of truth.

---

[155] This is a summary of the work, written apparently by a different hand.

12:11 *verba sapientium sicut stimuli et quasi clavi in altum defixi quae per magistrorum concilium data sunt a pastore uno*

The words of *a* wise man
are like goads,
and like nails fastened
high up,
which, by *the* council
of teachers
are given by one shepherd.[156]

12:12 *his amplius fili mi ne requiras faciendi plures libros nullus est finis frequensque meditatio carnis adflictio est*

More than this, my son,
do not require.
Of making of many books
there is no end,[157]
and frequent meditation
is *an* affliction to *the* body.

12:13 *finem loquendi omnes pariter audiamus Deum time et mandata eius observa hoc est enim omnis homo*

The end of speaking:
all is finished.
Let us hear.
Fear God
and observe His commands,
for this is all to *a* man.

12:14 *et cuncta quae fiunt adducet Deus in iudicium pro omni errato sive bonum sive malum sit*

And God brings to judgment
all things that are done,
whether they be good or evil,
on behalf of all.

---

[156] Compare the thrust of this statement to Hebrews 1:1: "*In many and various ways God spoke of old to our fathers by the prophets.*"

[157] Compare to John 21:25: "*But there are also many other things which Jesus did; were every one of them to be written, I suppose that the world itself could not contain the books that would be written.*"

The Song of Solomon

"The Song of Solomon" was written originally in Hebrew, centuries before the birth of Christ. In an age before computers or printing presses, this book, like all others, survived only by being copied manually by generations of scholars. This process took place for centuries among the Jews, the work's first custodians, who considered the book divinely inspired[158].

Its first known translation took place in the 3rd Century B.C.E. (Before the Common Era), in Alexandria, Egypt. At the behest of Ptolemy II Philadelphus,[159] Jewish scholars translated the Hebrew scriptures into Greek, the common language of the day. This translation, known as the Septuagint,[160] became the Bible of Greek-speaking Jewish synagogues scattered throughout the Greco-Roman world. As such, it became the Bible both of the first Gentile converts to Christianity, and of the writers of the New Testament.

The Song of Solomon was translated from Hebrew into Latin by Jerome some four centuries after Christ.[161] Jerome translated the work into the common Latin of his day, so-called "Vulgar Latin," rather into the more refined literary Latin. This made his translation accessible to ordinary hearers of the period, allowing it pass on from Jerome's translation into the canon of Western faith and culture. As with the Hebrew original, translations of the Song of Solomon had to be copied down by hand, until the invention of the printing press stabilized its form in the 15th Century C.E.[162]

---

[158] The Interpreter's Dictionary of the Bible: R-Z, George Buttrick, editor, Abingdon Press, Nashville, 1962, pgs. 420-426. (Hereafter cited as "Interpreter's")

[159] See http://en.wikipedia.org/wiki/Ptolemy_II_Philadelphus.

[160] "Interpreter's", pgs. 273-278

[161] See http://en.wikipedia.org/wiki/Jerome.

[162] See http://en.wikipedia.org/wiki/Printing_press.

The title of the book derives from the Hebrew inscription above the first line of poetry: "The Song of Songs, Which is Solomon's." In the Septuagint as well as most English translations, the phrase appears as Song of Solomon 1:1. The inscription is not found in the text of the Vulgate, and so does not appear in the text of this translation. Jerome begins the Vulgate translation with the first line of the first poem, rather than the inscription.

The doubled phrasing of the first phrase, "Song of Songs," reflects a Hebrew idiom which stresses that the thing in question is the supreme example of its type. Thus, the "Song of Songs" is the best of songs, even as the Holy of Holies is the most holy of all places.[163] Whether the inscription intends to tell us that Solomon composed the song, or merely that it was his favorite, is unclear from the language itself. Both Jewish and Christian traditions assert that Solomon wrote the poem as a young man, though many modern scholars dismiss the idea out of hand.

The book's date of composition is also disputed. Its association with Solomon makes it unlikely that the book was written earlier than his reign, which ended in the year 931 B.C.E.[164] Its inclusion in the Septuagint means it could not have been written later than the 3rd Century B.C.E. Given the length of time it must have taken for a work to have been accepted as canonical, one could argue logically for a date closer to the 9th than to the 3rd Centuries before Christ. The fact is that we know for sure neither the author's name nor the date of the work's composition.

The work is a series of passionate love poems, reflecting the courtship and marriage of a man and a woman. Because of the way the English language deals with gender, it is often difficult to follow who is

---

[163] See Hebrews 9:3.

[164] See http://en.wikipedia.org/wiki/Solomon.

speaking to whom in an English translation. Latin, like the Romance languages derived from it, handles gender differently. This makes it easier to follow the back-and-forth of the speakers.

In all, there seem to be four speakers:

> **The Man**, also referred to as the King and the Groom.
> **The Woman**, also referred to as the Wife, the Shulamite.
> **The Daughters of Jerusalem**, young women who are contemporaries of the Woman.
> **The Friends**, associates of the Man and Woman.

Scholars have debated through the centuries the meaning of the book. On an obvious level, it is about love between a woman and a man. That fact troubled later interpreters, shaped by the disdain for human sexuality that long shaped Jewish and Christian traditions. Jewish interpreters tended to see the book as an allegory for the relationship between God and Israel.[165] For Christians, the Man came to represent Christ or God, and the Woman the Church or the individual soul.[166]

It is not surprising that many interpreters refused to accept the literal interpretation of the book. The Song of Solomon is sexually graphic in ways that even jaded, modern readers are reluctant to discuss. It contains overt references to the woman's breasts (4:10), as well as "the joints of [her] thighs" (7:1). It mentions the location of her mother's first experience of intercourse (8:5). There are subtler allusions as well, which the reader will have to discover for herself.. Yet the love between the characters is as chaste and pure as it is passionate and graphic. "*All my fruits, old and new, I saved for you,*" the Woman assures the Man in 7:14.

---

[165] The New Oxford Annotated Bible: New Revised Standard Version, Michael Coogan, editor, Oxford Press, Oxford, 2001, pg. 959.

[166] Ibid., pg. 959.

Given its vivid content, why is the book in the Bible? In A. S. Herbert's words:

It is part of the glory of Israel's faith that it saw human life in all its aspects as having a full and rightful place in the divine purpose. Human love and marriage are part of God's will for man; through love's fulfillment in marriage human nature reaches the greatest heights of earthly experience. The horrors of man's perversion of love must be continually challenged by its true expression as God gave it to man, and as it is celebrated in [the Song of Solomon].[167]

The book is one of the most striking and brilliant literary works in the Old Testament canon. Whether it describes love physically or allegorically, few readers doubt the passion and inspiration of its composition. Rabbi Akiba, whose life and work helped provide the model for rabbinical Judaism after the destruction of the Jerusalem Temple in 70 C.E., said,

"*. . . all the ages are not worth the day on which the Song of Songs was given to Israel; for all the writings are holy, but the Song of Songs is the Holy of Holies.*"[168] [169]

[167] Peake's Commentary on the Bible, Matthew Black, editor, Thomas Nelson, Nashville, 1962, pg. 469.

[168] See http://en.wikipedia.org/wiki/Rabbi_Akiva.

[169] Peake's Commentary on the Bible, Matthew Black, editor, Thomas Nelson, Nashville, 1962, pg.468.

The Song of Songs, Which Is Solomon

Chapter 1

The Woman
1:1 *osculetur me osculo oris sui quia meliora sunt ubera tua vino*

Let him kiss me
with *the* kiss of his mouth,
because your body
is better than wine.[170]

1:2 *fraglantia unguentis optimis oleum effusum nomen tuum ideo adulescentulae dilexerunt te*

The passion of your scents
is *the* best;
your name *is* squeezed oil;
therefore young women
loved you.

1:3 *trahe me post te curremus introduxit me rex in cellaria sua exultabimus et laetabimur in te memores uberum tuorum super vinum recti diligunt te*

The Woman
Take me!

The Daughters of Jerusalem
We will run after you!

The Woman
The king brought me
into his cellar.

The Daughters of Jerusalem
We will exult
and be happy in you,
remembering your body
more than wine!

The upright will love you!

The Woman
1:4 *nigra sum sed formonsa filiae Hierusalem sicut tabernacula Cedar sicut pelles Salomonis*

I am black but beautiful!

The daughters of Jerusalem
are like *the* tabernacle
of Cedar,
like *the* pelts of Solomon.

1:5 *nolite me considerare quod fusca sim quia*

---

[170] Note the ambiguity of "Let him kiss me . . . because your body . . ." She doesn't seem to be addressing the one she is actually kissing.

decoloravit me sol filii matris meae pugnaverunt contra me posuerunt me custodem in vineis vineam meam non custodivi

Don't judge me
because I am darkened,
because *the* sun
discolored me.
My mother's sons fought
against me
and made me keeper
of *a* vineyard.

I have not tended my vine.

1:6 *indica mihi quem diligit anima mea ubi pascas ubi cubes in meridie ne vagari incipiam per greges sodalium tuorum*

Tell me, *you* who
delight my soul,
where do you feed *your
flock*?
Where do you eat at midday,
so I do not begin to wander
after *the* flocks
of your companions?

The Man
1:7 *si ignoras te o pulchra inter mulieres egredere et abi post vestigia gregum et pasce hedos tuos iuxta tabernacula pastorum*

If you don't know yourself,
O beautiful among women,
go out and pass beyond
the steps of *the* flock,
and graze your young goats
beside *the* shepherds'
tabernacle.

1:8 *equitatui meo in curribus Pharaonis adsimilavi te amica mea*

My love, I compared you
to my horsemen
in Pharaoh's chariots![171]

1:9 *pulchrae sunt genae tuae sicut turturis collum tuum sicut monilia*

Your cheeks are lovely,
like turtle-doves,
your neck like *a* necklace

1:10 *murenulas aureas faciemus tibi vermiculatas argento*

We will make golden bridles
for you,

---

[171] Physical prowess and grace are beautiful to him, not mere adornment.

studded with silver.

The Woman

1:11 *dum esset rex in accubitu suo nardus mea dedit odorem suum*

While the king reclined
to eat,
my scented oil gave its odor.

1:12 *fasciculus murrae dilectus meus mihi inter ubera mea commorabitur*

My lover to me *is*
like a little bundle of myrrh;
he will linger
between my breasts.

1:13 *botrus cypri dilectus meus mihi in vineis Engaddi*

A cluster of grapes
from Cyprus
is my lover to me,
in *the* vines of En-geddi.

The Man

1:14 *ecce tu pulchra es amica mea ecce tu pulchra oculi tui columbarum*

How beautiful you are,
my love!
How beautiful you are!
Your eyes *are* like doves!

The Woman

1:15 *ecce tu pulcher es dilecte mi et decorus lectulus noster floridus*

How handsome you are,
my love!
Our bed *is* blossoming!

1:16 *tigna domorum nostrarum cedrina laquearia nostra cypressina*

The beams of our house
are cedar,
our rafters of cypress.

Chapter 2

The Woman
2:1 *ego flos campi et lilium convallium*

I am *a* flower of *the* field,
and *a* lily of *the* valley.

The Man
2:2 *sicut lilium inter spinas sic amica mea inter filias*

Like *a* lily among thorns,
so *is* my love
among young women.

The Woman
2:3 *sicut malum inter ligna silvarum sic dilectus meus inter filios sub umbra illius quam desideraveram sedi et fructus eius dulcis gutturi meo*

Like an apple
among *the* trees of *the* forest,
so is my lover
among young men.
I sat under his shadow,
whom I desired,
and his fruit *was* sweet
to my throat.

2:4 *introduxit me in cellam vinariam ordinavit in me caritatem*

He brought me
into *the* wine cellar.
He commanded love in me.

2:5 *fulcite me floribus stipate me malis quia amore langueo*

Prop me up with flowers!
Press me with apples,
because I am sick with love!

2:6 *leva eius sub capite meo et dextera illius amplexabitur me*

His left *hand is*
under my head
and his right will caress me

The Man
2:7 *adiuro vos filiae Hierusalem per capreas cervosque camporum ne suscitetis neque evigilare faciatis dilectam quoadusque ipsa velit*

I adjure you,
daughters of Jerusalem,
by *the* roes and stags
of *the* field:
do not arouse or work
to awaken delight

until she chooses.[172]

The Woman
2:8 *vox dilecti mei ecce iste
venit saliens in montibus
transiliens colles*

The voice of my lover!
Look!
He comes, leaping
in *the* mountains,
crossing *the* hills!

2:9 *similis est dilectus meus
capreae hinuloque cervorum
en ipse stat post parietem
nostrum despiciens per
fenestras prospiciens per
cancellos*

My lover is like *a* roe
or *a* young deer.
He himself stands
behind our wall,
looking through *the* windows,
glancing through *the* shutters,

2:10 *et dilectus meus
loquitur mihi surge propera
amica mea formonsa mea et
veni*

and my lover speaks to me.

The Man
Rise up quickly,
my love, my beauty,
and come!

2:11 *iam enim hiemps
transiit imber abiit et recessit*

For winter is already past,
the storm has passed
and ebbed away.

2:12 *flores apparuerunt in
terra tempus putationis
advenit vox turturis audita
est in terra nostra*

Flowers have appeared
in *the* land.
The time of pruning
has come.
The voice of *the* turtle-dove
is heard in our land.

2:13 *ficus protulit grossos
suos vineae florent dederunt
odorem surge amica mea
speciosa mea et veni*

The fig tree has put forth
its green figs,
vines flower,
giving their odor!

---

[172] To adjure is to urge another to swear a legally binding oath. Compare this passage to 3:5, 5:8, and 8:4.

Rise up,
my love, my spectacular *one*,
and come!

2:14 *columba mea in foraminibus petrae in caverna maceriae ostende mihi faciem tuam sonet vox tua in auribus meis vox enim tua dulcis et facies tua decora*

My dove *is* in
the rooms of stone
in *the* hollows of *the* wall.
Show me your face!
Let your voice sound
in my ear,
for your voice is sweet
and your face lovely!

2:15 *capite nobis vulpes vulpes parvulas quae demoliuntur vineas nam vinea nostra floruit*

Capture for us *the* foxes,
the young foxes
who destroy our vines,
now that our vine
has flowered.

The Woman
2:16 *dilectus meus mihi et ego illi qui pascitur inter lilia*

My lover *is* mine
and I *am* his,
who feeds among *the* lilies,

2:17 *donec adspiret dies et inclinentur umbrae revertere similis esto dilecte mi capreae aut hinulo cervorum super montes Bether*

until *the* day breathes
and *the* shadows incline.
Come back!
My lover is like *a* roe
or *a* young deer
on *the* mountains of Bether.

Chapter 3

The Woman
3:1 *in lectulo meo per noctes quaesivi quem diligit anima mea quaesivi illum et non inveni*

In my bed at night
I sought him
whom my soul loves.
I sought him,
but I did not find him!

3:2 *surgam et circuibo civitatem per vicos et plateas quaeram quem diligit anima mea quaesivi illum et non inveni*

I rose and walked
through *the* city,
down rows of houses
and streets,
seeking him
whom my soul loves.
I sought him
but I did not find him!

3:3 *invenerunt me vigiles qui custodiunt civitatem num quem dilexit anima mea vidistis*

The watchmen
who keep *the* city found me.
Haven't you see
one whom my soul loves?

3:4 *paululum cum pertransissem eos inveni quem diligit anima mea tenui eum nec dimittam donec introducam illum in domum matris meae et in cubiculum genetricis meae*

A little while
after passing them,
I found him
whom my soul loves.
I took him and did not let go
until I brought him
to my mother's house
and into *the* bed of she
who gave birth to me.[173]

The Man
3:5 *adiuro vos filiae Hierusalem per capreas cervosque camporum ne suscitetis neque evigilare faciatis dilectam donec ipsa velit*

I adjure you,
daughters of Jerusalem,
by *the* roes and stags
of *the* field:

---

[173] Her mother's house is in Jerusalem. She is not a foreigner or stranger.

do not arouse or work
to awaken delight
until she chooses.

3:6 *quae est ista quae ascendit per desertum sicut virgula fumi ex aromatibus murrae et turis et universi pulveris pigmentarii*

Who is she who rises up
in *the* desert,
like *a* pillar of smoke
from aromatic myrrh,
and incense,
and all *the* powders
of *the* fragrance sellers?

The Friends
3:7 *en lectulum Salomonis sexaginta fortes ambiunt ex fortissimis Israhel*

Around Solomon's bed,
sixty strong men walk,
from *the* mightiest of Israel,

3:8 *omnes tenentes gladios et ad bella doctissimi uniuscuiusque ensis super femur suum propter timores nocturnos*

all having swords
and highly trained for war,
a weapon strapped
to each one's leg,
because of night's dangers.

3:9 *ferculum fecit sibi rex Salomon de lignis Libani*

King Solomon made *a*
carriage for himself
of *the* wood of Lebanon.

3:10 *columnas eius fecit argenteas reclinatorium aureum ascensum purpureum media caritate constravit propter filias Hierusalem*

He made its columns
of silver,
its seat of gold,
its frame of purple,
which he spread out,
full of love,
on account of *the* daughters
of Jerusalem.

3:11 *egredimini et videte filiae Sion regem Salomonem in diademate quo coronavit eum mater sua in die disponsionis illius et in die laetitiae cordis eius*

Go and see,
daughters of Zion,
King Solomon in *the* diadem
with which his mother

crowned him,
on *the* day of his coronation
and on *the* day of joy
of her heart.

Chapter 4

The Man
4:1 *quam pulchra es amica mea quam pulchra es oculi tui columbarum absque eo quod intrinsecus latet capilli tui sicut greges caprarum quae ascenderunt de monte Galaad*

How beautiful you are,
my love!
How beautiful you are!
Your eyes *are like* doves,
apart from that which
lies hidden within!
Your hair is like
a flock of goats,
which climb up
from Mount Gilead!

4:2 *dentes tui sicut greges tonsarum quae ascenderunt de lavacro omnes gemellis fetibus et sterilis non est inter eas*

Your teeth are like flocks
of shorn sheep,
who climb up
from *the* washing,
all with twin lambs,
and none among them
is sterile.

4:3 *sicut vitta coccinea labia tua et eloquium tuum dulce sicut fragmen mali punici ita genae tuae absque eo quod intrinsecus latet*

Your lips *are* like
a scarlet band,
and your speech sweet!
Your cheeks *are* like
a piece of pomegranate,
apart from that which
lies hidden within!

4:4 *sicut turris David collum tuum quae aedificata est cum propugnaculis mille clypei pendent ex ea omnis armatura fortium*

Your neck is like
the tower of David,
which is built with bulwarks.
A thousands shields hang
from it,
each one weapons
of *the* mighty.

4:5 *duo ubera tua sicut duo hinuli capreae gemelli qui pascuntur in liliis*

Your two breasts
like two young deer,
twins who graze
among *the* lilies.

4:6 *donec adspiret dies et inclinentur umbrae vadam ad montem murrae et ad collem turis*

Until *the* day breathes
and shadows incline,
let me go to
the mountain of myrrh
and to *the* hill of incense.

4:7 *tota pulchra es amica mea et macula non est in te*

You are totally beautiful,
my love!
There is no flaw in you!

4:8 *veni de Libano sponsa veni de Libano veni coronaberis de capite Amana de vertice Sanir et Hermon de cubilibus leonum de montibus pardorum*

Come from Lebanon,
my bride!
Come from Lebanon!
Come!
You will be crowned
from *the* top of Amana,
from *the* heights of Sanir
and Hermon,
from *the* lion’s dens,
from *the* leopards’
mountains!

4:9 *vulnerasti cor meum soror mea sponsa vulnerasti cor meum in uno oculorum tuorum et in uno crine colli tui*

You wounded my heart,
my sister, *my* wife!
You wounded my heart,
by one of your eyes alone,
by one lock from your neck!

4:10 *quam pulchrae sunt mammae tuae soror mea sponsa pulchriora ubera tua vino et odor unguentorum tuorum super omnia aromata*

How beautiful are
your nipples,
my sister, *my* wife!
Your breasts are more
beautiful than wine,
and *the* odor of your perfume
surpasses all aromas!

4:11 *favus distillans labia tua sponsa mel et lac sub lingua tua et odor vestimentorum tuorum sicut odor turis*

Your lips are *a* dripping
honeycomb, *my* wife!
Honey and milk are
under your tongue,
the odor of your garments
like *the* odor of incense!

4:12 *hortus conclusus soror mea sponsa hortus conclusus fons signatus*

An enclosed garden
is my sister, my wife,
an enclosed garden,
a sealed spring!

4:13 *emissiones tuae paradisus malorum punicorum cum pomorum fructibus cypri cum nardo*

Your emissions are
a paradise of pomegranates,
with *the* fruits of *an* orchard,
of *the* henna-tree,
with scented oil,

4:14 *nardus et crocus fistula et cinnamomum cum universis lignis Libani murra et aloe cum omnibus primis unguentis*

scented oil and saffron flower
and cinnamon,
with all *the* woods
of Lebanon,
myrrh and aloes,
with all *the* finest perfumes,

4:15 *fons hortorum puteus aquarum viventium quae fluunt impetu de Libano*

a garden spring,
a well of living waters,
which flow from *the* heights
of Lebanon,

4:16 *surge aquilo et veni auster perfla hortum meum et fluant aromata illius*

Rise, North Wind,
and come, South Wind!
Blow through my garden,
that its aromas might flow!

Chapter 5

The Woman
5:1 *veniat dilectus meus in hortum suum et comedat fructum pomorum suorum veni in hortum meum soror mea sponsa messui murram meam cum aromatibus meis comedi favum cum melle meo bibi vinum meum cum lacte meo comedite amici bibite et inebriamini carissimi*

Let my love come
into his garden
and eat *the* fruit
of his apple trees!

The Man
Come to my garden,
my sister, my wife!
I have trimmed my myrrh,
with all my aromatic spices,
I have eaten honeycomb
with my honey,
I have drunk my wine
with my milk!

Eat, friends!
Drink and be drunk,
my dearly loved!

The Woman
5:2 *ego dormio et cor meum vigilat vox dilecti mei*

pulsantis aperi mihi soror mea amica mea columba mea inmaculata mea quia caput meum plenum est rore et cincinni mei guttis noctium

I sleep and my heart watches
for *the* voice of my love
calling.

The Man
Open to me, my sister,
my lover,
my flawless dove!
My head is covered *with* dew,
my locks with *the* drops
of night!

The Woman
5:3 *expoliavi me tunica mea quomodo induar illa lavi pedes meos quomodo inquinabo illos*

I have taken off my tunic!
How will I put it *back* on?
I have washed my feet!
How will I dirty them *again*?

5:4 *dilectus meus misit manum suam per foramen et venter meus intremuit ad tactum eius*

My lover put his hand
through *the* opening
and my womb trembled
at his touch.

5:5 *surrexi ut aperirem dilecto meo manus meae stillaverunt murra digiti mei pleni murra probatissima*

I raised up that I might
open to my lover!
My hands dripped
with myrrh,
my fingers full
of costliest myrrh.

5:6 *pessulum ostii aperui dilecto meo at ille declinaverat atque transierat anima mea liquefacta est ut locutus est quaesivi et non inveni illum vocavi et non respondit mihi*

I opened the latch-key
to my beloved,
but he had turned aside
and gone.
My soul melted,
remembering his word.
I looked, but did not
find him.
I called him,
but he didn't call back.

5:7 *invenerunt me custodes qui circumeunt civitatem*

percusserunt me
vulneraverunt me tulerunt
pallium meum mihi custodes
murorum

The guards who walk around
the city found me.
They beat and wounded me.
The keepers of *the* wall
took my veil from me.

5:8 *adiuro vos filiae*
Hierusalem si inveneritis
dilectum meum ut nuntietis ei
quia amore langueo

I adjure you,
daughters of Jerusalem,
if you find my lover,
that you tell it,
because I am sick with love!

The Daughters of Jerusalem
5:9 *qualis est dilectus tuus*
ex dilecto o pulcherrima
mulierum qualis est dilectus
tuus ex dilecto quia sic
adiurasti nos

What is your lover like
among *the* loved,
O most beautiful of women?
What is your lover like
among *the* loved,
because you made us swear
thus?

The Woman
5:10 *dilectus meus candidus*
et rubicundus electus ex
milibus

My lover is radiant
and ruddy,
chosen from *a* thousand.

5:11 *caput eius aurum*
optimum comae eius sicut
elatae palmarum nigrae
quasi corvus

His head *is* finest gold;
his hair like *the* branches
of *the* palm tree,
black like *a* crow.

5:12 *oculi eius sicut*
columbae super rivulos
aquarum quae lacte sunt
lotae et resident iuxta fluenta
plenissima

His eyes *are* like
milk-washed doves
over streams of water,
who live beside
plentiful rivers.

5:13 *genae illius sicut*
areolae aromatum consitae a
pigmentariis labia eius lilia

distillantia murram primam

His cheeks are like
courtyards of aromatic spice,
sown by *the* fragrance sellers;
his lips *like* lilies
dripping finest myrrh.

5:14 *manus illius tornatiles*
aureae plenae hyacinthis
venter eius eburneus
distinctus sapphyris

His hands are like
lathed gold, full of hyacinths;
his stomach *like* ivory
inlaid with sapphires.

5:15 *crura illius columnae*
marmoreae quae fundatae
sunt super bases aureas
species eius ut Libani electus
ut cedri

His legs are like
marble columns
which are built on bases
of gold;
his appearance like Lebanon,
choice like cedars.

5:16 *guttur illius*
suavissimum et totus
desiderabilis talis est dilectus
meus et iste est amicus meus
filiae Hierusalem

His throat is most smooth
and totally desirable.
My lover is like this,
and this is my friend,
daughters of Jerusalem!

The Daughters of Jerusalem

5:17 *quo abiit dilectus tuus o*
pulcherrima mulierum quo
declinavit dilectus tuus et
quaeremus eum tecum

Where did your lover go,
O most beautiful of women?
Where did your lover
turn aside,
and we will seek him
with you?

Chapter 6

The Woman
6:1 *dilectus meus descendit*
in hortum suum ad areolam
aromatis ut pascatur in hortis
et lilia colligat

My lover came down
into his garden,
to *the* courtyard
of aromatic spices,
that he might dine in *the*
garden and gather lilies.

6:2 *ego dilecto meo et*
dilectus meus mihi qui
pascitur inter lilia

I *am* my lover's
and my lover is mine,
who feeds among the lilies!

The Man
6:3 *pulchra es amica mea*
suavis et decora sicut
Hierusalem terribilis ut
castrorum acies ordinata

My love is beautiful,
soft and elegant
like Jerusalem,
overwhelming like
the battle line of an army.

6:4 *averte oculos tuos a me*
quia ipsi me avolare fecerunt
capilli tui sicut grex
caprarum quae apparuerunt
de Galaad

Turn your eyes away
from me,
because they made me flee!
Your hair is like
a herd of deer,
which appeared from Gilead.

6:5 *dentes tui sicut grex*
ovium quae ascenderunt de
lavacro omnes gemellis
fetibus et sterilis non est in
eis

Your teeth *are* like
a herd of sheep,
who climb up
from *the* washing,
all with twin kids,
and no sterile *one*
is among them.

6:6 *sicut cortex mali punici*
genae tuae absque occultis
tuis

Like *the* skin of *a*
pomegranate *are* her cheeks,
apart from your hidden
charms.

6:7 *sexaginta sunt reginae et*

octoginta concubinae et adulescentularum non est numerus

There are sixty queens,
eighty concubines,
and numberless young women.

6:8 *una est columba mea perfecta mea una est matris suae electa genetrici suae viderunt illam filiae et beatissimam praedicaverunt reginae et concubinae et laudaverunt eam*

Yet my dove, my perfect *one*.
is unique *among them,*
only child of her mother
chosen of *the* one
who bore her.
The daughters saw her
and proclaimed her
most blessed.
Even queens and concubines
praised her!

6:9 *quae est ista quae progreditur quasi aurora consurgens pulchra ut luna electa ut sol terribilis ut acies ordinata*

Who is she who comes
like *the* dawn arising,
beautiful like *the* moon,
chosen like *the* sun,
fierce like *the* battle line
of *an* army?

6:10 *descendi ad hortum nucum ut viderem poma convallis ut inspicerem si floruisset vinea et germinassent mala punica*

I came down
to my nut garden,
to see *the* apples
of *the* valley,
to find out if
the vine flourished
and *the* pomegranate budded.

6:11 *nescivi anima mea conturbavit me propter quadrigas Aminadab*[174]

I did not know.
My soul troubled me,
because of *the* chariots
of Aminadab.[175]

---

[174] Nova Vulgata, *Non advertit animus meus,cum posuit me in quadrigas principis populi mei.*

[175] Passage is unclear. Compare to RSV: "*Before I was aware, my fancy set me in a chariot beside my prince.*" Aminadab was one of Solomon's ancestors. See Matthew 1:4.

The Friends
6:12 *revertere revertere*
Sulamitis revertere revertere
ut intueamur te

Come back, come back,
daughter of the Shulamites!
Come back, come back,
that we may admire you!

Chapter 7

The Man
7:1 *quid videbis in*
Sulamiten nisi choros
castrorum quam pulchri sunt
gressus tui in calciamentis
filia principis iunctura
feminum tuorum sicut
monilia quae fabricata sunt
manu artificis

Why would you stare
at *the* Shulamite,
if not like *a* dance
of armies?[176]

How beautiful are your steps,
daughter of *a* prince!
The joints of your thighs
are like *a* necklace,
which was made by *the* hands
of *an* artisan!

7:2 *umbilicus tuus crater*
tornatilis numquam indigens
poculis venter tuus sicut
acervus tritici vallatus liliis

Your navel is like
a beautifully-crafted bowl,
never lacking cups!

---

[176] The passage refers to the spectacle of ancient armies marching out to face each other in battle.

Your stomach is like
a pile of wheat,
surrounded by lilies!

7:3 *duo ubera tua sicut duo hinuli gemelli capreae*

Your two breasts *are*
like two fawns,
twins of *a* deer.

7:4 *collum tuum sicut turris eburnea oculi tui sicut piscinae in Esebon quae sunt in porta filiae multitudinis nasus tuus sicut turris Libani quae respicit contra Damascum*

Your neck is like
a dove of ivory!
Your eyes are like
pools in Heshbon,[177]
which are in *the* gate
of *the* daughter
of *a* multitude.
Your nose *is* like
the towers of Lebanon,
which watch
toward Damascus![178]

7:5 *caput tuum ut Carmelus et comae capitis tui sicut purpura regis vincta canalibus*

Your head *is* like Carmel,
and *the* hair of your head
like *the* purple cloth of kings,
bound in channels.

7:6 *quam pulchra es et quam decora carissima in deliciis*

How beautiful your are,
and how lovely *is*
my most beloved in delights!

7:7 *statura tua adsimilata est palmae et ubera tua botris*

Your height is like
palm trees,
and your breasts
like grape clusters.

7:8 *dixi ascendam in palmam adprehendam fructus eius et erunt ubera tua sicut botri vineae et odor*

---

[177] The city of Heshbon, on the far side of the Jordan River from Jerusalem, played an important part in Israel's history. It is first mentioned in scripture in Numbers 21:25.

[178] He compares his lover to the great fortifications that protected the kingdom from its enemies.

oris tui sicut malorum

I said, I will climb up
into *my* palm tree!
I will pick its fruit,
and your breasts will be like
clusters of grapes
from *the* vine,
and *the* fragrance of your
mouth like apples!

The Woman
7:9 *guttur tuum sicut vinum optimum dignum dilecto meo ad potandum labiisque et dentibus illius ruminandum*

Your throat *is* like
the finest wine,
worthy for my lover to drink,
and for his lips and teeth
to taste!

7:10 *ego dilecto meo et ad me conversio eius*

I *go to* my lover,
and his turning is to me!

7:11 *veni dilecte mi egrediamur in agrum commoremur in villis*

Come, my love!
Let us go into the field!
Let us stay in *the* villages!

7:12 *mane surgamus ad vineas videamus si floruit vinea si flores fructus parturiunt si floruerunt mala punica ibi dabo tibi ubera mea*

Let us rise up early
and go to *the* vineyards!
Let us see if
the vine blossoms,
if *the* flowers give forth fruit,
if *the* pomegranate blooms!
There, I will give
my breasts to you!

7:14 *mandragorae dederunt odorem in portis nostris omnia poma nova et vetera dilecte mi servavi tibi*

The mandrakes gave their
scent in our doorways!
All *my* fruits, old and new,
I saved for you![179]

---

[179] Her love is chaste, reserved for him alone.

Chapter 8

The Woman
8:1 *quis mihi det te fratrem meum sugentem ubera matris meae ut inveniam te foris et deosculer et iam me nemo despiciat*

Who will give you to me
as my brother,
sucking *the* breasts
of my mother,
so that if I find you outside
and kiss you,
no one now will despise me?

8:2 *adprehendam te et ducam in domum matris meae ibi me docebis et dabo tibi poculum ex vino condito et mustum malorum granatorum meorum*

I will take you
and lead you
to my mother's house!
There you will teach me
and I will give you *a* cup
of aged wine,
and new wine
from my pomegranates.

8:3 *leva eius sub capite meo et dextera illius amplexabitur me*

His left hand *will be*
under my head
and his right will caress me

The Man
8:4 *adiuro vos filiae Hierusalem ne suscitetis et evigilare faciatis dilectam donec ipsa velit*

I adjure you,
daughters of Jerusalem,
do not arouse or work
to awaken delight
until she chooses.

8:5 *quae est ista quae ascendit de deserto deliciis affluens et nixa super dilectum suum sub arbore malo suscitavi te ibi corrupta est mater tua ibi violata est genetrix tua*

Who is she who comes up
from *the* desert,
flowing with delights
and leaning on her lover?
Under *an* apple tree
I aroused you.
There your mother
was corrupted;
there she who bore you
was entered sexually.

8:6 *pone me ut signaculum*

super cor tuum ut signaculum
super brachium tuum quia
fortis est ut mors dilectio
dura sicut inferus aemulatio
lampades eius lampades ignis
atque flammarum

Place me as *a* seal
over your heart,
and *a* seal over your arm,
because delight is
as strong as death,
jealousy as hard
as destruction.
Its lamps *are* lamps of flame
and even fire.

8:7 *aquae multae non*
poterunt extinguere
caritatem nec flumina
obruent illam si dederit homo
omnem substantiam domus
suae pro dilectione quasi
nihil despicient eum

Many waters
cannot extinguish love,
nor *can* rivers overwhelm it.
If *a* man were to give
all *the* substance of his house
for delight,
they will despise it
as nothing.

The Friends
8:8 *soror nostra parva et*
ubera non habet quid
faciemus sorori nostrae in
die quando adloquenda est

Our sister is little
and has no breasts.
What shall we do
for our sister
on *the* day when she is
spoken for?

8:9 *si murus est aedificemus*
super eum propugnacula
argentea si ostium est
conpingamus illud tabulis
cedrinis

If she is *a* wall,
let us build
a bulwark of silver over her.
If she is *a* doorway
let us join it
with cedar boards.

The Woman
8:10 *ego murus et ubera*
mea sicut turris ex quo facta
sum coram eo quasi pacem
repperiens

I am *a* wall
and my breasts like *a* tower,
from which fact I am
before him
like one seeking peace.

The Friends
8:11 *vinea fuit Pacifico in ea quae habet populos tradidit eam custodibus vir adfert pro fructu eius mille argenteos*

The Peaceful One
had *a* vineyard
in that *land*
which has people.
He handed it over
to the keepers.
A man brings *a* thousand
pieces of silver for its fruit.

The Man
8:12 *vinea mea coram me est mille tui Pacifice et ducenti his qui custodiunt fructus eius*

My vineyard is before me.
A thousand to you,
Peaceful One,
and two hundred
to those who keep its fruit.

8:13 *quae habitas in hortis amici auscultant fac me audire vocem tuam*

You who live in *the* garden,
friends are listening!
Make me hear your voice!

The Woman
8:14 *fuge dilecte mi et adsimilare capreae hinuloque cervorum super montes aromatum*

Flee, my lover,
and be like *the* roe
and *the* young deer
over *the* mountains of spices.

A Note on Using Wikipedia

Some reviewers have raised a skeptical eyebrow at my references to Wikipedia, the online, cooperative encyclopedia. Certainly, there are better, more rigorous sources of information today. Yet, in my opinion, the advantages of using Wikipedia outweigh the disadvantages.

A July 2, 2008 story on CTV.ca, the online arm of Canadian National Television, explains the utility.[180] Jon Beasley-Murray, Professor of Latin American Studies at the University of British Columbia, gave students in his class an assignment of writing well-researched Wikipedia articles on topics relevant to his course.

According to the story, "Beasley-Murray still plans to tell students not to cite Wikipedia in work they hand in, but he says the site can provide valuable starting points if articles are properly cited."

Monica Freudenreich, one of Beasley-Murray's students, summed up how she came to see Wikipedia in the process: "Maybe you don't quote right off Wikipedia, but it's a great . . . list of academic sources that you can go and see. It cuts down the search process," she says.

Wikipedia is a handy springboard to more in-depth research. It is becoming increasingly a primary source for millions of internet users, who value its convenience and breadth. While it is far from perfect, it is improving steadily. These factors alone argue for its use, not to document specific information but as a starting point for further study. This is the sense in which I have cited it in my footnotes.

I value Wikipedia also for the democratization of knowledge it represents. As a living, self-correcting, collective, public-spirited effort to concentrate knowledge in accessible ways, it represents the best instincts of human scholarship. The same spirit that birthed libraries, schools, and all the public institutions of learning, has birthed Wikipedia also.

My advice to readers is, use Wikipedia, work to make it better, and pass on this invaluable resource to others.

---

[180] http://www.ctv.ca/servlet/ArticleNews/story/CTVNews/20080702/wikipedia_ubc_080702/20080702

Printed in the United States
147391LV00004B/17/P

9 780964 460973